Software Engineering Essentials

Volume III: The Engineering Fundamentals
FOURTH EDITION

Become a Certified Software Engineer

The *CSDA credential* is intended for graduating software engineers and entry-level software professionals

The *CSDP credential* is intended for mid-career software professionals looking to advance in their careers

The IEEE Computer Society (The world's largest organization of computer professionals) has launched an exam-based process for certifying software engineers as software engineering professionals.

This certificate establishes that the certificate holder is capable of using software engineering methods, tools, and techniques to develop and build software systems and, in addition, can fulfill the roles of:

- Software project manager
- Software architect and analysis
- Software designer
- Software configuration manager
- Software quality-assurance engineer
- V&V engineer
- Software test lead
- And so forth

The author team of Drs. Richard Hall Thayer and Merlin Dorfman has written a three-volume set of study guides to assist the potential certificate holder to pass the CSDP exam (you are currently reading Volume III).

In addition, Dr. Thayer has developed a self-teaching, multimedia CD training course, with both audio and visual components as an additional study guide to pass the certificate exam.

For more information go to www.CSDP-Training.com

Software Engineering Essentials

Volume III: The Engineering Fundamentals
FOURTH EDITION

A multi- text software engineering course or courses (based on the 2013 IEEE SWEBOK) for undergraduate and graduate university students

A self-teaching IEEE CSDP/CADA certificate exam training course based on the Computer Society's CSDP exam specifications

Edited & Written by

Richard Hall Thayer & Merlin Dorfman

Published by:
Software Management Training Press
Carmichael, California

2013

Copyright Notices

ISBN-13: 978-0-9852707-2-8
ISBN-10: 0-9852707-2-1

Acknowledgement

No successful endeavor has ever been done by one person alone. We would like to thank the people and organizations that supported us in this effort:

First we would like to thank our wives—Mildred Thayer and Sandy Dorfman—for their high degree of tolerance in putting up with us working many hours on this manuscript.

We would also like to thank the writers, proofreaders, and subject matter experts who wrote our overview papers on the various software engineering processes:

Friedrich L. Bauer, Keith H. Bennett, Antonia Bertolino, J. Glenn Brookshear, David Budgen, Richard E. Fairley, Stuart R. Faulk, Alfonso Fuggetta, Hassan Gomaa, Don Gotterbarn, Anne Matte Jensen Hass, Jill Macari, Eda Marchetti, Steven McConnell, National Aeronautics and Space Administration (NASA), Jed Scully, Laura Sfardini, Ian Sommerville, Steve Tockey, Leonard Tripp, and Gerard Voland.

In addition, we would like to thank: Steve Tockey for providing us with the current CSDP exam specifications in order to maximize the usefulness of our study guide, Ellen Sander for helping with proofing and copy editing our manuscript to make it ready for printing, Melville (Mel) Piercey of Copy Plus for providing printing and other graphic support, and Jim Tozza for giving us technical support to keep our computer equipment running. Dr. Thayer would like to give an extra special thanks to Big John Nelson and Iain Low of the *Technical Progress Limited* (TPL) of Cumbernauld, Scotland, for providing computer equipment and support services when Dr. Thayer was a resident at the University of Stirling, Scotland, during the 2000s.

And finally, Dr. Thayer would like to thank his little dog Maxwell (a.k.a. Max, Maxito, or Speedy) who kept him company in the evening hours when everybody else had gone to bed.

A curious Maxwell says that:

I have chewed on this manuscript and believe that it is a *bone*-a-fide study guide for the IEEE SWEBOK and the CSDP and CSDA exams

A Detailed Guide to the IEEE SWEBOK and the IEEE CSDP/CSDA Exam

A Three Volume Set

This is volume III of a three-volume document to (1) provide a more detailed understanding of the 2013 SWEBOK knowledge areas (KAs) and (2) use in preparing for the 2009 IEEE Software Engineering Certificates (called the Certified Software Development Associate and the Certified Software Development Professional, more commonly referred to as the CSDA and the CSDP). The *CSDA credential* is intended for graduating software engineers and entry-level software professionals. The *CSDP credential* is intended for mid-career software professionals looking to advance in their careers.

This study was divided into three volumes (1) because of its overall size (over 700 pages), (2) to provide a university-level textbook for an IEEE SWEBOK-based software engineering course or courses, and/or (3) to allow exam takers to buy and study only what they need in order to understand SWEBOK to take and pass the exam.

The Table of Contents for Volume III follows. This document also includes the Table of Contents for Volume I and Volume II. This information is provided so that interested software engineering exam takers can find additonal information about the test and dermine if the additional volumes are necessary. To aid in making this decision, the information in Table 1 (which follows) is also provided.

Table 1: The differences between the CSDP and the CSDA exams

Contains:	Volume I	Volume II	Volume III
Chapters in the study guides	1 through 5	6 through 11	12 through 16
Page counts in the study guides	260	256	204
Percent coverage of exam for CSDP	47%	35%	18%
Percent coverage of exam for CSDA	39%	24%	37%

The new CSDP/CSDA exam specifications are much more detailed than the earlier exams and contain 15 KAs that need to be defined and explained (plus a 16th KA added by the authors).

Since the exam is based on the IEEE SWEBOK 2013, this guide books can also serve as a textbooks for university-level software engineering courses.

The CSDA and the CSDP exams are similar and follow the same exam specification. The biggest difference is that the CSDA exam places a greater emphasis (and more questions) on the KAs of *computer economics, science, engineering, and mathematics* and therefore contains less emphasis on the other KAs. However, this new reference guide can be used to study for both exams.

Notes to Our Readers

One of the advantages of using a "print-on-demand" or an email publishing services is the ability to make relatively easy changes to the manuscript when errors or improvements are identified.

The authors encourage you to identify and send potential errors or suggested improvement to either Thayer or Dorfman at the below email addresses. We don't guarantee to make all the changes identified but we do promise to seriously consider all recommendations.

Note however that some things can't be changed. For example, the outline or contents of the exam specification, which are listed on the first page of all of the chapters labeled "n.2," are controlled by the Computer Society's *CSDP Certification Committee* and cannot be changed by us. Also we would have no real control over the papers written by the contributing software engineering experts (however we would notify them of your concerns).

These *three software-engineering books* were republished as "textbooks/guide book" in May 2013. One of the differences between a "guide book" and a "textbook" is that a textbook contains an "index" and a guide book usually does not. The index for this book is current under development and will be aided the textbook in the next printing. If you would like to have a copy of this index to use with this volume, please email Dr. Thayer, providing the volume number, and he will send you an electronic copy as soon as it is finished.

Thank you for listening to us.

Richard Hall Thayer
thayer@csus.edu

Merlin Dorfman
dorfman@computer.org

Disclaimer

While the Authors have more than 80 years of system and software engineering experience between us, we are not experts in all aspects of this very large discipline. We have made extensive use of material written by subject matter experts and have cross-checked the material with other sources to confirm its accuracy.

Every effort has been made to make this *Guidebook* as complete and accurate as possible. However, mistakes may remain, both typographical and in content. Furthermore, while the *Guidebook* is current as of the date of publication of the CSDP and CSDA exams, the state of the art advances on a daily basis. The reader should use his/her education and experience to supplement the *Guidebook*.

Table of Contents
Volume III: The Engineering Fundamentals

Volume I: The Development Process

Volume II: The Supporting Processes

Foreword

Much has happened in the software industry since Drs. Thayer, Dorfman, and Christensen originally published Volumes 1 and 2 of *Software Engineering.* For one, the software profession itself continues to mature. Ten years ago, Agile development was just gaining a foothold but could hardly be considered "generally accepted" in our industry. Today, virtually every software professional is well aware of Agile development and a significant fraction of today's professionals are successfully using it on a daily basis.

Another important change is that software is becoming ever more prevalent in everyone's everyday life, meaning the importance of software security is continually increasing. Private data about individuals and organizations must be kept private. And privileged functionality in specialized software systems must be access protected from unauthorized users. While there are software security specific methods and techniques, I claim that much of software insecurity is a direct result of sloppy, unprofessional software specification, development, and testing practices.

The IEEE Computer Society first published the Guide to the Software Engineering Body of Knowledge ("the SWEBOK Guide") in 2001 and published a revision in 2004. The SWEBOK Guide is essentially a catalog of the knowledge needed to be a professional-grade developer capable of delivering industrial-strength software products quickly and at low cost. To keep pace with these—and other—changes in the software industry, the SWEBOK Guide is undergoing another significant revision. Changes coming out in Version 3 of the SWEBOK Guide (planned for 2013) include:

- More obvious incorporation of Agile development techniques

- Incorporation of a new knowledge area (KA) on Professional Practice

- Incorporation of four new "foundation" KAs — the original ten knowledge areas describe how to develop software and the four new foundation KAs explain why we should be developing it the way we do. These new KAs include Engineering Economy Foundations, Computing Foundations, Mathematical Foundations, and Engineering Foundations.

- Incorporation of two supplemental KAs on Measurement and Security

In 2001, the IEEE Computer Society introduced the Certified Software Development Professional (CSDP) credential. CSDP is the only software certification that has all of the components of a professional certification:

- Exam-based verification of mastery of the software engineering body of knowledge

- Extensive experience based in the performance of the work or profession being certified

- Continuing professional education

CSDP is intended for mid-level software engineering professionals. The number of Certified Software Development Professionals (CSDPs) has grown steadily ever since. In 2008, the IEEE Computer Society also introduced the Certified Software Development Associate (CSDA), an entry-level certification for software professionals. The number of CSDAs also continues to grow steadily.

Another independent but related effort is the Curriculum Guidelines for Undergraduate Degrees in Software Engineering ("SE 2004") published in 2004. Developed concurrently, the SWEBOK Guide, CSDP/CSDA, and SE 2004 curriculum guide each provided a characterization of the discipline of software engineering. Despite nearly independent development, the three instruments agree to a remarkable extent.

The original intent of Thayer, Dorfman, & Christensen's Software Engineering set was a preparatory study guide for the CSDP examination. Both volumes covered the ten then-existing SWEBOK Guide knowledge areas. The study guide was necessary because the SWEBOK Guide itself is not intended to be of a tutorial nature. The SWEBOK Guide is intended to catalog software engineering concepts, not teach them. To keep up with evolution of the software industry (as expressed through evolution of the SWEBOK Guide, CSDP/CSDA, and the curriculum guidelines) a third volume in the Software Engineering series is needed. This third volume contains:

- Software Engineering Measurements
- Software Engineering Economics
- Computer Foundations
- Mathematics Foundations
- Engineering Foundations

In reality, the three-volume Software Engineering series is more than just a CSDP/CSDA study guide. It provides an overview snapshot of the software state of the practice in a form that is a lot easier to digest than the SWEBOK Guide. The three-volume set is also a valuable reference (useful well beyond undergraduate software engineering programs) that provides a concise survey of the breadth of software engineering.

Steven Tockey
Chair, CSDP Certification Committee
IEEE Computer Society

Honorary Foreword

To explain the origin of the term "Software Engineering," I submit the following story[1].

In the mid-1960s, there was increasing concern in scientific quarters of the Western world that the tempestuous development of computer hardware was not matched by appropriate progress in software. The software situation looked more to be turbulent. Operating systems had just been the latest rage, but they showed unexpected weaknesses. The uneasiness had been lined out in the NATO Science Committee by its U.S. representative, Dr. I.I. Rabi, the Nobel laureate and famous, as well as influential, physicist. In 1967, the Science Committee set up the Study Group on Computer Science, with members from several countries, to analyze the situation. The German authorities nominated me for this team. The study group was given the task of "assessing the entire field of computer science," with particular elaboration on the Science Committee's consideration of "organizing a conference and, perhaps, at a later date, ... setting up ... an International Institute of Computer Science."

The study group, concentrating its deliberations on actions that would merit an international rather than a national effort, discussed all sorts of promising scientific projects. However, it was rather inconclusive on the relation of these themes to the critical observations mentioned above, which had guided the Science Committee. Perhaps not all members of the study group had been properly informed about the rationale of its existence. In a sudden mood of anger, I made the remark, "The whole trouble comes from the fact that there is so much tinkering with software. It is not made in a clean fabrication process," and when I found out that this remark was shocking to some of my scientific colleagues, I elaborated the idea with the provocative saying, "What we need is *software engineering.*"

This remark had the effect that the expression "software engineering," which seemed to some to be a contradiction in terms, stuck in the minds of the members of the group. In the end, the study group recommended in late 1967 the holding of a Working Conference on Software Engineering, and I was made chairman. I had not only the task of organizing the meeting (which was held from October 7 to October 10, 1968, in Garmisch, Germany), but I had to set up a scientific program for a subject that was suddenly defined by my provocative remark. I enjoyed the help of my co-chairmen, L. Bolliet from France, and H. J. Helms from Denmark, and in particular, the invaluable support of the program committee members, A. J. Perlis and B. Randell in the section on design, P. Naur and J. N. Buxton in the section on production, and K. Samuelson, B. Galler, and D. Gries in the section on service.

Among the 50 or so participants, E. W. Dijkstra was dominant. He actually made not only cynical remarks like "the dissemination of error-loaded software is frightening" and "it is not clear that the people who manufacture software are to be blamed. I think manufacturers deserve better, more understanding users." He also said, already at this early date, "Whether the correctness of a piece of software can be guaranteed or not depends greatly on the structure of the thing made," and he had very fittingly named his paper "Complexity Controlled by Hierarchical Ordering of Function and Variability," introducing a theme that followed his life over the next 20 years.Some of his words have become proverbs in computing, like "testing is a very inefficient way of convincing oneself of the correctness of a program."

---

1. Dr. Bauer originally wrote this paper as an introduction to a 1993 IEEE tutorial, R.H. Thayer, and A.D. McGettrick (eds.), *Software Engineering: A European Perspective*, IEEE Computer Society Press, Los Alamitos, CA, 1993

With the wide distribution of the reports on the Garmisch Conference and on a follow-up conference in Rome, from October 27 to 31, 1969, it emerged that not only the phrase *software engineering,* but also the idea behind this became fashionable. Chairs were created, institutes were established (although the one which the NATO Science Committee had proposed did not come about because of reluctance on the part of Great Britain to have it organized on the European continent), and a great number of conferences were held.

The tutorial nature of the papers in this book is intended to offer readers an easy introduction to the topics and indeed to the attempts that have been made in recent years to provide them with the *tools,* both in a handcraft and intellectual sense that allow them now to honestly call themselves software *engineers.*

Friedrich L. Bauer
Professor Emeritus
Technical University of Munich, Germany

Preface

These software engineering books serves two separate but connected audiences and roles:

1. <u>**Software engineers**</u> **who wish to study for and pass either or both of the IEEE Computer Society's software engineering certification exams.**

   The Certified Software Development Professional (CSDP) and is awarded to software engineers who have 5 to 7 years of software development experience and pass the CSDP exam. This certification was instituted in 2001 and establishes that the certificate holder is a competent software engineer in most areas of software engineering such as:

   - Software project manager

   - Software developer

   - Software configuration manager

   - Software quality-assurance expert

   - Software test lead

   - And so forth

   The other certificate is for recent software engineering graduates or self-taught software engineers and is designated Certified Software Development Associate (CDSA). The CSDA also requires passing an exam, but does not require any professional experience.

2. <u>**University students**</u> **who are taking (or reading) a BS or MS degree in software engineering, or practicing software engineers who want to update their knowledge.**

   This book was originally written as a guide to help software engineers take and pass the IEEE CSDP exam. However several reviewers commented that this book would also make a good university text book for a undergraduate or graduate course in software engineering. So the original books were modified to be applicable to both tasks.

   The SWEBOK (Software Engineering Body of Knowledge) is a major milestone in the development and publicity of software engineering technology. However it needs to be noted that SWEBOK was NOT developed as a software engineering tutorial or textbook. *The SWEBOK is intended to catalog software engineering concepts, not teach them.*

   The new, three-volume, fourth edition, *Software Engineering Essentials*, by Drs. Richard Hall Thayer and Merlin Dorfman attempts to fill this void (you are now reading Volume III). This new software engineering text expands on and replaces the earlier two-volume, third-edition, *Software Engineering* books which was also written by Thayer and Dorfman and published by the IEEE Computer Society Press [2006].

   These new Volumes I and II offer a complete and detailed overview of software engineering as defined in IEEE SWEBOK 2013. These books provide a thorough analysis of *software development* in requirements analysis, design, coding, testing, and maintenance, plus the *supporting processes* of configuration management, quality assurance, verification and validation, and reviews and audits.

   To keep up with evolution of the software industry (as expressed through evolution of the SWEBOK Guide, CSDP/CSDA, and the curriculum guidelines) a third volume in the Software Engineering series is needed. This third volume contains:

- *Software Engineering Measurements*
- *Software Engineering Economics*
- *Computer Foundations*
- *Mathematics Foundations*
- *Engineering Foundations*

This three-volume, *Software Engineering* Essentials series, provides an overview snapshot of the software state of the practice in a form that is a lot easier to digest than the SWEBOK Guide. The three-volume set is also a valuable reference (useful well beyond undergraduate and graduate software engineering university programs) that provides a concise survey of the depth and breadth of software engineering.

These new KAs exist so that software engineers can demonstrate a mastery of scientific technology and engineering. This is in answer to the criticism of software engineering that it does not contain enough engineering to qualify it as an engineering discipline.

1. History

In 2000, the president of the Computer Society, Mr. Leonard L. Tripp, asked Dr. Richard Hall Thayer to develop a reference/text and a three-day CSDP Software Engineering course to aid software engineers in refreshing their knowledge of software engineering. Dr. Thayer is a Fellow of the IEEE, a member of the Computer Society's Golden Core, and a Certified Software Development Professional. Thayer teamed with Dr. Merlin Dorfman (Fellow of the AIAA and registered Professional Engineer) to develop these reference books. The first result was a book titled *Software Engineering,* 2nd edition, in two volumes. (Thayer and Dorfman also wrote the first edition in 1997; however it preceded the CSDP program.) The third edition was written in 2005 to update and improve the contents. In 2009, the exam was updated and made broader (containing more knowledge areas) and more difficult. Therefore, the CSDP exam reference needed to be rewritten yet again.

In 2004, the IEEE Computer Society initiated a reference book on software engineering to provide an overview of the discipline of software engineering. This book is entitled Software Engineering Body of Knowledge (SWEBOK). SWEBOK parallels the CSDP exam specifications. The SWEBOK is being updated for 2013 and is now the driving force behind the CSDP exams. The primary purpose of the current revision of the SWEBOK Guide is to add a Knowledge Area (KA) on professional practices—a subject currently covered by the CSDP exams—and to add "foundation" KAs on high-tech subject is technology and science.

To achieve alignment with the CSDP and to maintain the currency of the SWEBOK Guide, the IEEE Computer Society's Professional Practices Committee agreed in 2008 to the following changes in the CSDP exam:

- Add four new education KAs: *Engineering Economy Foundations, Computing Foundations, Mathematical Foundations,* and *Engineering Foundations*

- Remove three *Related Disciplines of Software Engineering (Chapter 12, SWEBOK 2004): Computer Science, Mathematics, and Software Ergonomics*

- Add four new education KAs: *Engineering Economy Foundations, Computing Foundations, Mathematical Foundations,* and *Engineering Foundations*

- Remove three *Related Disciplines of Software Engineering (Chapter 12, SWEBOK 2004): Computer Science, Mathematics, and Software Ergonomics*

- Add material about *Human-Computer Interfaces* in the *Software Design and Software Testing KA*

- *Remove the Software Tools* section from SWEBOK, *Software Engineering Tools and Methods,* and distribute the material to the other KAs

- Rename the *Software Engineering Tools and Methods* KA to *Software Engineering Methods KA* in SWEBOK 2013 to focus on methods that affect more than one KA

For additional information see http://www.computer.org/portal/web/swebok

In 2010, the Computer Society launched an additional initiative to set up a software development certificate for recent university graduates and other entry-level software engineers or computer scientists. This certificate was called the Certified Software Development Associate (CSDA). The CSDA credential is intended for graduating software engineers and entry-level software professionals and serves to bridge the gap between educational experience and real-world work requirements.

The CSDP and CSDA exams are similar and are based on the same exam specification. However, the CSDA exam places more emphasis on the basic knowledge areas of computer science and engineering.

2. The Book's Contents

In its role as a supporting text to the IEEE SWEBOK, this reference book greatly expands the SWEBOK outline to provide greater detail to the SWEBOK engineering concepts and as a result should make an above average university software engineering textbook or textbooks. As an example, this text greatly expands the coverage of the software engineering project management KA to provide the detail necessary to (1) properly manage a large-scale software project or (2) to study for a software engineering project management course.

The new CSDP/CSDA exam specifications (which are based on the SWBOK 2013) are much more detailed than the earlier CSDP 2004 exams specifications. The new specifications contain 15 KAs. The CSDA exam is similar to the CSDP exam and uses the same exam specifications. The biggest difference is that the CSDA exam places a greater emphasis (and more questions) on the KAs of *computer economics, science, engineering,* and *mathematics* (see Table 1 earlier) and therefore, less emphasis (and questions) on the other KAs.

This new reference guide can be used to study for both exams.

3. What Makes Our Book Unique?

This text makes use of the broad coverage of SWEBOK to ensure that all possible elements of the software engineering discipline are covered. We also asked *notable* software engineering authors to provide overview papers to provide a general look at some of the software engineering knowledge areas to help the student tie things together. By using the new print on demand (POD) business model to print our books and our decision to divide the extensive material into three parts we have provided one of the less expensive texts of it size and scope.

This is the fourth edition of this software engineering reference book and, in many ways, a better book than the earlier editions for upgrading a professional's software engineering knowledge.

Each chapter of the reference is divided into two parts. Part 1 consists of one or more papers written as an "overview tutorial" on one of the 16 KAs of the SWEBOK and the exam specifications. These authors are experts in their particular area and in many cases are also the authors of reference books recommended by the IEEE Computer Society to potential certification exam takers. Part 2 is an analysis of the certification exam specifications for that KA (written by the Drs. Thayer and Dorfman). Part 2 was based on the exam specifications that were furnished to the *Guides* authors by the Computer Society committee who wrote the exam questions. Note that the questions themselves have not been and will not be released to *guide book authors.*

The exam specification outlines 15 software engineering knowledge areas (KAs). Our book covers 16 KAs because we split one area into two—the Software Engineering Management KA was separated into Software Engineering Project Management KA and Software Measurement and Metrics Foundation KA. We have recommended to the Computer Society that they do the same for the next SWEBOK.

Richard Hall Thayer, PhD, CSDP
Emeritus Professor of Software Engineering
California State University, Sacramento

Merlin Dorfman, PhD, PE
Quality Systems Staff Engineer (Retired)
Cisco Systems, Inc.

Chapter 12.1
Software Measurements: Essential to Good Software Engineering[2]

Norman E. Fenton and *Shari Lawrence Pfleeger*
Professor of Computing Science   *Director of Research*
Centre for Software Reliability   *Institute for Information Infrastructure*
City University, London   *Protection, Dartmouth College*
                                       Hanover, New Hampshire

Software measurement, once an obscure and esoteric specialty, has become essential to good software engineering. Many of the best software developers measure characteristics of the software to get some sense of whether the requirements are consistent and complete, whether the design is of high quality, and whether the code is ready to be tested. Effective project managers measure attributes of process and product to be able to tell when the software will be ready for delivery and whether the budget will be exceeded. Informed customers measure aspects of the final product to determine if it meets the requirements and is of sufficient quality. Moreover, maintainers must be able to assess the current product to see what should be upgraded and improved.

1. Introduction

This document begins with a discussion of measurement in our everyday lives. In the first section, we explain how measurement is a common and necessary practice for understanding, controlling and improving our environment. In this section, you will see why measurement requires rigor and care. Later, we describe the role of measurement in software engineering. In particular, we look at how measurement needs are directly related to the goals we set and the questions we must answer when developing our software. Next, we compare software engineering measurement with measurement in other engineering disciplines, and propose specific objectives for software measurement.

2. Measurement in Everyday Life

Measurement lies at the heart of many systems that govern our lives. Economic measurements determine price and pay increases. Measurements in radar systems enable us to detect aircraft when direct vision is obscured. Medical system measurements enable doctors to diagnose specific illnesses. Measurements in atmospheric systems are the basis for weather prediction. Without measurement, technology cannot function.

Nevertheless, measurement is not solely the domain of professional technologists. Each of us uses it in everyday life. Price acts as a measure of value of an item in a shop, and we calculate the total bill to make sure the shopkeeper gives us correct change. We use height and size measurements to ensure that our clothing will fit properly. When making a journey, we calculate

---

2. This paper was derived from the Fenton and Pfleeger book, *Software Metrics: A Rigorous & Practical Approach,* 2nd Edition, PWS. Publishing Company, London. © 1997 Norman E. Fenton and Shari Lawrence Pfleeger.

distance, choose our route, measure our speed, and predict when we will arrive at our destination (and perhaps when we need to refuel). Therefore, measurement helps us to understand our world, interact with our surroundings and improve our lives.

2.1 What is measurement?

Measurements allow us to assign a descriptor to entities that then allow us to compare them with others like entities. In a shop, we can compare the price of one item with another. In the clothing store, we contrast sizes. In addition, on our journey, we compare distance traveled to distance remaining. The rules for assignment and comparison are made according to a well-defined set of rules. We can capture this notion by defining measurement formally in the following way:

> *Measurement is the process by which numbers or symbols are assigned to attributes of entities in the real world in such a way as to describe them according to clearly defined rules.*

Thus, measurement captures information about attributes of entities. An entity is an object (such as a person or a room) or an event (such as a journey or the testing phase of a software project) in the real world. We want to describe the entity by identifying characteristics that are important to us in distinguishing one entity from another. An attribute is a feature or property of an entity. Typical attributes include the area or color (of a room), the cost (of a journey), or the elapsed time (of the testing phase).

Often, we talk about entities and their attributes interchangeably, as in "It is cold today," when we really mean that the air temperature is cold today, or "she is taller than he" when we really mean, "her height is greater than his height." Such loose terminology is acceptable for everyday speech, but it is incorrect and unsuitable for scientific endeavors.

Thus, it is wrong to say that we measure things or that we measure attributes; in fact, we measure attributes of things. It is ambiguous to say that we "measure a room," since we can measure its length, area, or temperature. It is likewise ambiguous to say that we "measure the temperature" since we measure the temperature of a specific geographical location under specific conditions. In other words, what is commonplace in common speech is unacceptable for engineers and scientists.

When we describe entities by using attributes, we often define the attributes using numbers or symbols. Thus, price is designated as a number of dollars or pounds sterling, while height is defined in terms of inches or centimeters. Similarly, clothing size may be "small," "medium," or "large," while fuel is "regular," "premium," or "super." These numbers and symbols are abstractions that we use to reflect our perceptions of the real world. For example, in defining the numbers and symbols, we try to preserve certain relationships that we see among the entities.

Thus, someone who is six feet in height is taller than someone who is five feet in height. Likewise, a "medium" T-shirt is smaller than a "large" T-shirt. This number or symbol can be very useful and important. If we have never met a man we are going to see but are told that he is seven feet tall, we can imagine his height in relation to ourselves without our ever having seen him. Moreover, because of his unusual height, we know that he will have to stoop when he enters the door of our office. Thus, we can make judgments about entities solely by knowing and analyzing their attributes.

Measurement is a process whose definition is far from clear-cut. Many different authoritative views lead to different interpretations about what constitutes measurement. To understand what measurement is, we must ask a host of questions that are difficult to answer. For example:

- We have noted that color is an attribute of a room. In a room with blue walls, is "blue" a measure of the color of the room?

- The height of a person is a commonly-understood attribute that can be measured. Nevertheless, what about other attributes of people, such as intelligence? Is intelligence adequately measured by an IQ test score? Similarly, wine can be measured in terms of alcohol content ("proof"), but can wine quality be measured using the ratings of experts?

- The accuracy of a measure depends on the measuring instrument as well as on the definition of the measurement. For example, length can be measured accurately as long as the ruler is accurate and used properly. Nevertheless, some measures are not likely to be accurate, either because the measurement is imprecise or because it depends on the judgment of the person doing the measuring. For instance, proposed measures of human intelligence or wine quality appear to have likely error margins. Is this a reason to reject them as bona fide measurements?

- Even when the measuring devices are reliable and used properly, there is margin for error in measuring the best-understood physical attributes. For example, we can obtain vastly different measures for a person's height, depending on whether we make allowances for the shoes being worn or the standing posture. So how do we decide which error margins are acceptable and which are not?

- We can measure height in terms of meters, inches or feet. These different scales measure the same attribute. However, we can also measure height in terms of miles and kilometers —appropriate for measuring the height of a satellite above earth, but not for measuring the height of a person. When is a scale acceptable for the purpose to which it is put?

- Once we obtain measurements, we want to analyze them and draw conclusions about the entities from which they were derived. What kind of manipulations can we apply to the results of measurement? For example, why is it acceptable to say that Fred is twice as tall as Joe is, but not acceptable to say that it is twice as hot today as it was yesterday? In addition, why is it meaningful to calculate the mean of a set of heights (to say, for example, that the average height of a London building is 200 meters), but not the mean of the football jersey numbers of a team?

This rigorous approach lays the groundwork for applying measurement concepts to software engineering problems. However, before we turn to measurement theory, we examine first the kinds of things that can be measured.

2.2 Making things measurable.

The following are two measurement quotes from some very historic individuals.

1. Galileo Galilei (1564-1642) is credited with saying:

   Count what is countable, measure what is measurable, and what is not measurable, make measurable.

2. Baron William Thomson Kelvin (a.k.a. Lord Kelvin) (1824 - 1907) is credited with the following:

   I often say that when you can measure what you are speaking about, and express it in numbers, you know something about it; but when you cannot measure it, when you cannot express it in numbers, your knowledge is of a meager and unsatisfactory kind; it may be the beginning of knowledge, but you have scarcely in your thoughts advanced to the state of science.

These phrases are part of the folklore of measurement scientists. It suggests that one of the aims of science is to find ways to measure attributes of things in which we are interested. Implicit in this statement is the idea that measurement makes concepts more visible and, therefore, more understandable and controllable. Thus, as scientists, we should be creating ways to measure our world; where we can already measure, we should be making our measurements better.

In the physical sciences, medicine, economics, and even some social sciences, we are now able to measure attributes that were previously thought unmeasureable. Whether we like them or not, measures of attributes such as human intelligence, air quality, and economic inflation form the basis for important decisions that affect our everyday lives. Of course, some measurements are not as refined as we would like them to be; we use the physical sciences as our model for good measurement, continuing to improve measures when we can. Nevertheless, it is important to remember that the concepts of time, temperature and speed, once unmeasureable by primitive peoples, are now not only commonplace but also easily measured by almost everyone; these measurements have become part of the fabric of our existence.

To improve the rigor of measurement in software engineering, we need not restrict the type or range of measurements we can make. Indeed, measuring the unmeasureable should improve our understanding of particular entities and attributes, making software engineering as powerful as other engineering disciplines. Even when it is not clear how we might measure an attribute, the act of proposing such measures will open a debate that leads to greater understanding. Although some software engineers may continue to claim that important software attributes like dependability, quality, usability and maintainability are simply not quantifiable, we prefer to try to use measurement to advance our understanding of them.

Strictly speaking, we should note that there are two kinds of quantification: measurement and calculation (also known as metrics). *Measurement* is a direct quantification, as in measuring the height of a tree or the weight of a shipment of bricks. *Calculation* is indirect, where we take measurements and combine them into a quantified item that reflects some attribute whose value we are trying to understand. For example, when the city inspectors assign a valuation to a house (from which they then decide the amount of tax owed), they calculate it by using a formula that combines a variety of factors, including the number of rooms, the type of heating and cooling, and the overall floor space. The valuation is quantification, not a measurement, and its expression as a number makes it more useful than qualitative assessment alone. In this book, we use *direct* and *indirect* to distinguish *measurement* from *calculation*.

Sport offers us many lessons in measuring abstract attributes like quality in an objective fashion. Here, the measures used have been accepted universally, even though there is often discussion about changing or improving the measures. In the following examples, we highlight measurement concepts, showing how they may be useful in software engineering:

- **EXAMPLE 1.1:** In the decathlon athletics event, we measure the time to run various distances as well as the length covered in various jumping activities. These measures are subsequently combined into an *overall score,* computed using complex weighting scheme that reflects the importance of each component measure. The weights are sometimes changed as the relative importance of an event or measure changes. This score is widely accepted as a description of the athlete's all-round ability. In fact, the winner of the Olympic decathlon is generally acknowledged to be the world's finest athlete.

- **EXAMPLE 1.2:** The England soccer league (called "football" in the U.K) uses a points system is used to select the best all-round team over the course of a season. In 1981, the points system was changed; a win yielded three points instead of two, while a draw still yielded one point. This change was made to reflect the consensus view that the qualitative difference between a win and a draw was greater than that between a draw and a defeat.

- **EXAMPLE 1.3:** There are no universally recognized measures to identify the best individual soccer players (although number of goals scored is an accurate measure of quality of a striker). Although many fans and players have argued that player quality is an unmeasureable attribute, this issue was addressed prior to the 1994 World Cup games in the USA. To provide an objective (measurable) means of determining the "man of the match," several new measurements were proposed:

> To help FIFA [a.k.a. Fédération Internationale de Football Association (in English: International Federation of Association Football)] assess the best players, it will be necessary to add to the pitch markings. At ten-meter intervals, there will be lines both across and down the pitch. This will allow accurate pass yardage, sideways pass yardage, dribble yardage, and heading yardage to be found for each player.[3]

It was suggested that these measurements be added and weighted with the number of goals scored; tackles, saves or interceptions made; frequency and distance of passes (of various types), dribbles and headers. Notice that the proposed new measure of player quality required a change to the physical environment in which the game is played.

It is easy to see parallels in software engineering. In many instances, we want an overall score that combines several measures into a "big picture" of what is going on during development or maintenance. We want to be able to tell if a software product is good or bad, based on a set of measures, each of which captures a facet of "goodness." Similarly, we want to be able to measure an organization's ability to produce good software, or a model's ability to make good predictions about the software-development process. The composite measures can be controversial, not only because of the individual measures comprising it, but also because of the weights assigned.

Likewise, controversy erupts when we try to capture qualitative information about some aspect of software engineering. Different experts have different opinions, and it is sometimes impossible to get consensus.

Finally, it is sometimes necessary to modify our environment or our practices in order to measure something new or in a new way. It may mean using a new tool (to count lines of code or evaluate code structure), adding a new step in a process (to report on effort), or using a new method (to make measurement simpler). In many cases, change is difficult for people to accept; there are management issues to be considered whenever a measurement program is implemented or changed.

---

3. Translated from "Likely changes to the rules for the 1994 World Cup," *Nouveaux FIFA d'Arbitres* (FIFA Referees News), March 1990.

2. Measurement in Software Engineering

We have seen that measurement is essential to our daily lives, and measuring has become commonplace and well accepted. In this section, we examine the realm of software engineering to see why measurement is needed.

Software engineering describes the collection of techniques that apply an engineering approach to the construction and support of software products. Software engineering activities include managing, costing, planning, modeling, analyzing, specifying, designing, implementing, testing, and maintaining. By "engineering approach," we mean that each activity is understood and controlled, so that there are few surprises as the software is specified, designed, built, tested, and maintained. Whereas computer science provides the theoretical foundations for building software, software engineering focuses on implementing the software in a controlled and scientific way.

The importance of software engineering cannot be overstated, since software pervades our lives. From oven controls to airbags, from banking transactions to air traffic control, and from sophisticated power plants to sophisticated weapons, our lives and the quality of life depend on software. For such a young profession, software engineering has usually done an admirable job of providing safe, useful and reliable functionality. Nevertheless, there is room for a great deal of improvement. The literature is rife with examples of projects that have overrun their budget and schedules. Worse, there are too many stories about software that has put lives and businesses at risk.

Software engineers have addressed these problems by continually looking for new techniques and tools to improve both process and product. Training supports these changes, so that software engineers are better prepared to apply the new approaches to development and maintenance. However, methodological improvements alone do not make an engineering discipline.

2.1 Neglect of measurement in software engineering.

Engineering disciplines use methods that are based on models and theories. For example, in designing electrical circuits we appeal to theories—like Ohm's law, which describes the relationship between resistance, current and voltage in the circuit. However, the laws of electrical behavior have evolved by using the scientific method: stating a hypothesis, designing and running an experiment to test its truth, and analyzing the results.

Underpinning the scientific process is measurement: measuring the variables to differentiate cases, measuring the changes in behavior, and measuring the causes and effects. Once the scientific method suggests the validity of a model or the truth of a theory, we continue to use measurement to apply the theory to practice. Thus, to build a circuit with a specific current and resistance, we know what voltage is required and we use instruments to measure whether we have such a voltage in a given battery.

It is difficult to imagine electrical, mechanical and civil engineering without a central role for measurement. Indeed, science and engineering can be neither effective nor practical without measurement. But measurement has been considered a luxury in software engineering. For most development projects:

- We fail to set measurable targets for our software products. For example, we promise that the product will be user-friendly, reliable and maintainable without specifying clearly and objectively what these terms mean. As a result, when the project is complete, we cannot tell if we have met our goals. This situation has prompted Tom Gilb to state [Gilb 1988]:

> *Gilb's Principle of Fuzzy Targets: project without clear goals will not achieve their goals clearly.*

- We fail to understand and quantify the component costs of software projects. For example, most projects cannot differentiate the cost of design from the cost of coding or testing. Since excessive cost is a frequent complaint from many of our customers, we cannot hope to control costs if we are not measuring the relative components of cost.

- We do not quantify or predict the quality of the products we produce. Thus, we cannot tell a potential user how reliable a product will be in terms of likelihood of failure in a given period of use, or how much work will be needed to port the product to a different machine environment.

- We allow anecdotal evidence to convince us to try yet another revolutionary new development technology, without doing a carefully controlled study to determine if the technology is efficient and effective. Here are many examples or typical of promotional materials for automated software development tools and techniques.

  o "Our techniques guarantee 100% reliability"

  o "Our tool improves productivity by 200%"

  o "Build your code with half the staff in a quarter of the time"

  o "Cut your test time in half"

However, most of the time, these materials are not accompanied by reports detailing/offering scientific basis for the claims.

When measurements are made, they are often done infrequently, inconsistently, and incompletely. The incompleteness can be frustrating to those who want to make use of the results. For example, a developer may claim that 80% of all software costs involve maintenance, or that there are on average 55 faults in every 1000 lines of software code. But we are not always told how these results were obtained, how experiments were designed and executed, which entities were measured, and how and what were the realistic error margins. Without this additional information, we remain skeptical and unable to decide whether to apply the results to our own situations. In addition, we cannot do an objective study to repeat the measurements in our own environments. Thus, the lack of measurement in software engineering is compounded by the lack of a rigorous approach.

It is clear from other engineering disciplines that measurement can be effective, if not essential, in making characteristics and relationships more visible, in assessing the magnitude of problems, and in fashioning a solution to problems. As the pace of hardware innovation has increased, the software world has been tempted to relax or abandon its engineering underpinnings and hope for revolutionary gains. Now that software, playing a key role, involves enormous investment of energy and money, it is time for software engineering to embrace the engineering discipline that has been so successful in other areas.

2.2 Objectives for software measurement.

Even when a project is not in trouble, measurement is not only useful but also necessary. After all, how can you tell if your project is healthy if you have no measure of its health? So measurement is needed, at least for assessing the status of your projects, products, processes, and resources. Because we do not always know what derails a project, it is essential that we measure and record characteristics of good projects as well as bad. We need to document trends, the magnitude of corrective action, and the resulting changes. In other words, we must control our projects, not just run them. Tom DeMarco, a strong supporter of the need for measurement in software development, asserts that.

"You cannot control what you cannot measure" [DeMarco 1982].

There are compelling reasons to consider the measurement process scientifically, so that measurement will be a true engineering activity. Every measurement action must be motivated by a particular goal or need that is clearly defined and easily understandable. That is, it is not enough to assert that we must measure to gain control. The measurement objectives must be specific, tied to what the managers, developers and users need to know. Thus, these objectives may differ according to the kind of personnel involved and at which level of software development and use they are generated. Nevertheless, it is the goals that tell us how the measurement information will be used once it is collected.

Below are examples of the kinds of information needed to understand and control a software development project, separated by manager and developer perspectives:

2.2.1 Manager's perspectives:

- *What does each process cost?* We can measure the time and effort involved in the various processes that comprise software production. For example, we can identify the cost of eliciting requirements, the cost of specifying the system, the cost of designing the system, and the cost of coding and testing the system. In this way, we gain understanding not only of the total project cost but also of the contribution of each activity to the whole.

- *How productive is the staff?* We can measure the time it takes staff to specify the system, design it, code it, and test it. Then, using measures of the size of specifications, design, code, and test plans, for example, we can determine how productive the staff is at each activity. This information is useful when changes are proposed; the manager can use the productivity figures to estimate the cost and duration of the change.

- *How good is the code being developed?* By carefully recording faults, failures and changes as they occur, we can measure software quality, enabling us to compare different products, predict the effects of change, assess the effects of new practices, and set targets for process and product improvement.

- *Will the user be satisfied with the product?* We can measure functionality by determining if all of the requirements requested have actually been implemented properly. Moreover, we can measure usability, reliability, response time, and other characteristics to suggest whether our customers will be happy with both functionality and performance.

- *How can we improve?* We can measure the time it takes to perform each major development activity, and calculate its effect on quality and productivity. Then we can weigh the costs and benefits of each practice to determine if the benefit is worth the cost. Alternatively, we can try several variations of a practice and measure the results to decide which is best; for example, we can compare two design methods to see which one yields the highest-quality code.

2.2.2 Engineer's perspectives:

- *Are the requirements testable?* We can analyze each requirement to determine if its satisfaction is expressed in a measurable, objective way. For example, suppose a requirement states that a system must be reliable; the requirement can be replaced by one that states that "the mean time to failure must be greater than 15 elapsed hours of CPU time."

- *Have we found all the faults?* We can measure the number of faults in the specification, design, code, and test plans, and trace them back to their root causes. Using models of expected detection rates, this information can help us to decide whether inspections and testing have been effective and whether a product can be released for the next phase.

- *Have we met our product or process goals?* We can measure characteristics of the products and processes that tell us whether we have met standards, satisfied a requirement, or met a process goal. For example, certification may require that fewer than 20 failures have been reported per beta-test site over a given period of time. On the other hand, a standard may mandate that no module contain more than 100 lines of code. The testing process may require that unit testing must achieve 90% statement coverage.

- *What will happen in the future?* We can measure attributes of existing products and current processes to make predictions about future ones. For example, measures of size of specifications can be used to predict size of the target system, predictions about future maintenance problems can be made from measures of structural properties of the design documents, and predictions about the reliability of software in operational use can be made by measuring reliability during testing.

2.3 Measurement for understanding, control and improvement.

The lists above show us that measurement is important for three basic activities. First, there are measures that help us to *understand* what is happening during development and maintenance. We assess the current situation, establishing baselines that help us to set goals for future behavior. In this sense, the measurements make aspects of process and product more visible to us, giving us a better understanding of relationships among activities and the entities they affect.

Second, the measurement allows us to *control* what is happening on our projects. Using our baselines, goals and understanding of relationships, we predict what is likely to happen and make changes to processes and products that help us to meet our goals. For example, we may monitor the complexity of code modules, giving thorough review only to those that exceed acceptable bounds

Third, measurement encourages us to *improve* our processes and products. For instance, we may increase the number or type of design reviews we do, based on measures of specification quality and predictions of likely design quality.

No matter how measurements are used, it is important to manage the expectations of those who will make measurement-based decisions. Users of the data should always be aware of the limited accuracy of prediction and of the margin of error in the measurements. As with any other engineering discipline, there is room in software engineering for abuse and misuse of measurement. Management can pressure developers to produce precise measures with inadequate models, tools and techniques.

If you are expecting measurement to provide instant, easy solutions to your software engineering problems, be aware of our corollary to DeMarco's rule:

You can neither predict nor control what you cannot measure.

3. The Scope of Software Metrics

Software metrics is a term that embraces many activities, all of which involve some degree of software measurement:

- Cost and effort estimation

- Productivity measures and models

- Data collection

- Quality models and measures

- Reliability models

- Performance evaluation and models

- Structural and complexity metrics

- Capability-maturity assessment

- Management by metrics

- Evaluation of methods and tools

The following brief introduction will give you a sense of the techniques currently in use for each facet of measurement.

3.1 Cost and effort estimation.

Managers provided the original motivation for deriving and using software measures. They wanted to be able to predict project costs during early phases in the software life cycle. As a result, numerous models for software cost and effort estimation have been proposed and used. Examples include Boehm's COCOMO model [Boehm 1981], Boehm's COCOMO II model [Boehm 2000], Putnam's SLIM model [Putnam 1978] and Albrecht's function points model [Albrecht 1979]. These and other models often share a common approach: effort is expressed as a (pre-defined) function of one or more variables (such as size of the product, capability of the developers and level of reuse). Size is usually defined as (predicted) lines of code or number of function points (which may be derived from the product specification).

3.2 Productivity models and measures.

The pressing needs of management have also resulted in numerous attempts to define measures and models for assessing staff productivity during different software processes and in different environments.

Research efforts at RADC [1997] show productivity as a function of value and cost; each is then decomposed into other aspects, expressed in measurable form. The RADC model presents a significantly more comprehensive view of productivity than the traditional one, which simply divides size by effort. That is, many managers make decisions based on the rate at which lines of code are being written per person month of effort. This simpler measure can be misleading, if not dangerous [Jones 1986].

3.3 Data collection.

The quality of any measurement program is clearly dependent on careful data collection. However, collecting data is easier said than done, especially when data must be collected across a diverse set of projects. Thus, data collection is becoming a discipline in itself, where specialists work to ensure that measures are defined unambiguously, that collection is consistent and complete, and that data integrity is not at risk. Nevertheless, it is acknowledged that metrics data collection must be planned and executed in a careful and sensitive manner.

There are numerous examples of how the data collected can be distilled into simple charts and graphs that show managers the progress and problems of development. Basili and Weiss [1984] have described a general methodology for valid data collection, while Mellor [1992] describes the data collection necessary for reliability assessment.

Data collection is also essential for scientific investigation of relationships and trends. Good experiments, surveys, and case studies require carefully planned data collection, as well as thorough analysis and reporting of the results.

3.4 Quality models and measures.

Productivity cannot be viewed in isolation. Without an accompanying assessment of product quality, speed of production is meaningless. This observation has led software engineers to develop models of quality whose measurements can be combined with those of productivity models. For example, Boehm's advanced COCOMO cost-estimation model is tied to a quality model [Boehm et al. 1978], and similarly, the McCall quality model [McCall, Richards, & Walters 1977] commonly called the FCM (*Factor Criteria Metric)* model, is related to productivity.

These models are usually constructed in a tree-like fashion. The upper branches hold important high-level quality factors of software products, such as reliability and usability, which we would like to quantify. Each quality factor is composed of lower-level criteria, such as structuredness and traceability. The criteria are easier to understand and measure than the factors; thus, actual measures (metrics) are proposed for the criteria. The tree describes the pertinent relationships between factors and their dependent criteria, so we can measure the factors in terms of the dependent criteria measures. This notion of divide-and-conquer has been implemented as a standard approach to measuring software quality [ISO 9126].

3.5 Reliability models.

Most quality models include reliability as a component factor, but the need to predict and measure reliability itself has led to a separate specialization in reliability modeling and prediction. Littlewood [1989] and others provide a rigorous and successful example of how a focus on an important product quality attribute has led to increased understanding and control of our products.

3.6 Performance evaluation and models.

Performance is another aspect of quality. Work under the umbrella of performance evaluation includes externally observable system performance characteristics, such as response times and completion rates [Ferrari 1978]; [Ferrari, Serazzi, & Zeigner 1983] [Kleinrock 1975]. Performance specialists also investigate the internal workings of a system, including the efficiency of algorithms as embodied in computational and algorithmic complexity [Garey & Johnson 1979],

[Harel 1992]. The latter is also concerned with the inherent complexity of problems measured in terms of efficiency of an optimal solution.

3.7 Structural and complexity metrics.

Desirable quality attributes like reliability and maintainability cannot be measured until some operational version of the code is available. Yet we wish to be able to predict which parts of the software system are likely to be less reliable, more difficult to test, or require more maintenance than others, even before the system is complete. As a result, we measure structural attributes of representations of the software that are available in advance of (or without the need for) executions; then, we try to establish empirically predictive theories to support quality assurance, quality control, and quality prediction. Halstead [1977] and McCabe [1976] are two classic examples of this approach; each defines measures that are derived from suitable representations of source code.

3.8 Management by metrics.

Measurement is becoming an important part of software project management. Customers and developers alike rely on measurement-based charts and graphs to help them decide if the project is on track. Many companies and organizations define a standard set of measurements and reporting methods, so that projects can be compared and contrasted. This uniform collection and reporting is especially important when software plays a supporting role in the overall project.

That is, when software is embedded in a product whose main focus is a business area other than software, the customer or ultimate user is not usually well-versed in software terminology, so measurement can paint a picture of progress in general, understandable terms. For example, when a power plant asks a software developer to write control software, the customer usually knows a lot about power generation and control, but very little about programming languages, compilers or computer hardware. The measurements must be presented in a way that tells both customer and developer how the project is doing.

3.9 Evaluation of methods and tools.

Many articles and books describe new methods and tools that may make your organization or project more productive and your products better and cheaper. However, it is difficult to separate the claims from the reality. Many organizations perform experiments, run case studies or administer surveys to help them decide whether a method or tool is likely to make a positive difference in their particular situations. These investigations cannot be done without careful, controlled measurement and analysis. An evaluation's success depends on good experimental design, proper identification of the factors likely to affect the outcome, and appropriate measurement of factor attributes.

3.10 Capability maturity assessment.

In the 1980s, the U.S. Software Engineering Institute (SEI) proposed a capability maturity model [Humphrey 1989] to measure a contractor's ability to develop quality software for the US government. This model assessed many different attributes of development, including use of tools, standard practices and more. To use the first version of the model, called a *process maturity assessment,* a contractor answered over 100 questions designed to determine the contractor's actual practices. The resulting "grade" was reported as a five-level scale, from "1" *(ad hoc* development dependent on individuals) to "5" (a development process that could be optimized based on continuous feedback).

There were many problems with the first model, as described by Bollinger and McGowan [Bollinger & McGowan 1991] and the SEI has since revised its approach. The new model, called a *capability maturity assessment,* is based on key practices that every good contractor should be using. Other organizations, inspired by the SEI's goal, have developed other assessment models, in the hope that such evaluation will encourage improvement and enable organizations to compare and contrast candidate developers.

The notion of evaluating process maturity is very appealing.

4. Summary

This article has described how measurement pervades our everyday life. We have argued that measurement is essential for good engineering in other disciplines; it should likewise become an integral part of software engineering practice. In particular:

- The lessons of other engineering disciplines suggest that measurement must play a more significant role in software engineering.

- Software measurement is not a mainstream topic within software engineering. Rather it is a diverse collection of fringe topics (generally referred to as software metrics) that range from models for predicting software project costs at the specification stage to measures of program structure.

- Much software-metrics work has lacked the rigor associated with measurement in other engineering disciplines.

- General reasons for needing software-engineering measurement are not enough. Engineers must have specific, clearly stated objectives for measurement.

- We must be bold in our attempts at measurement. Just because no one has measured some attribute of interest does not mean that it cannot be measured satisfactorily.

- This rigorous basis will enable us to implement a scientific and effective approach to constructing, calculating and appropriately applying the metrics that we derive.

References

Additional information on the *software measurements* KA can be found in the following documents.

- [Albrecht 1979] A.J. Albrecht, "Measuring application development," Proceedings of IBM Applications Development Joint SHARE/GUIDE Symposium, Monterey, CA, pp. 83-92, 1979.

- [Basili & Weiss 1984] V.R. Basili, and D. Weiss, "A methodology for collecting valid software engineering data," *IEEE Transactions on Software Engineering*, SE-10(6), pp. 728-38, 1984.

- [Boehm et al. 2000] Barry W. Boehm, Chris Abts, A. Winsor Brown, Sunita Chulani, Bradford K. Clark, Ellis Horowitz, Ray Madachy, Donald J. Reifer, Bert Steece, *Software Cost Estimation with COCOMO II*. Addison-Wesley, Boston, MA, 2000.

- [Boehm 1981] B.W. Boehm, *Software Engineering Economics*, Prentice Hall, Englewood Cliffs, NJ, 1981.

- [Boehm 1978] B.W. Boehm, J.R. Brown, H. Kaspar, M. Lipow, G. McLeod, and M. Merritt, North Holland, *Characteristics of Software Quality, TRW Series of Software Technology*, Amsterdam, North Holland, 1978.

- [Bollinger & McGowan 1991] T.B Bollinger and C. McGowan, "A critical look at software capability evaluations," *IEEE Software*, 8(4), pp. 25-41, July 1991.

- [DeMarco 1982] T. DeMarco, *Controlling Software Projects*, Yourdon Press, New York, 1982.

- [Fenton & Pfleeger 1997] N. E. Fenton and S. L. Pfleeger, *Software Metrics: A Rigorous & Practical Approach*, 2nd Edition, PWS Publishing Company, London, 1997.

- [Ferrari 1978] D. Ferrari, *Computer System Performance Evaluation*, Prentice Hall, Englewood Cliffs, NJ, 1978.

- [Ferrari, Serazzi, & Zeigner 1983] D. Ferrari, G. Serazzi and A. Zeigner, *Measurement and Tuning of Computer Systems*, Prentice Hall, New York, 1983.

- [Garey & Johnson 1979] M.R. Garey and D.S. Johnson, *Computers and Intractability*, W.H. Freeman, San Francisco, CA, 1979.

- [Gilb 1988] T. Gilb, *Principles of Software Engineering Management*, Addison-Wesley, Reading MA, 1988.

- [Halstead 1977] M. Halstead, *Elements of Software Science*, Elsevier, N. Holland, 1977.

- [Harel 1992] D. Harel, *Algorithmics*, 2nd ed., Addison-Wesley, Reading, MA, 1992.

- [Humphrey 1989] W.S. Humphrey, *Managing the Software Process*, Addison-Wesley, Reading, MA, 1989.

- [ISO 9126] Software Engineering—Product Quality, International Organization for Standardization, 2001.

- [Jones 1986] C. Jones, *Programmer Productivity*, McGraw-Hill, New York, 1986.

- [Kleinrock 1975] L. Kleinrock, *Queuing Systems, Volume 1: Theory,* and *Volume 2: Computer Applications*, Wiley, New York, 1975.

- [Littlewood 1989] B. Littlewood, "Predicting software reliability," *Philosophical Transactions of the Royal Society of London*, A 327, pp. 513-27,1989.

- [McCabe 1976] T. McCabe, "A software complexity measure," *IEEE Transactions on Software Engineering*, SE-2(4), pp. 308-20, 1976.

- [McCall, Richards, & Walters 1977] J.A. McCall, P.K. Richards, and G.F. Walters, "Factors in Software Quality," *RADC TR-77-369*, 1977, Vols I, II, III, US Rome Air Development Center Reports NTIS AD/A-049 014, 015,055, 1977.

- [Mellor 1992] P. Mellor, "Failures, faults and changes in dependability measurement," *Information and Software Technology*, 34(10), pp. 640-54, 1992.

- [Putnam 1978] L.H. Putnam, "A general empirical solution to the macrosoftware sizing and estimating problem," *IEEE Transactions on Software Engineering*, SE-4(4), pp. 345-61, 1978.

- [RADC 1977] *RADC TR-77-369*, 1977, Vols I, II, III, US Rome Air Development Center Reports NTIS AD/A-049 014, 015, 055, 1977.

Chapter 12.2

Essentials of Measurements and Metrics

Richard Hall Thayer and Merlin Dorfman

This is the twelfth chapter of a textbook to aid individual software engineers in a greater understanding of the IEEE SWEBOK [2013] and a guide book to aid software engineers in passing the IEEE CSDP and CSDA certification exams.

This module presents a discussion of software measurements (a.k.a. software metrics). (An important note: Sometimes metric and measurement are used interchangeably. However, the best usage is that of measure for direct measure and metric for indirect measure.)

This chapter starts with the software engineering exam specification for the module on Software Engineering Measurement and Metrics Foundations. This list of exam specifications is reported to be the same list that the exam writers used to write the exam questions. Therefore it is the best source of help for the exam takers.

Note that this Measurement and Metrics Foundation exam specification was originally part of the Software Engineering Management exam specification module. The authors (Thayer & Dorfman) reasoned that the concept of measurement and metrics was universal to all software engineering knowledge areas and it was more accurately portrayed as universal to software engineering. Therefore, the measurement and metrics description was made part of a newly created Measurement and Metrics Foundation module. This change does not impact the reader's preparation for the CSDP exam. It does, however, clarify the study of software engineering in a university environment.

One of the IEEE standards involving software measurements is IEEE Standard 1061-1998, IEEE Standard for Software Quality Metrics. This standard provides a process to analyze the metrics primarily involved with productivity.

Key terms for software measures and measurement methods have been defined in *ISO Standard 15939, Systems and Software Engineering— Measurement Process* [ISO15939:2007], and in *Practical Software Measurement (PSM): A Foundation for Objective Project Management* [1998].

Note: The PSM is a large U.S. Government report by representatives of dozens of government agencies, government contractors, and experts in the field of measurements. This group is still active and has a users' group conference annually. Nevertheless, readers will encounter terminology differences in the literature; for example, the term "metrics" is sometimes incorrectly used in place of "measurements", but is technically different from measurement.

This article generally follows the PSM outline, which describes a process that defines the activities and tasks necessary to implement a software measurement process, and includes, as well, a measurement information model. Note that the PSM assumes an "acquirer-developer" model, in which a government "program office" manages the project while the actual development is done by a different organization. This chapter follows that terminology; the principles and conclusions are equally valid for situations where the developing and using organizations are the same.

Another good reference for this software maintenance chapter is Fenton's and Pfleeger's book, *Software Metrics: A Rigorous & Practical Approach* [1997]. This book is considered one of the primary measurement and metrics references in the United States and around the world. Norm Fenton is a leading researcher of measurements in the United Kingdom and Shari Lawrence Pfleeger is a leading specialist in the area of software engineering metrics in the U.S.

In this module, we introduce the following concepts and applications of measurement and metric activities in software engineering:

1. Managing a measurement program

2. Software measurement principles

3. Objectives of a software engineering measurement program

4. Fundamentals of measurement and metrics

5. Tailoring software measures

6. Applying software measurements

7. Implementing a measurement process

8. Reporting measurement status

12.1 Managing a Measurement Program

The importance of measurement and its role in better management practices is widely acknowledged, so its importance can only increase in the coming years. Effective measurement has become one of the cornerstones of organizational maturity [PSM 2001, pp. 8-9].

Measurement is most important at the project level. Software measurement helps the project manager do a better job. It helps:

- To define and implement more realistic project management plans

- To properly allocate scarce resources to put those plans into place

- To accurately monitor progress and performance against those plans

Software measurement provides the information required to make key project decisions and to take appropriate action. Measurement helps to relate and integrate the information derived from other project and technical management disciplines. In effect, it allows the software project manager to make decisions using objective information.

Specifically, software measurement provides objective information to help the project manager do the following [PSM 2001]:

- ***Communicate effectively*** — Measurement provides objective information throughout the software organization. This reduces the ambiguity that often surrounds complex and constrained software projects. Measurement helps managers to identify, prioritize, track, and communicate objectives and associated issues at all levels within the organization. It also is important to communicate between supplier and acquirer organizations.

- ***Track specific project objectives*** — Measurement can accurately describe the status of software project processes and products. It is key to objectively represent the progress of project activities and the quality of associated software products across the project life cycle. Measurement helps to answer crucial questions such as: "Is the project on schedule?" and "Is the software ready to be delivered to the user?"

- ***Identify and correct problems early*** — Measurement facilitates a proactive management strategy. Potential problems are objectively identified as risks to be assessed and managed. Existing problems can be better evaluated and prioritized. Measurement fosters the early discovery and correction of technical and management problems that can be more difficult and costly to resolve later. Managers use measurement as a resource to anticipate problems and to avoid being forced into a reactive, fix-on-fail approach.

- ***Make key trade-off decisions*** — Every software project is subject to constraints. Cost, schedule, capability, technical quality, and performance must be traded off against each other as well as managed together to meet established project objectives. Decisions in one area usually impact other areas, even if they seem unrelated. Measurement helps the decision maker to assess these impacts objectively and make informed trade-offs to best meet project objectives and to optimize software project and product performance.

- ***Justify decisions*** —The current software and information technology business environments demand successful project performance. Business, technical, and project managers must be able to defend the basis of their estimates and plans with historical performance data. Then, they must be able to justify changes to plans with current performance data. Measurement provides an effective rationale for selecting the best alternatives.

Just like any management or technical tool, measurement cannot guarantee that a project will be successful. However, it does help the decision maker take a proactive approach in dealing with the critical issues inherent in software-intensive projects. Measurement helps the project and consequently the organization to succeed.

12.2 Software Measurement Principles

Each project is described by different management and technical characteristics, and by a specific set of software issues and objectives. To address the unique measurement requirements of each project, PSM explains how to tailor and apply a generally defined software measurement process to meet specific project information needs. To help do this, PSM defines nine principles that describe the characteristics of an effective measurement process [PSM 2001, pp. 12-18].

The nine PSM software measurement principles are:

1. Program issues and objectives drive the measurement requirement

2. The developer's software process defines how the software is actually measured

3. Collect and analyze data at a level of detail sufficient to identify and isolate software problems

4. Implement an independent analysis capability

5. Use a systematic analysis process to trace the measures to the decisions

6. Interpret the measurement results in the context of other project information

7. Integrate software measurement into the project management process throughout the software life cycle

8. Use the measurement process as a basis for objective communication

9. Focus initially on project-level analysis

The following subsections discuss each of the nine principles. Experience has shown that a measurement process that adheres to these principles is more likely to succeed [PSM 2001, pp. 13-18].

12.2.1 Program issues and objectives. *Program issues and objectives drive the measurement requirements.* The purpose of software measurement is to help management achieve project *objectives* by identifying, tracking, and managing actual problems and potential obstacles to success. Project objectives are goals and requirements usually expressed in terms of functionality, cost, schedule, and quality. *Issues* are areas of concern that present obstacles to achieving project objectives. Issues include problems, risks, and the lack of information.

PSM emphasizes identifying project issues at the start of a project and then using the measurement process to provide insight into those issues throughout the project. Conducting a thorough risk analysis at the beginning of a project facilitates the initial identification and prioritization of issues. However, even if a formal risk analysis has not been performed, issues still can be identified. Note that not all risks or issues are quantifiable, nor are all risks covered by PSM.

While some issues are common to most projects, each project typically has some unique issues. Moreover, the priority of the issues usually varies from project to project. Most project-specific software issues fall into one of six classes of common software issues, as follows:

1. Schedule and progress

2. Resources and cost

3. Growth and stability

4. Product quality

5. Development performance

6. Technical adequacy

Focusing measurement attention on items that provide information about the project's issues minimizes the effort required for the measurement process. Resources are not expended on collecting data that may not be used.

12.2.2 Developer's software process. The developer's software process defines how the software is actually measured. The definition of a measurement process cannot be based solely on the objectives of the acquisition project manager. To collect measurement data in the most cost effective and useful manner, the software process of the developer and the management process of the acquirer must both be considered. Project issues identify the information that the measurement process must derive from the data. The developer's software process determines what specific data items are to be collected and how that can be accomplished.

Since one of the purposes of the measurement process is to provide insight into the performance of the developer, the measures that are collected must objectively represent the activities and products of the developer's software process. Measures that are normally collected by the software developer should be selected, if they are applicable. Measurement selection should also consider the software processes employed by any subcontractors.

12.2.3 Level of data collection and analysis. *Collect and analyze data at a level of detail sufficient to identify and isolate software problems.* The measurement process defined in PSM depends on the periodic collection, processing, and analysis of measurement data rather than on the review of pre-packaged analysis reports. This data includes plans, changes to plans, and counts of actual software activities, products, and expenditures. The acquisition project office should receive data from the developer at a low enough level of detail to allow for the isolation of problems by software components and activities. The software unit levels, as defined by the software component structure, and the software activity level, as defined by the work breakdown structure, are the levels of detail most commonly used.

12.2.4 Independent analysis capability. *Implement an independent analysis capability.* It is recommended that both the acquirer and the developer establish and maintain an independent measurement capability. This principle is motivated by the recognition that objective communication can only occur when both parties have achieved an understanding of the data under discussion. The ideal situation involves an independent measurement organization in the acquisition project office that regularly receives raw data from the developer, analyzes it, and presents the results to the project manager. Alternatively, the independent analysis function may be provided by an independent verification and validation (IV&V) organization, an engineering and management support contractor, or another third party organization independent of the developer.

The need for an independent analysis capability is applicable in both the government and commercial sectors. Each organization within a project team, especially the developer and the acquirer, generally has similar, but uniquely prioritized issues. An independent analysis capability allows each organization to focus its evaluation efforts on specific areas of concern. In some project organizations with effective and disciplined integrated project teams, measurement analysis responsibility can be assigned to a single project organization. In practice, however, these project organizations are rare. Best measurement practice dictates that an independent analysis capability be established for each organization.

12.2.5 Systematic analysis process. *Use a systematic analysis process to trace the measures to the decisions.* Measurement-based conclusions and recommendations must be generated in a systematic manner to be accepted as a basis for management decisions and subsequent action. Key concerns of management about such information are its traceability and repeatability. Traceability means that the conclusions and recommendations are generated from measurement data in a defined sequence of steps. Repeatability means that different analysts following the same sequence of steps are likely to arrive at the same conclusions and recommendations. An ad-hoc analysis approach does not provide management with the confidence necessary to act on measurement information.

PSM addresses three types of analysis. At the start of a project, or when major changes are implemented, *estimates* are developed as the basis for planning. The plans are then analyzed in terms of their *feasibility*. For example, the project manager may ask questions such as: "Is this a reasonably sized estimate?" or, "Can the software be completed with the proposed amount of effort and meet the delivery date?" Once the project is underway, the manager's concern turns to *performance*. The key questions focus on tracking against plans and may include: "Is the project on schedule?" or, "Are we developing a quality product?"

12.2.6 Project context. *Interpret the measurement results in the context of other project information.* Measurement provides an indication or warning that a problem may exist. No measurement result by itself is good or bad. For example, assume that the number of software unit designs completed to date is lower than planned. This situation might occur because the project is not fully staffed, yet while there is still time to add staff and recover. It might occur while the project is fully staffed because the developer's productivity is much lower than planned. The variance between planned and actual values indicates only that the project manager should pay attention to this issue *now*. Additional information must be collected to evaluate the cause and severity of the situation to assess its probable impact on project success.

12.2.7 Life-cycle integration. *Integrate software measurement into the project management process throughout the software life cycle.* The issue-driven software measurement approach described in PSM applies throughout the software life cycle. For purposes of this document, three major life-cycle phases are defined: project planning, development, and sustaining engineering. Four principal software activities occur within the development and sustaining engineering phases. These are requirements analysis, design, implementation, and integration and test. Measurement results must be provided periodically and at appropriate decision points throughout the life cycle.

Decisions made in one project phase or activity affect the results of other project phases and activities. Consequently, it is important to adopt a life-cycle perspective when implementing a measurement process. Over the course of the software life cycle, the issues of concern to the project managers may change. The measures used to monitor those issues should change accordingly. The basic measurement principles, however, still apply.

12.2.8 Objective communication. *Use the measurement process as a basis for objective communication.* Measurement activities cannot be conducted by either the development or acquisition organization in isolation. At each step of defining the measurement requirements and analyzing the measurement data, the project manager must communicate with the entire software project team. Most decisions that are based on the data will affect more than one party. A corrective action that is identified and planned in cooperation with the developer is more likely to succeed than one that appears to be arbitrarily imposed by the acquisition project manager.

While there may be some differences between the issues of concern to the software acquirer and the software developer, there should also be a high degree of commonality. The concept of integrated product and process development (IPPD) and the functioning of an integrated product team (IPT) depend on frequent and objective communication about technical and management issues among all team members. Measurement provides an effective vehicle for this.

It is important to ensure that all parties use the same data and have a common understanding of the data definitions, to know what the data represents. Most data comes from the developer; therefore, the burden falls primarily on the acquirer to understand the developer's software process and measurement data.

12.2.9 Project-level analysis. *Focus initially on project-level analysis.* Project success means meeting specific project objectives. While the larger organization of which the project is a part may have concerns and objectives that span multiple projects. The PSM guide [PSM 2001] stresses the need to measure and understand individual projects before attempting to make cross-project comparisons. Nevertheless, at several points in the measurement process, the analyst will need to refer to normative data and simple models based on the results derived from a large number of projects.

12.3 Objectives of a Software Engineering Measurement Program

Most projects begin with *objectives*. These objectives are typically defined in terms of budgets allocated, scheduled delivery milestones, required quality levels, business or mission performance targets, or overall system capability. Project success is based on achieving the defined objectives [PSM 2001, pp. 76-78].

The following paragraphs discuss some objectives for selecting and using the proper measurement for either an individual or a corporate project [Fenton & Pfleeger 1997, p. 13]:

- Managers and software engineers should *first* incorporate measurements into decision-making and process measurement in order to efficiently manage and control a software project. A predictive measurement approach to cost and schedule often amounts to guesswork, including inaccurate speculation. Journals continuously document project accounts that have missed their management estimate by 100% or 200%. The State of California missed several estimates by tens of millions of dollars [Neumann 1993].

- *Second*, software measurements provide managers and software engineers with insight into potential development or system problems. Without this insight, the manager will be forced to react to events as they occur. For example, when measuring the density of errors, he or she will see that as the error density percentages rise, problems increase. The time to address this problem is the present and not when the system is delivered. Otherwise, the system will probably never operate to everybody's satisfaction.

Below are examples of the kinds of information needed to understand and control a software development project, looking first at the perspectives of the manager and second at the perspectives of the software engineer [Fenton & Pfleeger 1977, pp. 12-13].

- From Managers
  - What is the total process cost?
  - How productive is the technical staff?
  - How effective/complete is the code being developed?
  - Will the end-user be satisfied with the product?
  - How can the management team reduce the cost or improve the product?
- From Engineers
  - What percent of requirements are untestable?
  - How many faults have been identified?
  - Have product or process goals been met?

12.4 Fundamentals of Measurements and Metrics

The fundamentals of measurements involve:

- Definitions of measurement
- Measurement scales
- Measurement classifications
- Goal-Question-Metric (GQM) paradigm

12.4.1 Definitions. Some measurement definitions are:

- *Measurement* — The process by which numbers or symbols are assigned (mapped) to entities of a given set in such a way as to describe an attribute of these entities.

- *Measure* — The number or symbol assigned to an entity by this mapping in order to characterize an attribute [Fenton & Pfleeger 1997].

- *Metric* — A quantitative measure of the degree to which a system, component, or process possesses a given attribute [IEEE Standard 610.12-1990].

12.4.2 Measurement scales. The following is a hierarchy of measurement beginning with *nominal* or *categorizing measurement*, then ordered from the simplest type of measurement to the most complex [Fenton and Pfleeger 1997, pp. 46-53].

- A *nominal* measurement is a simple categorization. This basic measurement deals with the assignment of a number or a symbol such as a letter assigned to a category; for example, the assignment of a country to a citizen of the world, e.g., American, English, Scottish, German, and so forth. There is no ranking implied, which is to say that Americans are not preferable to Englishmen.

- An *ordinal* measurement reflects a categorization accompanied by ranking. For example, Sears used to rank its appliances as *good, better*, and *best*.

- An *interval* measurement implies a fixed interval between numbers or symbols. One example is the assignment of a determined size to a person. A six-foot tall man is two inches taller than a 5 foot-10-inch man.

- A *ratio* measurement implies a measurement with a defined starting point. A basketball team can win with a score that is 50% better than its opponent because both teams started with a zero score.

- Lastly, an *absolute* measurement is the assignment of a measure to an artifact, normally in the form of counting. There are 55 persons in the classroom.

The above five measurements are ordered from simplest (lower level) to most complex (higher level). Each higher level scale possesses the properties of the lower. A higher-level scale can be reduced to a lower level.

12.4.3 Software engineering measurements classifications. While the application of measurement to software engineering can be complex, particularly in terms of modeling and analysis methods, there are several aspects of software engineering measurement that are fundamental and that underlie many of the more advanced measurement and analysis processes.

The following paragraphs list several generally accepted classifications of metrics. They are presented in pairs, such as direct and indirect, project and process, quality and quantity, and reflective and predictive. Sometimes *metric* and *measurement* are used interchangeably. However, the most common use is that of *measure* for direct measure and *metric* for indirect measure.

A direct metric is the mapping of a real world entity to a measurement, for example:

- Length of a program module in source lines of code (SLOC)

- Number of defects discovered during peer reviews

- Labor hours used on a specific job control number

An indirect measurement (a.k.a. a *calculated measurement* or *metric*) is calculated from two or more direct measurements. For example:

- Programmer productivity = SLOC/effort spent per month

- Module defect density = number of defects/module size

- Requirements growth = total number of requirements minus initial number divided by initial number of requirements

A process metric supports the software development process. These metrics provide information supporting the visibility of progress, i.e., how many additional months or years are required to complete the project/process? *Product metric* relates to amount, size, or volume. For example, the estimated number of lines of code contained in a software product, the number of pages of requirements specifications, the number of change requests received from internal engineering or a customer, and the number of errors in a configuration item. *Quality metric* provides a quantitative measure of software quality. For example, reliability is a quality metric. The expected *time to repair* a fault is a quality metric. Usability is also a quality metric, although measuring usability is subject to disagreements among technical persons. Another example of a quality metric is the number of errors per thousand lines of code (the indirect measurement of error density).

The opposite of quality metric is *quantity* metrics. *Quantity metrics* provide quantifiable measurements relating to specific aspects of software development. Total project size, estimated system cost, and number of change requests received are examples of quantity metrics.

The last two metrics carry the unusual names of *predictive and reflective metrics. Predictive metrics* look to the future. They are necessary for managers to ensure the project reaches cost and schedule goals. For example, what is the expected size of a system once it is finished? How many modules will it contain? How many lines of code will be written? What is the expected system cost? What is the expected delivery date of the system?

Reflective metrics measure specific project aspects once the development process is complete. For example, how many software engineering developers, engineers, and programmers worked on the project? How many designed, coded, and tested units were delivered?

All of these metrics are essential to the management of a software engineering project.

12.4.4 Goal-Question-Metrics paradigm. It has been pointed out that management often collects measurement data without a clear understanding of how it will be used to improve management or engineering activities. The Goal-Question-Metric paradigm (GQM) is one of the best-known methods of selecting software measurements and metrics that will be useful. GQM is an approach to software metrics that has been promoted by Victor Basili of the University of Maryland, College Park and the Software Engineering Laboratory at the NASA Goddard Space Flight Center. The GQM concept was developed by Dr. David M. Weiss as a PhD dissertation under the supervision of Dr. Victor Basili. Dr. Weiss's work was inspired by the work of Albert Endres at IBM Germany [http://en.wikipedia.org/wiki/GQM].

GQM defines a measurement model on three levels [http://en.wikipedia.org/wiki/GQM]:

- ***Conceptual level (goal)*** — A *goal* is defined for an object for a variety of reasons, with respect to various models of quality, from various points of view and relative to a particular environment.

- *Operational level (question)* — A set of questions is used to define models of the object of study and then focuses on that object to characterize the assessment or achievement of a specific goal.

- *Quantitative level (metric)* — A set of metrics, based on the models, is associated with every question in order to answer it in a measurable way.

The literature typically describes GQM in terms of a six-step process where the first three steps are about using business goals to drive the identification of the right metrics and the last three steps are about gathering the measurement data and making effective use of the measurement results to drive decision making and improvements. Basili described his six-step GQM process as follows:

1. Develop a set of corporate, division and project business goals and associated measurement goals for productivity and quality.

2. Generate questions (based on models) that define those goals as completely as possible in a quantifiable way.

3. Specify the measures needed to be collected to answer those questions and track process and product conformance to the goals.

4. Develop mechanisms for data collection.

5. Collect, validate and analyze the data in real time to provide feedback to projects for corrective action.

6. Analyze the data in a post mortem fashion to assess conformance to the goals and to make recommendations for future improvements.

12.4.5 USAF software metrics policy. On 16 February 1994, the US Air Force adopted Policy 93M-017. The policy mandates that size, effort, schedule, software quality, and rework be measured for all software intensive systems (20,000 SLOC or greater). The specific metrics to be collected shall be decided upon by the managers. It is strongly encouraged that all managers of software systems, regardless of size, collect metrics throughout the entire system life cycle. The following core metrics are mandatory [ftp://ftp.cs.tut.fi /pub/tut /object /metrics.txt]:

- Size

- Effort (staff)

- Schedule

- Software quality

- Rework

These metrics were developed primarily for the U.S. Department of Defense for the monitoring of software suppliers.

12.5 Tailoring Software Measures

As described in Part 1 of the *PSM Guide* [2001], PSM provides a systematic method for identifying project issues, selecting and specifying measures, and integrating them into the developer's software process. The objective of the measurement tailoring process is to define the measures that provide the greatest insight into project issues at the lowest cost. The PSM tailoring approach focuses effort and resources on getting the most important project information first.

Project objectives and issues drive the entire measurement process. Issues are real or potential obstacles to the achievement of project objectives. The PSM tailoring process begins with identifying and prioritizing project-specific issues. Issues are derived from project-context information, management experience, and risk assessment results. Priorities are assigned to each issue to establish its relative importance as a factor in selecting appropriate measures.

The second tailoring activity is selecting appropriate measures to address the project-specific issues. The selection activity employs a PSM-defined framework that maps common software issues to measurement categories to measures. Detailed tables in Part 3 of the *PSM Guide* [PSM 2001] provide criteria for making these selections. These selections result in measurement data requirements that can be incorporated into a Request for Proposal. These initial data requirements are refined in the final tailoring activity based on the developer's process.

The final tailoring activity is integrating the measures into the developer's software process. The suitability of the selected measures in the context of the developer's software process and the overall technical approach must be considered. Measurement requirements should not be used to change the developer's software process, but to gain insight into it. When implementing measurement on an existing project, special consideration should be given to existing data sources and ongoing measurement activities.

The results of the tailoring process are documented in a project measurement plan. The plan may be formal or informal, depending on the nature of the project and the relationship between the developer and the project office. The developer's proposed measurement approach may also be a factor in source selection.

The tailoring process is iterative. New issues may be discovered or refinements may be proposed in the course of examining the developer's process. Alternative measures may be proposed to satisfy the project office's information needs while minimizing cost. Tailoring may also occur after the initial software measurement plan has been developed. New issues and new opportunities for measurement may be discovered as the project matures. Previously identified issues may decrease in importance.

The PSM tailoring guidance focuses on selecting the "best" measures to address the identified software issues. Each measure is initially aligned with a single issue to help simplify the selection process. However, most measures actually are used in conjunction with others to provide insight into a wide set of project issues.

12.6 Applying Software Measurements

This paragraph shows how the measurement plan that results from the tailoring process, described earlier, is applied during the project planning, development, and sustaining engineering phases of the project life cycle [PSM 2001, pp. 40-42]. We continue to discuss the collection of the data, generation of measurement indicators and reports, analysis of results, and the use of measurement information to support project management decisions and actions. Management support and participation throughout these activities are essential to the success of the measurement process.

These are the major activities by which data is collected and converted into the information that provides a basis for action by the project manager. During measurement application, the specified measures are collected and analyzed to provide the feedback on the issues needed for effective decision-making. Risk and financial status must also be considered during decision-making. During this process, questions may be raised and new issues may be identified, causing the process to iterate.

12.6.1 Collect and process data. Collecting and understanding measurement data is the first activity in analyzing project issues. Getting good data is the foundation of any measurement process. Almost all data originates with the software developer, including planned, actual, and historical data. As explained earlier, the data collected should reflect the nature of the software product and the developer's software process. Be sure to include all contractors and subcontractors in the data collection effort. The key tasks in collecting and processing data are accessing the data, verifying the data, and normalizing the data.

12.6.2 Access data. Software data comes from many sources. The project's software development plan, status reports, and engineering databases are primary sources. The software development plan typically contains the budgets and schedules against which progress and expenditures will be compared. Data must be collected from both initial plans and later replans, including incremental changes to plans. As the project evolves, the corresponding actual data on problems, progress, size, and effort will become available.

The developer may collect data more frequently than it is reported to the acquirer. The most common reporting intervals are monthly for requirements analysis, design, and implementation, and weekly for integration and test activities. Integration and test data is typically reported more frequently because the analysis period is relatively short. When developing the data delivery schedule, remember to allow adequate time for analysis between data delivery and reporting. The lag between data analysis and reporting should be as short as possible.

One approach that helps to assure timely provision of detailed data is to provide the acquisition project office with on-line access to the developer's software engineering databases that contain the necessary information. For most projects, data will be reported using a combination of electronic, on-line, and hard-copy methods.

12.6.3 Verify data. Getting useful measurement results depends on getting good data for the analysis and reporting process. Data verification must consider the accuracy of the data as it is recorded, as well as the fidelity with which it is transmitted. Data verification is complicated because some of the assumptions underlying the measurement process can change during the project. Aggregation structure of product components, processes, and even definitions of measures may be updated as the project evolves. Sometimes, estimates and actuals are measured differently. Consider these possibilities during the data-verification task.

Even valid software engineering data is likely to be "noisy." Software engineering is a human-intensive activity; things seldom go exactly as planned. Because performance varies from week to week, be wary of "actual" data that exactly matches the "plan."

12.6.4 Normalize data. During analysis, it may be necessary to combine or compare measurement data from different activities or from software components with different characteristics, such as language type. In order to combine or compare data, the data must be "normalized." Normalizing measurement requires defining conversion rules or models. For example, to compare the productivity of different developers, it may be necessary to use a model that takes into account the effect of project schedule and size on productivity. Normalization has to be performed carefully. Any rules or models used must be documented and validated with historical data.

Not all of the data needs to be reported to the project manager at the detailed level at which it is received. Consequently, it is often necessary to combine raw data from low-level components into higher levels. Aggregating data requires defining the relationships among the measured objects based on defined attributes. For effective communication to occur, both the developer and project manager must understand and use the same aggregation and normalization rules.

The data collection and processing activity is actually where insight into the project issues begins. The availability, consistency, validity, and overall quality of the measured data provide information that helps to initiate analysis.

12.6.5 Analyze issues. During the analysis activity, measurement indicators are generated from the data collected in the data collection activity as part of a systematic analysis process. This process results in quantifying the project status relative to the *known issues,* calculating estimates to complete analyses, and assessing risk exposure. This analysis is based on both measurement and project-context information. Measurement results cannot usually stand alone. Only the integration of quantitative and qualitative data produces true project insight. The results of the analysis are the basis for identifying *new issues* and taking corrective action with respect to known issues.

The measurement process must be able to respond quickly to the information needs of project managers. Typical questions asked by project managers include the following:

- Can I trust the data?

- Is there really a problem?

- How big is the problem?

- What is the scope of the problem?

- What is causing the problem?

- Are there related problems?

- What should I expect to happen?

- What are my alternatives?

- What is the recommended course of action?

- When can I expect to see the results?

The measurement process should generate the answers to these questions.

The *credibility* and *completeness* of the analysis process are enhanced when the analysis follows a *repeatable* process. Analysis results are more likely to be *useful* and the project manager will have a higher degree of *confidence* in them. PSM [2001] presents the analysis activity from three perspectives: 1) a model of relationships between issues that helps to guide the analysis, 2) measured indicators used to present measurement information about issues for analysis, and 3) the types of analyses conducted. The three types of analyses include estimation, feasibility, and performance.

12.7 Implementing a Measurement Process

Previously we described the software measurement process, including tailoring and applying software measures to address specific project issues. A well-defined measurement process is of little value if it is not properly implemented within the organization. We discuss how to do this, and describe four key measurement implementation activities. We also address how measurement information can be used to support overall organizational requirements [PSM 2001, pp. 53-61].

12.7.1 Measurement implementation overview. Implementing a measurement process within an organization is similar to implementing any new initiative or function. Measurement represents a significant change in how an organization does business, and the issues and concerns related to this change must be directly addressed.

There are four key activities that must take place to effectively introduce software measurement into an organization (see Figure 1). They are as follows:

1. ***Obtain organizational support*** — The objective of this activity is to generate support for software measurement at all levels within the organization. Management-mandated measurement without organizational buy-in and multilevel support will seldom succeed. Members of the organization at all levels need to understand how measurement will directly benefit their projects and their own work processes.

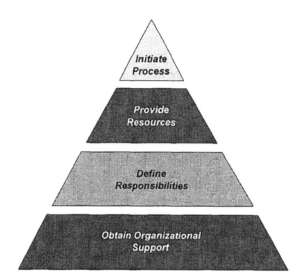

Figure 1: Measurement Implementation Activities

2. ***Define measurement responsibilities*** — During this activity, measurement-related responsibilities within the organization are established and assigned. The key positions generally responsible for software measurement include the organizational and project managers, the measurement analyst or analysis team, and other members of the technical and management staff who are involved with software acquisition and development activities. Clear definitions of who is responsible for what parts of the measurement process are important to successful implementation.

3. ***Provide measurement resources*** — During this activity, the measurement resources required to implement the measurement process within the organization are established. These resources include tools and funding for the measurement effort.

4. ***Initiate the measurement process*** — During this activity, the focus transitions from *establishing* the measurement process to actually *applying* it within the context of a software project.

The following sections explain these activities in more detail.

12.7.2 Obtain organizational support. *Implementing measurement* in an organization often requires a major cultural change. Fear generally exists that the measurement results will be used improperly to evaluate individual performance or to arbitrarily rank development organizations. There may be concern that measurement will highlight problems in a project or in organizations that were not visible before the measurement process was implemented. For example, the measurement analysis may show that the software development plan was unrealistic, or that only a portion of the software functionality will actually be delivered. These concerns are real, and to overcome them requires an understanding of measurement, as well as how to use the measurement results properly at all levels within the organization.

Management support is critical to successfully implement a measurement process. This support goes beyond the senior managers saying that software measurement is "a good idea." Management must take an active and visible interest in the measurement process. Senior managers must be perceived as supporting the process by providing adequate resources, asking for data and analyses, and acting on these analyses. The entire organization will then understand that measurement is important, and begin to actively support it as well. A measurement process requires enthusiastic leadership at the highest levels of the organization to make it work.

Many managers first learn about software measurement when some significant software "event" brings into question the way a project or organization is being managed. Others learn about it as a result of a policy directive or initiative. Few managers are first introduced to software measurement as an effective project management process that can help to achieve project and organizational objectives. In many cases, management views measurement as "another thing to do" and as something that will require resources that are already committed. The benefits of measurement to the organization should be clearly identified.

In addition to management support, measurement has to be adopted and supported at lower levels in the organization. Most people want to do a good job, and measurement can help them to do this. Evaluating acquisition alternatives, assessing the feasibility of proposed software plans, and identifying the key areas of technical concern are all activities that involve the use of measurement. One of the important aspects of obtaining support for measurement throughout the organization is to ensure that everyone understands that the measurement results will be used to support the organization's objectives, and not used to evaluate individual performance.

12.7.3 Define measurement responsibilities. *The size and structure of each specific organization is directly related to how measurement responsibility is assigned.* How many people are involved, and how the measurement tasks are actually allocated, vary considerably from organization to organization. In general, responsibility for implementing the measurement process takes place at different levels.

The primary responsibility for the measurement process is at the management level. In many government and industry organizations, two types of managers are involved in the acquisition and support of software-intensive systems:

- **Executive manager** — *The executive manager,* who in many cases is the government Program Executive Officer (PEO) or business sector manager, *generally has responsibility for an organization that controls more than one project.* The executive manager's decisions materially affect all of the projects within the organization. Measurement helps the executive manager determine the status of individual projects, and make decisions that apply across the organization.

- **Project manager** — The *project manager has direct responsibility for the success of a software-intensive project.* In most cases, the project manager is the primary user of the measurement results. This person is responsible for identifying and managing the software issues and communicating with the developer and senior levels of executive management. The project manager uses measurement to make project decisions.

In some organizations, the project manager is also the executive manager. It is the project manager's responsibility to ensure that measurement is integrated into the project. Integration includes all of the activities that make measurement part of the overall project management and technical processes, including the identification of resources to support the measurement effort.

While management is responsible for integrating and using measurement within the organization, the project technical staff is usually assigned the day-to-day tasks related to tailoring and applying the measures. Generally, an individual or team has the primary responsibility for tailoring the measures, collecting and processing the measurement data, analyzing the measurement results, and reporting the results to management.

Depending on the size and scope of the project, the measurement team can consist of a part-time measurement analyst or a multi-person team. The important thing is to have the primary measurement responsibility for the project assigned to a specific individual, and to allow that individual to interface directly with the project development organization. If a software engineering or measurement integrated product team (IPT) is established, the measurement analyst or measurement team should be represented. Above all, the personnel responsible for measurement must be able to independently arrive at objective answers and alternatives, and be able to provide results directly to the project decision makers.

Other members of the project technical staff also have responsibility within the measurement process. Each should understand how the process works and what information it can provide to them. They should also support measurement analysis efforts by helping to identify project events that may have an impact on interpreting the measurement data.

The development organization plays an important role in the measurement process. Most of the software data used by both the developer and the acquirer comes from the developer. All users must understand how each measure is defined and what the data represents. For example, what project work breakdown structure (WBS) elements are included in the reported software effort data?

The measurement results are most effective when used by the software development team on a day-to-day basis. In addition to helping to communicate issues and solutions, the development team uses the measurement results to identify and correct problems quickly as a part of their day-to-day work.

12.7.4 Provide measurement resources. Experience suggests that the measurement process will require from *one to five percent of the total software project cost.* The actual cost of a software measurement process depends on the specific data that is collected, and whether that data already exists in the developer's software engineering process. Measurement costs include personnel and tools, as well as the cost for the developer to assemble and report the data. Most developers use software data internally to manage their projects. As such, there should be little additional cost for the data to be provided. If the developer does not collect software data, there should be some concern about the maturity of the underlying software development process.

As with any initiative, there are some non-recurring startup costs associated with implementing a measurement process. These costs, which include both training and tools, diminish as measurement becomes a day-to-day activity within the organization. It is important to view the measurement process as a long-term resource within the organization. It should become self-supporting, saving as much as it costs, within a relatively short period after it is established.

In some organizations, the measurement costs for individual projects may be reduced by establishing the measurement team as an organizational resource. As long as there is a primary analyst assigned to work independently on each project, the measurement team can share resources, tools, and expertise.

12.7.4.1 Measurement tools. Once the specific measurement requirements and practices have been established, the tools used to collect, process, and analyze the data should be identified. On many smaller projects, the measurement process can be adequately supported using a personal computer with common off-the-shelf office software. On larger projects, or on projects that need to implement more advanced analysis techniques, additional measurement tools are usually required. When deciding what resources are required, the wrong thing to do is to purchase a specific tool before determining if it supports the information needs of the project. The types of software issues that need to be addressed and the characteristics of the measurement process drive the support tool requirements. No measurement process should ever be implemented around a predefined set of measurement tools.

Several different classes of tools are commonly applied in the measurement process, as described below. Many of these tools are used by the developer, but may also be accessed by the project office.

- *Database, graphing, and reporting tools* manage and store the measurement data and produce graphical and text-based reports. Commercial personal computer database applications are generally adequate for most projects. For larger projects with extensive data management and storage requirements, consideration should be given to using more powerful tools.

- *Software analysis and modeling tools* provide enhanced graphics and software analysis capabilities generally unavailable from databases or spreadsheets. The category includes software cost estimation models, software reliability models, statistical analysis tools, and similar applications. These tools can be extremely valuable when implemented as part of the overall measurement process.

- *Measurement application tools* are specifically designed to help implement a measurement process and support user interaction at all levels of the organization by providing real-time access to both measurement data and analysis results. They are useful for summarizing and providing measurement information at the management level.

- *Schedule and project management tools* assist in project scheduling, progress tracking, and critical path analysis. Some tools in this category can also track resource allocations and expenditures for identified activities.

- *Financial management tools* help to collect and store data related to labor and to fund expenditures. Some tools in this category include cost accounting and earned value functions. In some cases, existing financial management systems may not provide software specific data at an adequate level of detail. These systems may be difficult to modify.

- *Software product analysis tools* generate software product related data through automatic analysis of specific software products. Examples include software complexity analyzers, software size counting utilities, and software test coverage analyzers.

- *Software data collection tools* automatically extract software measurement data from systems that support the developer's software process. They can be commercial or locally developed utilities that access the developer's CASE tools, configuration management tools, and other software related systems. They are useful for providing the project office with direct access to the developer's measurement data.

General guidelines for selecting tools to support the measurement process include:

- Select tools that support the measurement process as tailored to meet specific project needs. Do not build a process around the tools.

- Evaluate tools that may already be available within the organization.

- Select tools that automate as much of the measurement process as possible. Automated data collection, data processing, analysis, and reporting tools can considerably improve the efficiency of the measurement process.

- Work closely with the developer to coordinate measurement tool selection and implementation, especially with respect to electronic data transfer.

- Select tools that simplify importing and exporting data between different formats.

- Select tools that run on a common platform.

On most projects, some manual data entry will usually be required. This should be kept to a minimum. It is usually more cost effective to implement commercially available tools and applications instead of developing them in-house. Data transfer utilities that provide direct access to the developer's measurement data, in many cases, are unique to each project. It is usually more cost effective to implement these utilities, rather than relying on manual data transfer and entry.

12.7.4.2 Measurement training. Personnel at all levels of the organization require appropriate software measurement training.

Table 1 summarizes the general training requirements for different personnel in the project organization.

Project managers require a good foundation in the basic concepts of software engineering and software measurement. They need to understand the capabilities and limitations of the measurement process and how it can help them meet their objectives.

Project office technical managers and engineers require training in the basic concepts of software engineering and measurement. They must understand how the data will be used within the project organization and how measurement will influence their own work.

Members of the measurement analysis team need appropriate training and experience in software engineering, the measurement process, and in specific software measurement disciplines. Software engineering expertise is critical to success. It provides the basis for interpreting and analyzing the data. Project personnel assigned to the analysis team should understand the activities and products inherent to the software development process, and be able to relate project software issues to specific measures and analysis activities. Software estimation and modeling skills and statistical analysis experience is required for more advanced analysis.

Table 1: Measurement training requirements for project personnel

Job Function			Measurement Training Requirements
Project Manager	**Technical Manager & Engineers**	**Measurement Analysis & Team Members**	
Yes	Yes	Yes	Software engineering
Yes	Yes	Yes	Management overview
No	Yes	Yes	Data collection & management
No	No	Yes	Management analysis

12.7.5 Initiate the measurement process. On most projects, some data collection and analysis occurs immediately after the decision is made to implement a measurement process. It is not unusual for all of the implementation activities to be taking place concurrently. A key requirement is to show how the measurement process can help address even the basic software issues and start to answer the project manager's questions. Even if the project is large, initially implementing a few key measures to address the highest-priority issues will provide important information that was not previously available.

One of the most important things to do is to establish an interface between the project office and the developer with respect to software measurement. Once established, this interface will become one of the most important tools in the measurement process. Direct access to the developer allows the measurement analyst to freely address data issues, and allows analysis feedback to be provided to the developer at the working level. In many instances, the acquirer/developer interface can be established as part of an IPT.

Just establishing a measurement process will not have an immediate impact on the project. As the measurement process is implemented, the measurement results will need to be "marketed" within the organization. At this point in time it is especially important to use the measurement results correctly. The data should be well defined, the analysis should be accurate, and the developer should have an opportunity to address the results.

The measurement information and analysis results should be made available to the entire project team, including both the acquisition and development organization. Discussion of the measurement results within the project team should focus on how the measurement results reflect what is actually happening on the project, and if new issues identified by the analysis are valid. The developer is important to the measurement process. If the developer is punished for poor measurement results, then the flow of data may be impeded or manipulated, resulting in a loss of project insight and communication.

The measurement process tends to impose a discipline on project software management activities. If the measurement process is properly implemented, the results will be used throughout the organization. It will provide insight into the project issues and help management to make informed software decisions.

12.7.6 Using the measurement results. The primary user of software measurement information is the individual software project team. The team includes the acquisition project office and technical support organizations, as well as the software developer and associated development organizations. Other organizations, particularly those with responsibility within the acquisition structure, have a need for information that is provided by the project's measurement process. Each of these information needs is somewhat unique, because each level within the organization has a different role with respect to business and technical management and must address different issues and questions.

The bases for addressing the requirements at the organizational and enterprise levels are the data and analysis results from the individual project level. These are aggregated using an issue-driven measurement process to address cross-project issues and objectives. When fully implemented, a common integrated risk management approach is established to assess and manage risk at all organizational levels using measurement data.

12.8 Reporting

When reporting a project status containing measurements and metrics, the reports should include dates, past history, and future measurement forecasts.

Since one can expect neither management nor a reviewer to remember the report from month to month, the metrics report needs to contain past history in the same form as the current data (for example, a plot on a graph). The report should contain (again using the same form) a forecast of future progress based on the past metrics. Lastly, make sure to indicate the date of a particular plan for this report. Do not allow people to misconstrue when and where the data was collected and what it represents.

12.9 Summary

Some important aspects of this article are:

- Measurement is the assigning of numbers or symbols to an artifact. Metrics is the computation of a number from two or more measurements.

- The best method of establishing a measurement program is through the GQM paradigm.

- Measurement is essential in providing feedback to managers as to the potential success or failure of the project.

- Measurement data needs to be reviewed and acted upon.

- A plan for data collection and reporting of measurement data is essential for a meaningful metrics system.

References

Additional information on the *software measurement and metrics KA* can be found in the following documents:

- **[Fenton & Pfleeger 1997]** Norman E. Fenton and Shari Lawrence Pfleeger. *Software Metrics: A Rigorous & Practical Approach,* London, 1997.

- **[ISO 15939:2007]** ISO/IEC 15939:2007, *Systems and software engineering -- Measurement process,* ISO/IEC, 2007.

- **[Neumann 1993]** P.G. Neumann, "System Development Woes," Communications of the ACM, Vol. 36, No. 10, Oct 1993, p. 146.

- **[PSM 2001]** *Practical Software Measurement (PSM): A Foundation for Objective Project Management*, Office of the Undersecretary of Defense for Acquisition and Technology and the Joint Logistics Commanders. Joint Group on Systems Engineering, Washington D.C., 2001.

Chapter 13.1[4]

Software Engineering Economics

Steve Tockey
Construx Software
10099 NE Eighth Street, #1350
Bellevue, WA 98004

Software professionals are faced with choices every day. Some choices are big, like whether to do Project A or Project B when there's only enough money for one of them, whether to use the Rational Unified Process [Kruchten 00], or an Agile development process [Cockburn 02], or maybe even what programming language to use. Other choices may seem relatively small, like whether it would be better to fix bugs #47, #58, and #66 or to include a particular new feature in the next product release. Maybe it's choosing an algorithm or data structure within a particular module. Regardless of how large or small a choice is, it will affect the costs and revenues of the organization.

. . . Software economics has often been misconceived as the means of estimating the cost of programming projects. But economics is primarily a science of choice, and software economics should provide methods and models for analyzing the choices that software projects must make. — Leon Levy [1987]

1. Introduction

This paper highlights some of those methods and models to help you better analyze the choices a typical software organization faces. The methods and models covered in this paper are:

- Cash flow streams
- Interest
- Present worth
- Break-even analysis
- Optimization analysis

For a more comprehensive discussion of engineering economy and its relevance to software see [Tockey 99] or [Tockey 04].

2. Cash-Flow Streams

In for-profit companies—where most software professionals work—the primary goal of the company is to make money for its owners. To be sure, other decision criteria are relevant (environmental impact, well-being of employees, social welfare, and so on) but the primary determinant will almost always be profit. Companies that don't make a profit don't stay in business very long no matter how good they are to the environment or how well they treat their employees. In government and not-for-profit organizations, the goal isn't to make a profit; it's to

---

4. Based on the article by Steve Tockey, "An Introduction to Engineering Economics for Software," first published in *Software Engineering: The Supporting Processes*, (Vol. II). Edited by Richard Hall Thayer and Merlin Dorfman, IEEE Computer Society Press, Los Alamitos, CA, © 2005 IEEE.

maximize the benefit to some population while using a minimum of resources. Since money is a scarce resource in these organizations, the financial implications of technical decisions are still relevant.

Whether you work in a for-profit or a not-for-profit organization, you should align your software technical decisions with the goals of your organization. Simply:

> *"Is it in the best interest of the organization to invest its limited resources this way, or would the same investment produce a higher return elsewhere?"*

To answer this question you'll need to look at proposed alternative actions in financial terms, i.e., from a cash flow perspective. A cash flow stream is the financial view of some proposed alternative. There are a number of ways to develop a cash flow stream; one is to start with a work breakdown structure (WBS) and estimate the schedule & costs of each WBS item. The timings and amounts of revenues also need to be estimated. Note that revenues could be a result of (increased) product sales and/or a result of cost reductions within the organization. The cash flow stream is the sum, by period, of all costs and revenues in that period.

For this paper, a mythical company, XYZSoft, is considering two alternatives. The first alternative is to make improvements to their internally developed inventory management software. The second alternative is to develop and deploy a Customer Relationship Management (CRM) system.

XYZSoft doesn't have the resources to do both projects and must choose between them. They've decided that a 5-year planning horizon is appropriate for this decision. Table 1 shows the estimated cash flow stream for the inventory management project. By convention, an initial investment—the money it takes just to start an alternative—is shown as being "at the end of year zero." Table 1 shows that XYZSoft expects to spend $40,000 on things like development hardware and software just to get this project started.

Table 1: Estimated cash flow stream for the Inventory Management project

End of Year	Net Cash Flow
0	-$40,000
1	-150,000
2	100,000
3	80,000
4	80,000
5	60,000

3. Interest

Given the cash flow streams for the alternatives, various techniques can be used to analyze them from a financial perspective and find out which is better for the business.

The estimated cash flow stream for the CRM project is shown in Table 2.

3. Interest

A very important factor in business decision analysis is the notion of interest. Literally, it's a rental fee for money. It's just like renting a house or a car; the renter takes possession of the thing being rented and returns it later with some amount of money. In this case, the thing being rented is also money. The renter (borrower) takes possession of some amount of money now, using it to start a business, buy a computer, take a Caribbean cruise, etc., and pays back a larger amount of money later.

Table 2: Estimated cash flow stream for the CRM project

End of Year	Net Cash Flow
0	-$40,000
1	-150,000
2	30,000
3	70,000
4	120,000
5	130,000

From a software organization's perspective, there are two situations to consider:

- The organization doesn't already have the money available—if the organization is really interested in doing some proposed alternative then the cost of borrowing the money to finance it needs to be factored into the decision. At a minimum, the alternative had better return at least the interest expense on the borrowed money.

- The organization already has the money—in this situation the question is, "Can we get the best return by using it this way or could we get a better return doing something else?" That something else could mean lending it to someone else; this is the net effect of putting it into a bank account, a certificate of deposit (CD), or in the stock market. An organization would be highly unlikely to lend money without requiring the borrower to promise giving back more than was lent; the money over and above what was lent is the interest. The interest that could be earned by investing the money elsewhere needs to be factored into this decision.

3.1 Minimum attractive rate of return

To support financial decision making, companies often establish a "Minimum Attractive Rate of Return" (MARR). The MARR is just that, it's the lowest rate of return that the organization would consider to be a good business investment. The MARR is the interest rate used in the financial analysis. Factors typically considered in setting the MARR include:

- **What type of organization is it** — For-profit industries are free to set the MARR as they please. Regulated public utilities often have their MARR set by a Public Utilities Commission or other governing entity. Government organizations often use the prevailing bond rate.

- **What the prevailing interest rate for typical investments like savings accounts, stocks, bonds, money market, etc. is established** — The MARR should be at least as high as the best prevailing interest rate; otherwise the organization could get more income from just putting its money in these more typical investments?

- **How much money is available** — When there is less money available for investment, the MARR should go up to focus the organization on activities with the highest profits?

- **Where the money comes from** — If it's borrowed capital, the MARR should be set to at least the interest rate on the borrowed money. If it's equity funding, the MARR should be comparable to what the organization is typically able to get through other operations?

- **How many competing proposals are there** — As the number of proposals goes up, the organization might want to be more selective and express this through a higher MARR?

Assume that XYZSoft has set their MARR at 17%.

3.2 Interest formulas

Interest causes an amount of money at one point in time to have a different value than the same amount of money at a different point in time. One hundred dollars in your pocket today is worth more than the promise of $100 in your pocket next year. What's needed is a way of equating money at one point in time to an amount of money that has the same essential value at some other point in time. Several such formulas exist; three of them will be discussed here.

3.2.1 Single-payment compound-amount (F/P). The single-payment compound-amount formula takes a known amount of money at the present (P), an interest rate (i), and a length of time (n), and tells how much it would be worth at that future time (F). The formula is:

$$F = P(1 + i)^n$$

Given that XYZSoft has set their minimum attractive rate of return at 17%, any amount of money three years from now that's less than $100(1 + 0.17)^3$, or about $160, is less interesting to them than $100 today. They'd rather have the $100 today because they are confident they can grow it to be worth at least $160 in three years.

3.2.2 Single-payment present-worth (P/F). The single-payment present-worth formula takes a known amount of money in the future (F), an interest rate (i), and a length of time (n), and tells how much it would be worth at the present (P). The formula is

$$P = F\left[\frac{1}{(1 + i)^n}\right]$$

3.2.3 Equal-payment-series capital-recovery (A/P). The equal-payment-series capital-recovery formula is the standard way to compute loan payments. The formula takes a known amount of money at the present (P), an interest rate (i), and a length of time (n), and tells how much needs to be paid as a series of n equal payments (A) to recover the lender's money with interest. The formula is:

$$A = P\left[\frac{i(1 + i)^n}{(1 + i)^n - 1}\right]$$

If XYZSoft wanted to borrow $100,000 for five years at 9% interest with annual payments, their payments would be:

$$A = \$100{,}000\left[\frac{0.09(1+0.09)^5}{(1+0.09)^5 - 1}\right] = \$29{,}709$$

3.2.4 Solving interest problems using tables of interest factors. Given a fixed interest rate (i) and a fixed length of time (n), the ratio between the known and unknown amounts is fixed. When the interest rate is 17% and the length of time is three years, a future value (F) will always be $(1+0.17)^3$ or 1.6016 times the present value (P). People aren't normally able to compute exponents in their head, let alone even remember all of the different interest formulas. They're also unlikely to have memorized the literally thousands of ratios they might need. One common way to address interest problems is to use tables of interest factors. Table 3 is an excerpt of one such table of factors.

Using the single-payment compound-amount (F/P) factor for 17% at 8 years as an example (see Table 3), the steps for solving interest problems using tables is:

Table 3: An example table of interest factors, in this case for 17%

	17.00% Interest Factors for Discrete Compounding					
	Single-payment		Equal-payment Series			
	Compound-amount	Present-worth	Compound-amount	Sinking-fund	Present-worth	Capital-recovery
n	Find F given P $(F/P,i,n)$	Find P given F $(P/F,i,n)$	Find F given A $(F/A,i,n)$	Find A given F $(A/F,I,n)$	Find P given A $(P/A,i,n)$	Find A given P $(A/P,i,n)$
1	1.1700	0.8547	1.0000	1.0000	0.8547	1.1700
2	1.3689	0.7305	2.1700	0.4608	1.5852	0.6308
3	1.6016	0.6244	3.5389	0.2826	2.2096	0.4526
4	1.8739	0.5337	5.1405	0.1945	2.7432	0.3645
5	2.1924	0.4561	7.0144	0.1426	3.1993	0.3126
6	2.5652	0.3898	9.2068	0.1086	3.5892	0.2786
7	3.0012	0.3332	11.7720	0.0849	3.9224	0.2549
8	3.5115	0.2848	14.7733	0.0677	4.2072	0.2377
9	4.1084	0.2434	18.2847	0.0547	4.4506	0.2247
10	4.8068	0.2080	22.3931	0.0447	4.6586	0.2147

XYZSoft believes that they can take $100.00, or about $62 today, and turn it into at least $100 within three years.

$$\$100\left[\frac{1}{(1+0.17)^3}\right]$$

1. Find the table corresponding to the interest rate needed. In this example, start with the table for 17% interest.

2. Select the row for the number of periods needed. In this example select the row for $n = 3$.

3. Identify the column in that table for the interest function needed. Single-payment compound-amount is the first column on the left.

4. The factor needed is at the intersection of the identified column and the selected row. The single-payment compound-amount (F/P) factor for 17% at 3 years is 1.6016.

Tables for various interest rates can be found in books such as [Tockey 04], [Eschenbach 03], [Thuesen 93], [DeGarmo 93], and [Grant 90]. Spreadsheet software and higher-end calculators often have built-in functions for computing interest factors.

4. Present Worth

The effect of interest means we can't simply add up the values in a cash flow stream to find out how much a proposed action is worth. We also can't just compare cash flow streams on a year-by-year basis. Unless *every* year in one cash flow stream is greater than or equal to another, we can't be certain which alternative is better without doing more work.

That additional work involves translating the cash flow values for each alternative, using the MARR as the interest rate, into a common timeframe. Only then can the cash flow streams be compared in a meaningful fashion. One of the most common timeframes is "present worth," or PW (i). Present Worth is sometimes called "Net Present Value." PW (i) means that the cash flow stream has the same value as some amount of cash today at the given interest rate "i." The formula for calculating the PW (i) of a cash flow stream is:

$$PW(i) = \sum_{t=0}^{n} F_t (1+i)^{-t}$$

where F_t is the net cash flow amount at time t.

The PW (i) formula uses single-payment present-worth (P/F) to translate each separate cash flow instance to its equivalent end-of-year-zero amount and then sums up all of those end-of-year-zero amounts. Table 4 shows the calculation of PW (i) for the Inventory Management software project. The F_t values are from Table 1 and the $(1+i)^{-t}$ values are from the third column of Table 3. The PW (17%) of the Inventory Management project is $24,855 meaning that this project is financially equivalent to XYZSoft receiving a one-time net income of $24,855 today.

It should now be clear that the Inventory Management project is the better choice for XYZSoft because of its PW (17%) is higher by more than $4,000.

Table 5 shows PW (17%) calculated for the CRM project. This project is financially equivalent to XYZSoft receiving a one-time net income of $20,749 today.

Notice that if the original cash flow streams were simply summed up—which is essentially PW(*i*) with a MARR of 0%—the recommendation is opposite from the recommendation at a MARR of 17%. The PW (0%) of the Inventory Management project is $130,000 while the PW (0%) of the CRM project is $160,000. Even though the CRM project may have appeared to earn $30,000 more, interest—what XYZSoft can do with money in the meantime—causes those dollars to be worth less than the dollars from the Inventory Management project. This example highlights the effect that interest can have on business decisions; any significant business decision, be it also a technical decision or not, that doesn't address interest could be suspect.

5. Break-Even Analysis

Another application of engineering economy to software is break-even analysis. Break-even analysis—and optimization analysis, which is explained below—typically doesn't need to include the time-value of money.

Suppose XYZSoft is also trying to choose between two different connection plans offered by Internet Service Providers (ISPs). The amount of data transferred each month could be an important factor in the decision. If only a little data will be transferred then one plan might be better but if lots of data will be transferred then another plan might be better.

Table 4: PW(i) for the inventory management project

Year	F_t	$(1+i)^{-t}$	$F_t(1+i)^{-t}$
0	-$40,000	1.0000	-$40,000
1	-150,000	0.8547	-128,205
2	100,000	0.7305	73,051
3	80,000	0.6244	49,950
4	80,000	0.5337	42,692
5	60,000	0.4561	27,367

$$\sum = \$24,855$$

Table 5: PW(i) for the CRM project

Year	F_t	$(1+i)^{-t}$	$F_t(1+i)^{-t}$
0	-$40,000	1.0000	-$40,000
1	-150,000	0.8547	-128,205
2	30,000	0.7305	21,915
3	70,000	0.6244	43,706
4	120,000	0.5337	64,038
5	130,000	0.4561	59,294

$$\sum = \$20,749$$

Break-even analysis helps choose between two or more alternatives by figuring out which points, if any, would be indifferent between those alternatives. Below the break-even point one alternative is better and above that point another alternative is better.

5.1 Decision variables and objective functions

In break-even analyses, the choice being made is represented in terms of one or more decision variables and one or more objective functions. A decision variable represents a set of possible values for some factor in a given decision. The amount of data to be transferred through the ISP each month would be a decision variable: different amounts of data transfer are possible.

An objective function is an equation that relates the values of one or more decision variables to the performance of an alternative. An objective function that relates values of decision variables to income (e.g., income as a function of units sold) is called an income function while an objective function that relates decision variables to cost is called a cost function. If one ISP plan charges $50 per month plus $0.50 per gigabyte transferred then its cost function would be:

$$C = \$50.00 + \$0.50G$$

where G is the amount of data in gigabytes—the decision variable—and C is the resulting cost.

In software projects, examples of cost functions can be:

- The cost of some quantity of CD-ROM copies
- The cost of Internet access through an ISP based on connect time
- How long it takes to process a data set based on the number of entries
- The size of a memory-resident data structure based on the amount of data
- The cost of a multi-user software tool based on the number of seats

Cost doesn't always need to be in terms of money, it could be expressed in terms of execution time, memory used, or any other critical resource.

5.1 Break-even analysis with two alternatives

Break-even analysis is simplest when there are only two alternatives. Consider an ISP that offers two pricing plans. Suppose Plan A is the same as given above, a fixed monthly rate of $50 plus $0.50 per gigabyte transferred:

$$\text{Cost under Plan A} = \$50.00 + \$0.50G$$

Plan B has a higher fixed monthly rate, say $100, but has a lower per-gigabyte charge, $0.10.

$$\text{Cost under Plan B} = \$100.00 + \$0.10G$$

If XYZSoft doesn't plan on transferring much data, then Plan A would be better than Plan B. At 25 gigabytes per month Plan A would cost $62.50 while Plan B would cost $102.50. If XYZSoft intends to transfer a lot of data each month then Plan B would be better. At 500 gigabytes per month Plan A would cost $300 while Plan B would cost $150. Somewhere between 25 gigabytes and 500 gigabytes per month is a point where the costs would be identical for both plans. This is the essence of break-even analysis.

Since we are looking for the value of G where both plans have the same cost, we can set the Plan A cost equal to the Plan B cost and solve for the number of gigabytes of data transfer where this happens. Specifically, the same cost under both plans happens when:

$$\$50.00 + \$0.50G = \$100.00 + \$0.10G$$

Solving for G

$$\$0.50G - \$0.10G = \$100.00 - \$50.00$$

$$\$0.40G = \$50.00$$

$$G = 125$$

The break-even point, 125 gigabytes per month, is where the two alternatives have exactly the same cost. Knowing that, XYZSoft can choose their ISP plan intelligently. If they expect to transfer less than 125 gigabytes per month their bill will be less if they sign up for Plan A. If, on the other hand, they expect to transfer more than 125 gigabytes per month, their monthly bill will be less under Plan B.

Break-even problems can also be solved graphically by plotting the objective functions and finding the intersection point. Figure 1 shows the graphical solution to XYZSoft's ISP plan break-even analysis.

6. Optimization Analysis

Optimization studies objective functions to find the point where overall performance is best. Optimization is useful when the functions being studied have two or more competing components: one of the components increases as the decision variable increases while the other component decreases. Software's classic space-time trade-off is a good example; an algorithm that runs faster will often use up more memory. The optimum point balances the value of the faster run time against the cost of the additional memory.

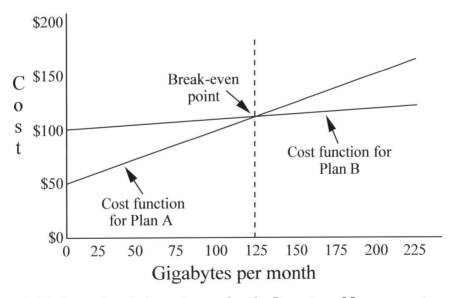

Figure 1: Estimated cash flow stream for the Inventory Management project

6.1 Optimizing a single alternative with a single decision variable

The simplest optimization analysis is when there is only one alternative and its value is determined by a single decision variable.

$$Cost = F(DecisionVariable)$$

Suppose that XYZSoft is in the middle of upgrading their Inventory Management system. One of the modifications to increase performance is to distribute the application and run the parts on separate processors. A network communication link will be needed to connect the parts. One part of the application generates requests but the requests are created at a rate that would cause too much network overhead if each request were sent separately. XYZSoft developers decide to queue the requests. The developers realize that making the data packets bigger cuts down on the network overhead but it also increases the average queue time per request. They want to balance the reduced network overhead with the longer queue time.

After studying the performance of the network and the Inventory Management software, they've determined that the overall queuing delay is described by the cost function.

$$TD = 20r + \frac{320}{r} + 50$$

Where TD is the overall delay in milliseconds and r is the number of requests in a data packet. The $20r$ component is the cost of waiting for another request before sending; this increases with r. The $320/r$ component is the network overhead, which decreases as r increases. The XYZSoft developers need to find the value of r that minimizes TD.

There are two ways of finding the optimum point. The brute force approach is to simply run different sample values for the decision variable through the function and narrow in on the best result. The elegant approach uses differential calculus; the objective function will be at a minimum or maximum whenever its first derivative equals zero. Setting the first derivative function to zero and solving for the values of the decision variable where this happens identifies those minimum or maximum points.

The first derivative of the queuing delay cost function is:

$$\frac{dTD}{dr} = 20 - \frac{320}{r^2}$$

Setting this first derivative to zero and solving for the decision variable:

$$\frac{dTD}{dr} = 20 - \frac{320}{r^2} = 0$$

$$r = \sqrt{\frac{320}{20}} = 4$$

The optimum number of requests per data packet is 4.

In the general case there can be multiple local minimum or maximum points on the function being studied. If you identify more than one minimum or maximum point using differential calculus you'll need to run those points back through the original function to find which one is the overall minimum or maximum. When the brute force approach is used, the overall minimum or maximum will usually be obvious by simply looking at the computed values.

7. There's More to this Story

This is literally the tip of the iceberg on engineering economics for software. Many more methods and models are necessary for general case decision analysis. These include:

- Future worth, annual equivalent, internal rate of return, discounted payback period
- Proposals that aren't mutually exclusive
- Economic life, replacement, and retirement of assets
- Inflation and deflation
- Accounting, depreciation, and cost accounting
- Income taxes and after-tax cash flow analysis
- Not-for-profit decision analysis
- Break-even analysis with more than two alternatives
- Optimization analysis with more than two alternatives or multiple decision variables
- Decisions involving risk or uncertainty
- Decisions involving multiple decision attributes (criteria)

More complete coverage of these topics can be found in books such as [Tockey 04], [Eschenbach 03], [Thuesen 93], [DeGarmo 93], and [Grant 90].

8. Summary

Software professionals are faced with choices every day. Some choices are big, like whether to do Project A or Project B when there's only enough money for one. Other choices may seem relatively small, like choosing an algorithm or data structure within a particular module. Regardless of how large or small a choice is, it *will* affect the costs and revenues of the organization. Remember Leon Levy's statement [Levy 87].

> . . . *software economics has often been misconceived as the means of estimating the cost of programming projects. But economics is primarily a science of choice, and software economics should provide methods and models for analyzing the choices that software projects must make.*

This paper highlighted some of those methods and models to help you better analyze the choices a typical software organization faces. The methods and models covered in this paper were:

- Cash flow streams
- Interest
- Present worth
- Break-even analysis
- Optimization analysis

References

Additional information on the *software economics* KA can be found in the following documents.

- **[Cockburn 02]** Alistair Cockburn, *Agile Software Development*, Addison-Wesley, Reading, MA, 2002.

- **[DeGarmo 93]** E. DeGarmo, W. Sullivan, J. Bontadelli, *Engineering Economy*, 9th Edition, Prentice Hall, Upper Saddle River, NJ, 1993.

- **[Eschenbach 03]** Ted G. Eschenbach, *Engineering Economy: Applying Theory to Practice*, 2nd Edition, Oxford University Press, England, 2003.

- **[Grant 90]** Grant, Ireson, and Leavenworth, *Principles of Engineering Economy,* Eighth Edition, Wiley, Hobroken, NJ, 1990.

- **[Kruchten 00]** Philippe Kruchten, *The Rational Unified Software Development Process: An Introduction*, 2nd Edition, Addison-Wesley, Reading, MA, 2000.

- **[Levy 87]** Leon Levy, *Taming the Tiger - Software Engineering and Software Economics*, Springer-Verlag, London, 1987.

- **[Thuesen 93]** G. J. Thuesen and W. J. Fabrycky, *Engineering Economy*, 8th Edition, Prentice Hall, Upper Saddle River, NJ, 1993.

- **[Tockey 99]** Steve Tockey, "Recommended Skills and Knowledge for Software Engineers," *Proceedings of the 12th Conference on Software Engineering Education and Training*, IEEE, March 22-24, 1999.

- **[Tockey 04]** Steve Tockey, *Return on Software*, Addison-Wesley, Reading, MA, 2004.

Chapter 13.2
Essentials of Software Engineering Economics

Richard Hall Thayer and Merlin Dorfman

This is the thirteenth chapter of a textbook to aid individual software engineers to a greater understanding of the IEEE SWEBOK [2013] and a guide book to aid software engineers in passing the IEEE CSDP and CSDA certification exams.

The engineering economics book by Steve Tockey [2005] is the main source of information for this chapter. This is an excellent book and easy to read, and therefore its review might be worth your investment in time and money.

Chapter 13 covers the CSDP exam specifications for the software engineering economics module [Software Exam Specification, Version 2, 18 March 2009]. This list of exam specifications is reported to be the same list that the exam writers used to write the exam questions. Therefore it is the best source of help for the exam takers.

This part of the study guide involves:

1. Software engineering economic fundamentals
2. For-profit decision making
3. Not-for profit decision making
4. Present economy
5. Estimation risks and uncertainty
6. Multiple attribute decisions

13.1 Software Engineering Economics Fundamentals

- Proposals
- Cash flow
- Business decision-making process
- Time value of money
- Equivalence
- Basis for comparison
- Mutually exclusive alternatives

13.1.1 Proposals. A *proposal* is a single, separate, considered option, such as whether or not to carry out a particular software development project. A proposal may enhance an existing program, or it may develop the same software from scratch. Each proposal represents a unit of choice, meaning one can choose whether or not to carry out the proposal. The whole purpose of business decision-making, given the current business circumstances, is to decide which proposals should be accepted and which ones should be rejected [Tockey 2005, p. 23].

13.1.2 Cash flow. *Cash flow* is a specific amount of money flowing into or out of an organization as a direct result of an agreed-upon proposal. A single occurrence of this procedure is called a *cash flow incident*. A *cash flow stream* refers to the set of cash flow instances, over time, used to fund the proposal. There are a number of categories of cash flows [Tockey 2005, pp. 24-26]:

- *Initial investment* — Captures all of the one-time, non-recurring costs associated with the start-up proposal.

- *Operation and maintenance costs* — These costs occur only after the activity has started and continue through its retirement.

- *Sales income* — The cash flow-sales income refers to the direct income generated by the proposal.

- *Cost avoidance* — Cost avoidance is a process of reducing expenses needed to produce products and/or services. This procedure leaves more of the revenue as profit.

- *Salvage value* — Salvage value refers to the remaining value of assets (e.g., equipment and facilities) remaining at the end of the project.

13.1.3 Business decision-making process. The *business decision-making process* is an approach to selecting the most cost-effective and technically viable solution to a business problem. The technical person (frequently called the chief engineer or technical lead) should choose the solution that maximizes the return for the organization's software investment [Tockey 2005, pp. 35-44].

Several steps involved in selecting the most technically viable solution are:

- To understand the business problem

- To prioritize the selection criteria relevant to the business decision

- To identify reasonable technically feasible solutions contained in the proposals

- To evaluate each proposal against the selection criteria

- To select a preferred solution

- To monitor performance of the selected solution in order to learn and improve from the project experience

13.1.4 Time value of money. One of the fundamental concepts of business and associated business decisions is that money has a time value, i.e., a dollar today is worth more than a dollar a year from now. Money is indexed to a value that changes over time. Borrowers lend money to investors and invested money accrues interest. This concept is rooted in human history and is commonly known as *monetary policy*. Anyone making a business decision needs to understand monetary policy, interest, and how each affects debt decisions [Tockey 2005, pp. 47-53].

13.1.5 Simple equivalence. A simple equivalent is determined by calculating the future value "F" of an investment's present value "P," assuming simple interest at an interest rate of "n." This means that as long as the interest rate is competitive (i.e., in line with other potential sources), future money is equivalent to present day money times the interest rate [Tockey 2005, p. 100].

13.1.6 Basis for comparison. A *basis for comparison* is simply a common framework of methods for consistently comparing two or more cash-flow streams. This allows for the meaningful comparison of multiple proposals. The following represent five examples of bases for comparison [Tockey 2005, pp. 111-124]:

- *Present worth* — This basis for comparison translates a cash-flow stream into an equivalent single cash-flow instance at the beginning of the planning horizon. The present worth of a cash-flow stream shows the present value of the future stream, *right now* at the current interest rate.

- *Future worth* — The basis for comparison that translates a cash-flow stream into an equivalent single cash-flow instance at the end of the planning horizon.

- *Internal rate of return* — The internal rate of return (IRR) expresses the cash-flow stream in terms of an interest rate. The IRR is the interest rate that causes the present worth of the expenses to equal the present worth of the income.

- *Payback period* — The basis for comparison that represents the value of a cash-flow stream in terms of the time it will take to recover the proposal's initial value.

- *Capitalized equivalent amount* — A dollar amount now (at the given interest rate) that will be equivalent to the net difference of the income and payment if the cash-flow pattern is repeated indefinitely.

13.2 For-Profit Decision-Making

13.2.1 For-profit organizations (are just that). For-profit organizations and companies ensure a constant, reliable source of profit for the owners or shareholders. Therefore, business decisions are selected based on their profitability over the expected lifetime of the company. The essence of getting the "biggest bang for your technical buck" in for-profit companies is to align the technical decision with the goal of *maximizing profits*. All other things being equal, the role of the software individual – whether manager or technician – in a "for-profit" company should be to choose the best technical solution to solve the problem. The best technical solution is defined as the one that produces the highest profit [Tockey 2005, pp. 18-19].

This section of software engineering economics covers the following economic attributes:

- For-profit decision analysis

- Minimum attractive rate of return (MARR)

- Economic life

- Planning horizon

- Replacement and retirement decisions

- Inflation

- Depreciation

- General accounting and cost accounting

- Income taxes

13.2.2 For-profit decision analysis. A for-profit decision analysis involves taking a set of *mutually exclusive alternatives* and finding the best single alternative to carry out a for-profit organizational goal (i.e., to maximize the profit for the organization).

Mutually exclusive alternatives are a collection of two or more proposals, each one representing a unique and mutually exclusive potential course of action. Exclusive of course means that one proposal does not interact with or influence another proposal. Likewise, it ignores tendencies between proposals such as using a common staff and similar or identical interest rates. In order to compare alternative courses of action, it is important to remove all invalid proposals. This process involves [Tockey 2005, pp. 129-131]:

- Removing any alternative that contains mutually exclusive proposals

- Removing any alternative that contains contingencies that cannot be satisfied

- Removing any alternative that exceeds budget or resource constraints

13.2.3 Minimum attractive rate of return (MARR). An organization's *minimum attractive rate of return* (MARR) is the lowest internal rate of return the organization will consider to be a good investment. The MARR is a statement verifying an organization's confidence that it will reach the established minimum rate of return. The MARR is literally set by a policy decision originating with the proposal developer and approved by the organization's management. The setting of the MARR needs to be carefully thought out. If set too high, alternatives with a good return might not be selected. If set too low, marginally profitable or even unprofitable alternatives may be chosen [Tockey 2005, p. 141].

13.2.4 Economic life. The total *lifetime costs* of an asset are driven by two components [Tockey 2005, pp.160-164]:

1. Capital recovery with returns

2. Operation and maintenance costs

Capital recovery with returns will usually start off with high assets and decrease over time. On the other hand, the *operation and maintenance costs* for an asset usually begin low and increase over time.

13.2.5 Planning horizon. The *planning horizon* is a consistent time span used to compare two or more proposals and is sometimes called a *study period* [Tockey 2005, p. 158].

The planning horizon is based on the following:

- Company policy

- How far into the future a reasonable effort can be made

- The economic life of the short-lived assets

- The economic life of the longer-lived assets

- The best judgment of the person performing the decision analysis

13.2.6 Replacement and retirement decisions. *Replacement decisions* are necessary when an organization has a particular asset and considers replacing it with something else. Replacement decisions use the same decision process as represented by the initial investment of assets. However, additional challenges such as sunk costs and salvage value complicate the decision analysis.

- *Sunk cost* is any cost that is irrecoverable by future actions. Psychologically, people tend to pay attention to sunk costs even though they are irrelevant in business decisions. The sunk cost of an asset is equal to the acquisition cost minus the salvage value.

- Salvage value is any remaining value in an asset at the end of its useful life.

13.2.6.1 Retirement decisions. *Retirement* decisions are made when it is determined that an activity will be discontinued, such as when a software company considers no longer selling a software product or a hardware manufacturer considers retiring a particular model of computers [Tockey 2005, pp. 171-172].

13.2.6.2 Replacement decisions. As long as an organization is involved in an activity and is dependent upon one or more assets, and the lifetime of those assets is shorter than the duration of those activities, the organization will eventually be faced with a replacement decision. The two causes for replacement—*deterioration* and *obsolescence*—may happen separately or concurrently [Tockey 2005, p. 172].

- *Deterioration* — One reason for replacement is *deterioration*. A well-used machine or equipment simply wears out.

- *Obsolescence* — *Obsolescence* occurs when products have been changed within their environments and their assets are now worth less than before. More capable assets become available or demand for the asset changes significantly; i.e., the demand may have risen rendering the asset incapable of providing the necessary service. Alternatively, demand may have decreased, and therefore a less capable or less costly asset can replace the existing one.

13.2.7 Inflation. *Inflation* occurs when the purchasing power of money is reduced. The inflation rate and the drop in purchasing power, although closely related, are not exactly the same. *Inflation* exists when the same amount of money has reduced purchasing power, or with a general price increase. *Purchasing power* refers to the real buying power of a given monetary unit [Tockey 2005, p. 194].

Accounting for inflation is a business decision. There are two approaches to making this decision [Tockey 2005, p. 196]:

1. *Actual dollar analysis* — Every cash-flow instance represents the actual out-of-pocket dollars received or paid at that point in time

2. *Constant dollar analysis* — Every cash-flow instance represents a hypothetical constant purchasing power referred to a fixed point in time

If the interest rate is higher than the inflation rate, money will appreciate in value over time.

13.2.8 Depreciation. *Depreciation* has two different meanings when pertaining to business [Tockey 2005, pp. 212-214]:

1. Actual or physical depreciation means the asset is aging. The more an item is used, the more it wears out. Physical depreciation also includes such physical characteristics as rust, corrosion, or theft.

2. Functional depreciation is the result of a modified or changed work environment such that the asset is either obsolete or unable to keep up with demand.

13.2.9 General accounting and cost accounting. *Accounting* entails the tracking of money received by a company, financial transactions within the company, and financial obligations leaving the company [Tockey 2005, p. 233].

13.2.10 Income taxes. A tax is a charge, usually of money, imposed by authority on persons or property for public purposes, or a sum levied on members of an organization to defray expenses.

These ordinary taxes can be simply included in an expense cash-flow occurrence. Expense cash-flow occurrences should be cited in the main proposal.

Income taxes are a different matter. The term "income tax" is misleading and is not exactly a tax on total income, but is a tax on net income (revenue minus expenses). Income tax can be extremely high, as much as 50% in some states. Therefore, it should be obvious that a decision analysis that does not include accounting for income tax can lead to an incorrect business plan. Income tax is more complex than other taxes because the amount of tax owed is difficult to compute. The accounting office must have access to both gross income and proposed expenses. *Income taxes* are charged against a corporation's net income [Tockey 2005, pp. 265-266].

13.3 Not-For-Profit Decision-Making

A *not-for-profit organization* is an organization that may produce services or products without the long-term intent to make a profit. Government operates as a not-for-profit organization. The role of individuals in not-for-profit organizations is to solve a problem by choosing from a set of possible technical solutions. The chosen solution maximizes the organization's objective, which is to provide the greatest benefit at the least cost [Tockey 2005, pp. 19-20].

This section of the study guide involves:

- Benefit-cost analysis
- Cost–effectiveness analysis

13.3.1 Benefit-cost analysis. A *benefit-cost analysis* for a non-profit organization is one aspect in the selection process for projects to be developed based on which alternative will benefit the customer. A customer in this environment might be a government agency, an organization, an individual, a foreign government with whom the U.S. has an agreement to provide assistance, or a corporation.

The costs are defined as all expenses minus all savings incurred by the sponsor (who may or may not be the customer). This includes any initial investment expenses plus any ongoing operating and maintenance costs. A project proposal is desirable only when its net benefits are greater than its net costs.

13.3.2 Cost-effectiveness analysis. Originating in the defense and space communities, cost-effectiveness analysis is known as "getting the biggest bang for the buck." This analytical process shares similar philosophies and methodologies with benefit-cost analysis. The three requirements of cost-effectiveness analysis to be used in decisions are as follows [Tockey 2005, p. 311]:

1. The problem must have well-defined parameters.

2. Multiple solutions should be considered and evaluated.

3. The proposal under consideration should present at least two valid solutions.

These three requirements of cost-effectiveness analysis are supported by two versions:

1. *Fixed-cost version* — The fixed-cost version is an attempt to maximize benefits given maximum available costs. In this case, a fixed cost is the dollar amount allocated for the project and available to the developer to design as much usability for that amount of money.

2. *Fixed-effectiveness version* — The fixed-effectiveness version refers to a fixed end goal in which the costs needed to achieve this goal are minimized. The fixed-effectiveness approach anticipates what the project has to accomplish while taking cost into account.

13.4 Present Economy

Present economy introduces break-even and optimization analysis. These two forms of decision analysis are collectively referred to as "present economy" because they don't involve the time value of money (also called "future economy").

This section of the study guide involves:

1. Break-even analysis
2. Optimization analysis

13.4.1 Break-even analysis. A *break-even analysis* is the requisite analysis when a decision is required between two developing alternatives, particularly if the two alternatives use different metrics to measure costs. The decision variable and the object function are two components of a break-even analysis [Tockey 2005, p. 319].

1. A *decision variable* represents a set of possible values to be considered and some choices to be made in a given decision analysis. A break-even point is a method of choosing between two alternatives. For example, below the break-even point one supplier may be cheaper, while above that point the other supplier charges less than the first.

2. An *object function* is an equation that rates the values of decision variables according to the performance of an alternative.

13.4.2 Optimization analysis. Optimization analysis refers to the use of *optimization* to study an objective function over a range of values. The object is to find the point in which the overall performance is most favorable. Optimization is useful when the objective function being studied has two or more *competing* components, e.g., one of the components increases as the decision variable increases, whereas the other component decreases.

13.5 Estimation, Risk, and Uncertainty

Business decisions depend on accurate estimates while accounting for possible risk and uncertainty. It is rare that a business fact or measurement is known with certainty. The best a project developer can hope for is a well-calculated estimate based on sound judgment and analytical decisions [Tockey 2005, p. 343].

Also, perhaps a "sensitivity analysis," showing how much the results would change if some of the assumptions changed, would strengthen the decision making process.

An *estimate* is a prediction. Business decisions always look into the future; they are always based on factors that are not yet known. So the best that a given manager can do is to try to get as close as possible to what the actual factor outcome will be, while understanding the remaining level of uncertainty.

This section of the study guide involves:

- Estimation techniques
- Addressing uncertainty
- Decisions under risk

- Decisions under uncertainty

13.5.1 Estimation techniques. An *estimate* is a prediction of a future value plus some indication of accuracy. For example, an estimate may include acceptable percentage amounts over or under the initial projected cost [Tockey 2005, pp. 343-345].

As already stated, an estimate is a prediction. It is a quantitative prediction outlining how much a project will cost to develop, expected development time, and the number of problem reports to be filed by the customer. Successful business decisions depend on accurate estimates. A poor estimate can of course lead to ineffective business decisions. Because business decisions speculate on future circumstances, a calculated estimate is necessary. Business decisions take into account future factors and values that cannot be known with certainty. Therefore, estimates provide a tool to best analyze a proposed business decision and closely predict the expected actual outcome of the project. As the project progresses, the scope of the decisions becomes smaller and smaller, yet decision-making continues for the duration of the project [Tockey 2005, p. 343-344].

13.5.2 Estimates vary in scope. Although they cover numerous subjects, estimates provide support for decision-making based on factors containing values with less than 100% certainty. Software business decisions contain a number of different sources of uncertainty [Tockey 2005, p. 345]:

- *The business environment* — Some kinds of business ventures are inherently more uncertain than others.

- *Novelty of the activity* — If you have never done anything like this before, there is probably no sound basis for an estimate.

- *Very long planning horizon* — Do not look too far into the future to develop a basis for uncertainty. A 25-year planning effort will have far greater uncertainty than a 5-year planning horizon.

13.5.3 Addressing uncertainty. *Uncertainty* means lack of certainty about an issue, idea, or problem. Reasons for uncertainty can range from lack of sureness to almost complete lack of definite subject knowledge. In some situations, the factors being estimated may have a broad range of possible outcomes, while a very narrow range may exist in another situation. This disparity of range is called a *variance*. The more uncertainty contained in an estimate, the less likely you are to calculate an accurate figure [*Webster's Ninth New Collegiate Dictionary 1987*].

13.5.4 Decision under risk. Sometimes an organization knows, through past experience or some other basis, where problems are likely to occur during development or operations, and what the consequences of those problems might be. Therefore, management will make decisions taking into consideration these known *risks*.

13.5.4.1 Monte Carlo analysis. Expected value is based on the idea that the value of an alternative with multiple possible outcomes can be thought of as the average of individual outcomes. The decisions are based on the average number of random individual outcomes that would likely occur if the alternatives were repeated a large number of times, e.g., the Monte Carlo analysis [Tockey 2005, pp. 403-407].

13.5.4.2 Decision trees. A decision tree maps out possible results from a sequence of decisions containing a series of future random events with associated known probabilities. Decision trees are useful when working with a number of possible future situations and when taking into account decisions that can be made in stages. Decision trees are built with three basic building blocks: decision nodes, chance nodes, and arcs. Figure 2 shows an example of a decision tree. Each connector is a yes/no question [Tockey 2005, pp. 411-412].

Figure 2: Example of a decision tree

13.5.5 Decision under uncertainty. Decision under uncertainly refers to techniques used when it is impossible to assign probabilities to outcomes. These techniques can be used when probabilities are not linked to the outcome. For example, given the case of a safety-critical software system in which failure could threaten human life, customers will not react well to the assignment of failure probabilities [Tockey 2005, p. 425].

There are a number of different techniques for addressing uncertainty. A few examples are [Tockey 2005, pp. 426-431]:

- *Laplace rule* — Also called "the principle of insufficient reason," this rule assumes that each outcome is equally likely. It simply uses equal probability for each proposed outcome. Therefore, the selection of the optimum proposal is based on specific factors such as the "highest payoff."

- *Maximum rule* — The maximum rule is the most pessimistic of the uncertainty techniques. Maximum rule assumes that the worst outcome will occur (also called Murphy's Law). Maximum rule assumes that occurrences will transpire at the most inopportune time. So, one must pick the alternative proposal offering the *best* payoff from among the *worst* possible payoffs.

- *Maximax rule* — The maximax rule is the most optimistic of the uncertainly techniques. Select the alternative proposal that offers the best payoff from all proposed positive payoffs.

- *Hurwicz rule* — The Hurwicz rule assumes that without guidance, a manager will focus on uncertainty extremes (see maximum and maximum rules). The manager must then choose a degree of optimism (between 0 and 1) with a remainder indicating pessimism. This will allow blending of the most optimistic payoff with the most pessimistic payoff using the selected degree of optimism as a weighting factor.

- *Minimax regret rule* — The minimax regret rule bases its decision on minimizing the regret endured (cost incurred) by choosing the wrong alternative. The regret would surface due to external influences caused by selection of the wrong alternative. Therefore, the alternative with the smallest maximum regret should be chosen.

13.6 Multiple Attribute Decisions

Money, although almost always the most important decision criterion, is definitely not the sole criterion. Essential decision criteria one might consider for a new computer purchase include technical features, processor speed, memory capacity, disk size, size of screen, and reliability. A monetary value must be assigned to each of these parameters; otherwise there is no rational basis for a decision. You can't trade cost vs. reliability as apples and oranges; they can only be traded off if the value of reliability has been quantified.

This section of the chapter will discuss:

- Value and measurement scales

- Compensatory and non-compensatory techniques

13.6.1 Value and measurement scales. The decision making process—be it a financial decision or not—is about maximizing values. You should always choose, from among an available set of alternatives, the value and measurement scale that maximizes total value; e.g., the largest memory, the faster processor, the widest screen. However, total cost is simply a way of quantifying value. Examine the following two kinds of value scales [Tockey 2005, p. 440].

1. *Use-value* — Use-value refers to the ability to get things done and takes into account the properties that cause the project to perform. For example, use-value related to a computer derives from its capacity to do work. A computer is given input and provides useful output. A CPU with a higher clock speed and greater output efficiency is worth more in total value. A computer with a larger memory can perform more calculations and is therefore of greater value to the project.

2. *Esteem-value* — Esteem-value refers to properties that make things desirable. Note that esteem-value is far more difficult, if not downright impossible, to qualify especially in terms of money. Esteem-value for a computer might include whether it carries a brand name or is manufactured by an off-brand company. For example, in the 1960s, software research laboratories strived to own an IBM 7094. This computer represented the status of a "quality" laboratory. Research centers using the IBM 7094 were considered to be great laboratories, whether or not any useful products were created and marketed.

13.6.2 Compensatory and non-compensatory techniques. Compensatory and noncompensatory techniques are two families of decision techniques that differ in their use of decision attributes [Tockey 2005, pp. 447-449].

1. One family is the *"compensatory"* or "single-dimensioned technique." This family collapses into a single figure of merit. It is called compensatory because for any given alternative, a lower score in one attribute can be compensated by a higher score in another attribute.

2. The other family is the *"non-compensatory"* technique. This family does not allow tradeoffs among the attributes. Each attribute is treated as a separate entity in the decision process.

13.6.2.1 Non-compensatory techniques. In the non-compensatory family of techniques, each of the favored attributes is created as a separate entity. A comparison is made on an individual attribute-by-attribute basis. The following are three specific techniques described in this family [Tockey 2005, p. 447-449].

- ***Dominance*** — The dominance technique compares each pair of alternatives on an attribute-by-attribute basis, looking for one of the alternatives to be at least as good in every attribute and better in at least one. When that kind of relationship between alternatives is found, there's no problem deciding between the two. One alternative is clearly superior to the other. The inferior alternative can be discarded.

  The dominance technique is unlikely to select a single alternative, but in some situations it could.

- ***Satisficing*** — The satisficing technique is sometimes called "the method of feasible ranges," because it is based on establishing an acceptable range of values. Any alternative with one or more attributes outside the range is discarded. Like the dominance technique, the satisficing technique may not lead to accepting a single alternative. However, satisficing is effective when filtering through a set of alternatives and reducing the amount of work to be done using other techniques.

- ***Lexicography*** — The two previous non-compensatory techniques don't treat any given decision attributes as more important than any other. Lexicography assumes that all attributes have equal importance. Supposing that one attribute is known to be more important than the others, a final choice could probably be made based on that one decision alone. If it turns out that two alternatives do not have equal non-compensatory techniques, simply move to the second most important attribute to break the tie.

13.6.2.2 Compensatory techniques. The noncompensatory techniques don't allow for tradeoffs between the attributes. Even though Thai Buffet and Hamburger Heaven have the same speedy service, maybe Thai Buffet has better food than Hamburger Heaven but Hamburger Heaven is less expensive than Thai Buffet. Maybe Hamburger Heaven's prices are so low that it makes up for the difference in food quality. The compensatory family of techniques allows better performance on one attribute to compensate for poorer performance in another; tradeoffs between the attributes will be allowed [Tockey 2005, pp. 449-452].

Under the compensatory family of techniques, values for the attributes are converted into a common measurement scale. The units for that common scale will usually be entirely arbitrary, but as long as the common scale is at least an interval scale (the difference between the values have the same significance at all points on that scale), different scores on that scale can be compared in a meaningful way. Three compensatory decision techniques are presented here:

- ***Nondimensional scaling*** — The non-dimensional scaling technique converts the attribute values into a common scale where they can be added together to make a composite score for each alternative. The alternative with the best composite score is selected. In non-dimensional scaling, all attributes are defined to have equal importance, so the common scale will need to have the same range, 0.0 to 1.0, 0 to 10, 0 to 100, etc., for all attributes.

- ***Additive weighting*** — The additive weighting technique is the most popular compensatory technique. The process is identical to non-dimensional scaling with the exception that the attributes can have different "weights" or degrees of influence on the decision. An attribute that's judged to be more important than another will have more influence on the outcome.

- ***Analytic hierarchy process*** — Dr. Thomas Saaty [1980, 1994], a pioneer in the field of operations research, developed the analytic hierarchy process (AHP) in the late 1960s. AHP is an enhancement of the additive weighting technique and has these features:

- o AHP can convert ordinal-scaled values into ratio scales.
- o AHP can help derive meaningful weights instead of just arbitrarily assigning them.
- o AHP not only allows inconsistency, AHP provides a measure of that inconsistency.

References

Additional information on the *software economics* KA can be found in the following documents:

- **[Saaty 1980]** Thomas Saaty. *The Analytic Hierarchy Process,* McGraw-Hill, New York, 1980.

- **[Saaty 1994]** Thomas Saaty. *Fundamentals of Decision Making and Priority Theory with the Analytic Hierarchy Process.* RWS Publications, Pittsburgh, PA, 1994. See also: Ernest H. Forman, *Decision by Objectives*, http://mdm.gwu.edu/forman/dbo.pdf.

- **[Tockey 2005]** Steve Tockey, *Return on Software: Maximizing the Return on Your Software Investment* (Hardcover), 1st Edition. Addison Wesley, Boston, 2005, 656 pages. ISBN-13: 978-0321228758. (Recommended as a CSDP/CSDA exam reference book by the IEEE Computer Society).

- **[*Webster's Ninth New Collegiate Dictionary 1987*]** Merriam-Webster Inc, Springfield, MA, 1987.

Chapter 14.1

Computer Science: An Introductory Survey[5]

J. Glenn Brookshear
Marquette University
Milwaukee WI 53201-1881

This paper is based on J. Glenn Brookshear's "Computer Science: An Overview" to provide an introduction to and overview of Computing Foundations for the benefit of individual software engineers who are hoping to take and pass the Certified Software Development Professional (CSDP) or the Certified Software Development Associate (CSDA) exam. This paper supports the Computer Fundamentals knowledge area (KA). Brookshear's book is well organized and easy to read.

The paragraph numbering and naming is based on the CSDP exam specifications and not on the original paragraph numbering and names from Brookshear's book [R. Thayer and M. Dorfman].

14.1 Programming Fundamentals

14.1.1 Machine language. Programs for modern computers consist of sequences of instructions that are encoded as numeric digits (usually binary). Such an encoding system is known as a *machine language*. Unfortunately, writing programs in a machine language is a tedious task that often leads to errors that must be located and corrected (a process known as *debugging*) before the job is finished.

The development of complex software systems such as operating systems, network software, and the vast array of application software available today would likely be impossible if humans were forced to write programs in machine language. Dealing with the intricate detail associated with such languages while trying to organize complex systems would be a taxing experience, to say the least. Consequently, programming languages were developed allowing algorithms to be expressed in a form that is both palatable to humans and easily convertible into machine language instructions.

14.1.2 Assembly language. In the 1940s, researchers simplified the programming process by developing notational systems by which instructions could be represented in mnemonic rather than numeric form. For example, the instruction "move the contents of register 5 to register 6" would be expressed as using the machine language whereas in a mnemonic system it might appear as "4056."

As a more extensive example, the machine language routine that adds the contents of memory cells 6C and 6D and stores the result at location 6E might be expressed as using mnemonics. Moreover, we have used the descriptive names Price, Shipping Charge, and Total Cost to refer to the memory cells at locations 6C, 6D, and 6E, respectively. (Such descriptive names are often called *identifiers*.) Note that the mnemonic form, although still lacking, does a better job of representing the meaning of the routine than does the numeric form.

---

5. This paper was based on J. Glenn Brookshear, *Computer Science: An Overview*, 10th edition, Pearson/Addison-Wesley, Boston, © 2009 Pearson Education, Inc. (This book is recommended by the IEEE Computer Society as a reference book for the CSDP exam.)

Once such a mnemonic system was established, programs called *assemblers* were developed to convert mnemonic expressions into machine language instructions. Thus, rather than being forced to develop a program directly in machine language, a human could develop a program in mnemonic form and then have it converted into machine language by means of an assembler. A mnemonic system for representing programs is collectively called an *assembly language.* At the time assembly languages were first developed, they represented a giant step forward in the search for better programming techniques. In fact, assembly languages were so revolutionary that they became known as *second-generation languages,* the first generation being the machine languages themselves.

Although assembly languages have many advantages over their machine-language counterparts, they still fall short of providing the ultimate programming environment. After all, the primitives used in an assembly language are essentially the same as those found in the corresponding machine language. The difference is simply in the syntax used to represent them. Thus a program written in an assembly language is inherently machine-dependent—that is, the instructions within the program are expressed in terms of a particular machine's attributes. In turn, a program written in assembly language cannot be easily transported to another computer design because it must be rewritten to conform to the new computer's register configuration and instruction set.

Another disadvantage of an assembly language is that a programmer, although not required to code instructions in numeric form, is still forced to think in terms of the small, incremental steps of the machine's language. The situation is analogous to designing a house in terms of boards, nails, bricks, and so on. It is true that the actual construction of the house ultimately requires a description based on these elementary pieces, but the design process is easier if we think in terms of larger units such as rooms, windows, doors, and so on.

In short, the elementary primitives in which a product must ultimately be constructed are not necessarily the primitives that should be used during the product's design. The design process is better suited to the use of high-level primitives, each representing a concept associated with a major feature of the product. Once the design is complete, these primitives can be translated to lower-level concepts relating to the details of implementation.

14.1.3 Complier language. Following this philosophy, computer scientists began developing programming languages that were more conducive to software development than were the low-level assembly languages. The result was the emergence of a *third generation* of programming languages that differed from previous generations in that their primitives were both higher level (in that they expressed instructions in larger increments) and machine independent (in that they did not rely on the characteristics of a particular machine). The best-known early examples are FORTRAN (FORmula TRANslator), which was developed for scientific and engineering applications, and COBOL (COmmon Business-Oriented Language), which was developed by the U.S. Navy for business applications.

In general, the approach to third-generation programming languages was to identify a collection of high-level primitives in which software could be developed. Each of these primitives was designed so that it could be implemented as a sequence of the low-level primitives available in machine languages. For example, the statement:

assign TotalCost *the value* Price + ShippingCharge

expresses a high-level activity without reference to how a particular machine should perform the task, yet it can be implemented by the sequence of machine instructions discussed earlier. Thus, our programming structure

$$identifier \leftarrow expression$$

is a potential *high-level primitive*.

Once this collection of high-level primitives had been identified, a program, called a *translator*, was written that translated programs expressed in these high-level primitives into machine-language programs. Such a translator was similar to the second-generation assemblers, except that it often had to compile several machine instructions into short sequences to simulate the activity requested by a single high-level primitive. Thus, these translation programs were often called *compilers*.

An alternative to translators, called *interpreters*, emerged as another means of implementing third-generation languages. These programs were similar to translators except that they executed the instructions as they were translated instead of recording the translated version for future use. That is, rather than producing a machine-language copy of a program that would be executed later, an interpreter actually executed a program from its high-level form.

14.1.4 Machine independence and beyond. With the development of third-generation languages, the goal of machine independence was largely achieved. Since the statements in a third-generation language did not refer to the attributes of any particular machine, they could be compiled as easily for one machine as for another. A program written in a third-generation language could theoretically be used on any machine simply by applying the appropriate compiler.

Reality, however, has not proven to be this simple. When a compiler is designed, particular characteristics of the underlying machine are sometimes reflected as conditions on the language being translated. For example, the different ways in which machines handle I/O operations have historically caused the "same" language to have different characteristics, or dialects, on different machines. Consequently, it is often necessary to make at least minor modifications to a program to move it from one machine to another.

Compounding this problem of portability is the lack of agreement in some cases as to what constitutes the correct definition of a particular language. To aid in this regard, the American National Standards Institute (ANSI) and the International Organization for Standardization (ISO) have adopted and published standards for many of the popular languages. In other cases, informal standards have evolved because of the popularity of a certain dialect of a language and the desire of other compiler writers to produce compatible products.

However, even in the case of highly standardized languages, compiler designers often provide features, sometimes called *language extensions*, that are not part of the standard version of the language. If a programmer takes advantage of these features, the program produced will not be compatible with environments using a compiler from a different vendor.

In the overall history of programming languages, the fact that third-generation languages fell short of true machine independence is actually of little significance for two reasons. First, they were close enough to being machine independent that software could be transported from one machine to another with relative ease. Second, the goal of machine independence turned out to be only a seed for more demanding goals. Indeed, the realization that machines could respond to such high-level statements as:

assign TotalCost *the value* Price + ShippingCharge

led computer scientists to dream of programming environments that would allow humans to communicate with machines in terms of abstract concepts rather than forcing them to translate these concepts into machine-compatible form. Moreover, computer scientists wanted machines that could perform much of the algorithm discovery process rather than just algorithm execution. The result has been an ever-expanding spectrum of programming languages that challenges a clear-cut classification in terms of generations.

14.1.5 Programming paradigms. The generation approach to classifying programming languages is based on a linear scale on which a language's position is determined by the degree to which the user of the language is freed from the world of computer gibberish and allowed to think in terms associated with the problem being solved.

14.2 Algorithms, Data Structures/Representation and Complexity

We begin with the most fundamental concept of computer science—that of an algorithm. Informally, an algorithm is a set of steps that defines how a task is performed. Before a machine such as a computer can perform a task, an algorithm for performing that task must be discovered and represented in a form that is compatible with the machine. A representation of an algorithm is called a program. For the convenience of humans, computer programs are usually printed on paper or displayed on computer screens.

For the convenience of machines, programs are encoded in a manner compatible with the technology of the machine. The process of developing a program, encoding it in machine-compatible form, and inserting it into a machine is called programming. Programs, and the algorithms they represent, are collectively referred to as software, in contrast to the machinery itself, which is known as hardware. (In some environments software includes people, data structures, and user documentation.)

We have seen that before a computer can perform a task, it must be given an algorithm telling it precisely what to do; consequently, the study of algorithms is the cornerstone of computer science. In this paper we introduce many of the fundamental concepts of algorithms. We begin by reviewing the concept of an algorithm.

14.2.1 The concept of an algorithm. We define an *algorithm* as a set of steps that define how a task is performed. In our study we have encountered multitudes of algorithms. We have found algorithms for converting numeric representations from one form to another, detecting and correcting errors in data, compressing and decompressing data files, controlling multiprogramming in a multitasking environment, and many more.

In fact, many researchers believe that every activity of the human mind, including imagination, creativity, and decision making, is actually the result of algorithm execution.

But before we proceed further, let us consider the formal definition of an algorithm.

14.2.2 The formal definition of an algorithm. Informal, loosely-defined concepts are acceptable and common in everyday life, but a science must be based on well-defined terminology. Consider, then, this formal definition of an algorithm:

> *An algorithm is an ordered set of unambiguous, executable steps that define a terminating process.*

Note that the definition requires that the set of steps in an algorithm be ordered. This means that the steps in an algorithm must have a well-established structure in terms of the order of their execution. This does not mean, however, that the steps must be executed in a sequence consisting of a first step, followed by a second, and so on.

Some algorithms, known as parallel algorithms, contain more than one sequence of steps, each designed to be executed by different processors in a multiprocessor machine. In such cases the overall algorithm does not possess a single thread of steps that conforms to the first-step, second-step scenario. Instead, the algorithm's structure is that of multiple threads that branch and reconnect as different processors perform different parts of the overall task.

Next, consider the requirement that an algorithm must consist of executable steps. To appreciate this condition, consider the instruction:

"Make a list of all the positive integers"

that would be impossible to perform because there are infinitely many positive integers. Thus any set of instructions involving this instruction would not be an algorithm. Computer scientists use the term *effective* to capture the concept of being executable. That is, to say that a step is effective means that it is doable.

Another requirement imposed by our earlier definition of an algorithm is that the steps in an algorithm be unambiguous. This means that during execution of an algorithm, the information in the state of the process must be sufficient to determine uniquely and completely the actions required by each step. In other words, the execution of each step in an algorithm does not require creative skills. Rather, it requires only the ability to follow directions.

The definition of an algorithm also requires that an algorithm define a terminating process, which means that the execution of an algorithm must lead to an end. The origin of this requirement lies in theoretical computer science, where the goal is to answer such questions as "What are the ultimate limitations of algorithms and machines?"

Here computer science seeks to distinguish between problems whose answers can be obtained algorithmically and problems whose answers lie beyond the capabilities of algorithmic systems. In this context, a line is drawn between processes that culminate with an answer and those that merely proceed forever without producing a result.

There are, however, meaningful applications for non-terminating processes, including monitoring the vital signs of a hospital patient and maintaining an aircraft's altitude in flight. The term *algorithm* is often used in applied or informal settings in reference to sets of steps that do not necessarily define terminating processes.

14.2.3 The abstract nature of algorithms. It is important to emphasize the distinction between an algorithm and its representation—a distinction that is analogous to that between a story and a book. A story is abstract, or conceptual, in nature; a book is a physical representation of a story. If a book is translated into another language or republished in a different format, it is merely the representation of the story that changes—the story itself remains the same.

In the same manner, an algorithm is abstract and distinct from its representation. A single algorithm can be represented in many ways. As an example, the algorithm for converting temperature readings from Celsius to Fahrenheit is traditionally represented as the algebraic formula:

$$F = (9/5) C + 32$$

But it could be represented by the instruction:

Multiply the temperature reading in Celsius by 9/5 and then add 32 to the product,

or even in the form of an electronic circuit. In each case the underlying algorithm is the same; only the representations differ.

The distinction between an algorithm and its representation presents a problem when we try to communicate algorithms. A common example involves the level of detail at which an algorithm must be described. Among meteorologists, the instruction "Convert the Celsius reading to its Fahrenheit equivalent" suffices, but a layperson, requiring a more detailed description, might argue that the instruction is ambiguous. The problem, however, is not with the underlying algorithm but that the algorithm is not represented in enough detail for the layperson. In the next section we will see how the concept of primitives can be used to eliminate such ambiguous problems in an algorithm's representation.

Finally, while on the subject of algorithms and their representations, we should clarify the distinction between two other related concepts—programs and processes. A *program* is a representation of an algorithm. We define a *process* to be the activity of executing a program.

14.2.4 Algorithmic representation. The following are algorithmic representations of data structures.

14.2.4.1 Arrays. Two types of data structures are known as homogeneous and heterogeneous arrays. Recall that a *homogeneous array* is a "rectangular" block of data whose entries are of the same type. In particular, a two-dimensional homogeneous array consists of rows and columns in which positions are identified by pairs of indices—the first index identifies the row associated with the position, the second index identifies the column. An example would be a rectangular array of numbers representing the monthly sales made by members of a sales force—the entries across each row representing the monthly sales made by a particular member and the entries down each column representing the sales by each member for a particular month. Thus, the entry in the third row and first column would represent the sales made by the third salesperson in January.

In contrast to a homogeneous array, a *heterogeneous array* is a block of data items that are of different types. The items within the block are usually called *components*. An example of a heterogeneous array would be the block of data relating to a single employee, the components of which might be the employee's name (of type *character*), age (of type *integer*), and skill rating (of type *real*).

14.2.4.2 Lists, stacks, and queues. Another basic data structure is a list, which is a collection whose entries are arranged sequentially. The beginning of a list is called the *head* of the list. The other end of a list is called the *tail*.

Almost any collection of data can be envisioned as a list. For example, text can be envisioned as a list of symbols, a two-dimensional array can be envisioned as a list of rows, and music recorded on a CD can be envisioned as a list of sounds. More traditional examples include guest lists, shopping lists, class enrollment, and inventory lists. In some cases we may need to remove entries from a list one at a time, change the arrangement of the entries in a list or perhaps search to see if a particular item is in a list.

By restricting the manner in which the entries of a list are accessed, we obtain two special types of lists known as stacks and queues. A *stack* is a list in which entries are inserted and removed only at the head. An example is a stack of books where physical restrictions dictate that all additions and deletions occur at the top. Following colloquial terminology, the head of a stack is called the *top* of the stack.

The tail of a stack is called its *bottom* or *base*. Inserting a new entry at the top of a stack is called *pushing* an entry. Removing an entry from the top of a stack is called *popping* an entry. Note that the last entry placed on a stack will always be the first entry removed—an observation that leads to a stack being known as a *last in-first-out,* or *LIFO* (pronounced "LIE-foe") structure.

A *queue* is a list in which the entries are removed only at the head and new entries are inserted only at the tail. An example is a line, or queue, of people waiting to buy tickets at a theater, i.e., the person at the head of the queue is served while new arrivals step to the rear (or tail) of the queue.

Queues are often used as the underlying structure of a buffer. A *buffer* is a storage area for the temporary placement of data being transferred from one location to another. As the items of data arrive at the buffer, they are placed at the tail of the queue. Then, when it comes time to forward items to their final destination, they are forwarded in the order in which they appear at the head of the queue. Thus, items are forwarded in the same order in which they arrived.

14.2.4.3 Trees. A *tree* is a collection whose entries have a hierarchical organization similar to that of an organizational chart of a typical company. The president is represented at the top, with lines branching down to the vice presidents, who are followed by regional managers, and so on. To this intuitive definition of a tree structure we impose one additional constraint, which (in terms of an organizational chart) is that no individual in the company reports to two different superiors. That is, different branches of the organization do not merge at a lower level.

Each position in a tree is called a *node*. The node at the top is called the *root node* (if we turned the drawing upside down, this node would represent the base or root of the tree). The nodes at the other extreme are called *terminal nodes* (or sometimes *leaf nodes*). We often refer to the number of nodes in the longest path from the root to a leaf as the *depth* of the tree. In other words, the depth of a tree is the number of horizontal layers within it.

At times we refer to tree structures as though each node gives birth to those nodes immediately below it. In this sense, we often speak of a node's ancestors or descendants. We refer to its immediate descendants as its *children* and its immediate ancestor as its *parent*. Moreover, we speak of nodes with the same parent as being *siblings*. A tree in which each parent has no more than two children is called a *binary tree.*

If we select any node in a tree, we find that that node together with the nodes below it also have the structure of a tree. We call these smaller structures *subtrees*. Thus, each child node is the root of a subtree below the child's parent. Each such subtree is called a *branch* from the parent. In a binary tree, we often speak of a node's left branch or right branch in reference to the way the tree is displayed.

14.2.4.4 Static versus dynamic structures. An important distinction in constructing abstract data structures is whether the structure being simulated is static or dynamic, that is, whether the content of the structure changes over time. For example, in a data structure that contains a list of names, it is important to consider whether the list will remain a fixed size throughout its existence or expand and shrink as names are added and deleted.

As a general rule, static structures are more easily managed than dynamic ones. If a structure is static we need merely to provide a means of accessing the various data items in the structure and perhaps a means of changing the values at designated locations. But, if the structure is dynamic, we must also deal with the problems of adding and deleting entries as well as finding the memory space required by a growing data structure. In the case of a poorly designed structure, adding a single new entry could result in a massive rearrangement of the structure, and excessive growth could dictate that the entire structure be transferred to another memory area where more space is available.

14.2.4.5 Pointers. Recall that the various cells in a machine's main memory are identified by numeric addresses. Being numeric values, these addresses themselves can be encoded and stored in memory cells. A *pointer* is a storage area that contains such an encoded address. In the case of data structures, pointers are used to record the location where data items are stored. For example, if we must repeatedly move an item of data from one location to another, we might designate a fixed location to serve as a pointer. Then, each time we move the item, we can update the pointer to reflect the new address of the data. Later, when we need to access the item of data, we can find it by means of the pointer. Indeed, the pointer will always "point" to the data.

14.2.5 Complexity. In this section we are interested in the question of whether a solvable problem has a practical solution. We will find that some problems that are theoretically solvable are so complex that they are unsolvable from a practical point of view.

14.2.5.1 Measuring a problem's complexity. We can measure the efficiency of algorithms by classifying algorithms according to the time required to execute them. We now use this classification system to help us identify the complexity of problems. Our goal is to develop a classification system that tells us which problems are more complex than others and ultimately which problems are so complex that their solutions lies beyond practicality.

The reason that our present study is based on our knowledge of algorithm efficiency is that we wish to measure the complexity of a problem in terms of the complexity of its solutions. We consider a simple problem to be one that has a simple solution; a complex problem is one that does not have a simple solution. Note that the fact that a problem has a difficult solution does not necessarily mean that the problem itself is complex. After all, a problem has many solutions, one of which is bound to be complex. Thus to conclude that a problem itself is complex requires that we show that none of its solutions are simple.

In computer science, the problems of interest are those that are solvable by machines. The solutions to these problems are formulated as algorithms. Thus the complexity of a problem is determined by the properties of the algorithms that solve that problem. More precisely, the complexity of the simplest algorithm for solving a problem is considered to be the complexity of the problem itself.

But how do we measure the complexity of an algorithm? Unfortunately, the term *complexity* has different interpretations. One deals with the amount of decision making and branching involved in the algorithm. In this light, a complex algorithm would be one that involves a twisted, entwined set of directions. This interpretation might be compatible with the point of view of a software engineer who is interested in issues relating to algorithm discovery and representation, but it does not capture the concept of complexity from a machine's point of view. A machine does not really make decisions when selecting the next instruction for execution but merely follows its machine cycle over and over, each time executing the instruction that is indicated by the program counter. Consequently, a machine can execute a set of tangled instructions as easily as it can execute a list of instructions in a simple sequential order. This interpretation of complexity, therefore, tends to measure the difficulty encountered in an algorithm's representation rather than the complexity of the algorithm itself.

14.3 Problem-Solving Techniques

The techniques of problem solving and the need to learn more about them are not unique to computer science but rather are topics pertinent to almost any field. The close association between the process of algorithm discovery and that of general problem solving has caused computer scientists to join with those of other disciplines in the search for better problem-solving techniques.

As evidence of the elusive, artistic nature of problem solving, the following loosely-defined problem-solving phases presented by the mathematician G. Polya [1973] in 1945, are the basic principles on which many attempts to teach problem-solving skills are based today.

- Phase 1. Understand the problem

- Phase 2. Devise a plan for solving the problem

- Phase 3. Carry out the plan

- Phase 4. Evaluate the solution for accuracy and for its potential as a tool for solving other problems

Translated into the context of program development, these phases become

- Phase 1. Understand the problem

- Phase 2. Get an idea of how an algorithmic procedure might solve the problem

- Phase 3. Formulate the algorithm and represent it as a program

- Phase 4. Evaluate the program for accuracy and for its potential as a tool for solving other problems

Having presented Polya's list, we should emphasize that these phases are not steps to be followed when trying to solve a problem but rather phases that will be completed sometime during the solution process. The key word here is followed. You do not solve problems by following. Rather, to solve a problem, you must take the initiative and lead. If you approach the task of solving a problem in the frame of mind depicted by "Now I've finished Phase 1, it's time to move on to Phase 2," you are not likely to be successful. However, if you become involved with the problem and ultimately solve it, you most likely can look back at what you did and realize that you performed Polya's phases.

14.4 Use and Support for Abstraction

The concept of abstraction so permeates with the study of computer science and the design of computer systems that it behooves us to address it in this preliminary section. The term abstraction, as we are using it here, refers to the distinction between the external properties of an entity and the details of the entity's internal composition. It is abstraction that allows us to ignore the internal details of a complex device such as a computer, automobile, or microwave oven and use it as a single, comprehensible unit. Moreover, it is by means of abstraction that such complex systems are designed and manufactured in the first place. Computers, automobiles, and microwave ovens are constructed from components, each of which is constructed from smaller components. Each component represents a level of abstraction at which point the use of the component is isolated from the details of the component's internal composition.

It is by applying abstraction that we are able to construct, analyze, and manage large, complex computer systems, which would be overwhelming if viewed in their entirety at a detailed level. At each level of abstraction, we view the system in terms of components, called abstract tools, whose internal composition we ignore. This allows us to concentrate on how each component interacts with other components at the same level and how the collection as a whole forms a higher-level component. Thus we are able to comprehend the part of the system that is relevant to the task at hand rather than being lost in a sea of details.

Abstraction is a recurring theme in our study. We will learn that computing equipment is constructed using levels of abstract tools. We will also see that the development of large software systems is accomplished in a modular fashion in which each component is used as an abstract tool in larger components. Moreover, abstraction plays an important role in the task of advancing computer science itself, allowing researchers to focus attention on particular areas within a complex field.

14.4.1 Support for abstraction

- ***Information hiding*** — In computer science, *information hiding* is the principle of segregation of the *design decisions* in a computer program that are most likely to change, thus protecting other parts of the program from extensive modification if the design decision is changed. The protection involves providing a stable *interface* that protects the remainder of the program from the implementation (the details that are most likely to change) [http://en.wikipedia.org/wiki/Information_hiding].

- ***Encapsulation*** — The term *encapsulation* is often used interchangeably with information hiding. Not all agree on the distinctions between the two though; one may think of information hiding as being the principle and encapsulation being the technique. A software module hides information by encapsulating the information into a module or other construct which presents an interface. "The process of compartmentalizing the elements of an abstraction that constitute its structure and behavior; encapsulation serves to separate the contractual interface of an abstraction and its implementation" [http://en.wiki pedia.org/wiki/Information_hiding].

- ***Hierarchy*** — A *hierarchy* is an arrangement of items (objects, names, values, categories, etc.) in which the items are represented as being "above," "below," or "at the same level as" one another [http://en.wikipedia.org/wiki/Hierarchy].

14.5 Computer Organization

The modern definition of a computer is an electronic device that performs calculations on data, presenting the results to humans or other computers in a variety of (hopefully useful) ways. Computer organization refers to the level of abstraction above the digital logic level, but below the operating system level. At this level, the major components are functional units or subsystems that correspond to specific pieces of hardware built from the lower level building blocks described in the previous module.

The generic computer contains input devices (keyboard, mouse, A/D [analog-to-digital] converter, etc.), a computational unit, and output devices (monitors, printers, D/A converters). The computational unit is the computer's heart and usually consists of a central processing unit

(CPU), a memory, and an input/output (I/O) interface. I/O devices present on a given computer vary greatly.

A simple computer operates fundamentally in discrete time. Computers are clocked devices, in which computational steps occur periodically according to ticks of a clock. This description belies clock speed: When one has "a one-GHz computer," the computer takes one nanosecond to perform each step. That is incredibly fast! A "step" does not, unfortunately, necessarily mean a computation like an addition; computers break such computations down into several stages, which mean that the clock speed need not express the computational speed. Computational speed is expressed in units of millions of instructions/second (MIPS). A one-GHz computer (clock speed) may have a computational speed of 200 MIPS.

Computers perform integer (discrete-valued) computations. Computer calculations can be numeric (obeying the laws of arithmetic), logical (obeying the laws of an algebra), or symbolic (obeying any selected law). Each computer instruction that performs an elementary numeric calculation—an addition, a multiplication, or a division—does so only for integers. The sum or product of two integers is also an integer, but the quotient of two integers is likely to not be an integer. How does a computer access numbers that have digits to the right of the decimal point? This problem is addressed by using the so-called floating-point representation of real numbers.

14.5.1 Floating point representation of real numbers. In computing, *floating point* describes a system for representing real numbers that supports a wide range of values. Numbers are in general represented approximately to a fixed number of significant digits and scaled using an exponent. The base for the scaling is normally 2, 10 or 16. The typical number that can be represented exactly is of the form:

$$Significant\ digits \times base^{exponent}$$

The term *floating point* refers to the fact that the radix point (decimal point, or, more commonly in computers, binary point) can "float;" that is, it can be placed anywhere relative to the significant digits of the number. This position is indicated separately in the internal representation, and floating-point representation can thus be thought of as a computer realization of scientific notation. Over the years, several different floating-point representations have been used in computers; however, for the last ten years the most commonly encountered representation is that defined by IEEE 754-2008, *IEEE Standard for Floating-Point Arithmetic* [http://en.wikipedia.org/wiki/Floating_point]).

14.6 Basic Concept of a System

A system is a purposeful collection of interrelated components that work together to achieve an objective. This general definition embraces a vast range of systems. For example, a very simple system such as a pen may only include three or four hardware components. By contrast, an air traffic control system includes thousands of hardware and software components in addition to human users who make decisions based on information transmitted via the computer system. See Chapter 14.2 in this volume [Sommerville 2007, p. 21-23].

14.7 Basic User Human Factors

One of the tasks during requirements specification is to define how the proposed software system will interact with its environment. In this section we consider topics associated with this interaction when it involves communicating with humans—a subject with profound significance. After all, humans should be allowed to use a software system as an abstract tool. This tool should be easy to apply and designed to minimize (ideally eliminate) communication errors between the system and its human users. This means that the system's interface should be designed for the convenience of humans rather than merely the expediency of the software system.

The importance of good interface design is further emphasized by the fact that a system's interface is likely to make a stronger impression on a user than any other system characteristic. After all, a human tends to view a system in terms of its usability, not in terms of how cleverly it performs its internal tasks. From a human's perspective, the choice between two competing systems is likely to be based on the system's interfaces. Thus, the design of a system's interface can ultimately be the determining factor in the success or failure of a software engineering project.

For these reasons, the human-machine interface has become an important concern in the requirements specification stage of software development projects and is a growing subfield of software engineering. In fact, some would argue that the study of human-machine interfaces is an entire field in its own right.

Research in human-machine interface design draws heavily from the areas of engineering called *ergonomics*, which deals with designing systems that harmonize with the physical abilities of humans, and *cognetics*, which deals with designing systems that harmonize with the mental abilities of humans. Of the two, ergonomics is the better understood, largely because humans have been interacting physically with machines for centuries. Examples are found in ancient tools, weaponry, and transportation systems.

Mental interaction with machines, in contrast, is a relatively new phenomenon, and thus it is cognetics that offers the higher potential for fruitful research and enlightening insights. The formation of habits may also cause problems when a human is required to use several application software packages. The interfaces of such packages may be similar yet different. Similar user actions may result in different system responses or similar system responses may require different user actions. In these cases habits developed in one application may lead to errors in the other applications.

Another human characteristic that concerns researchers in human-machine interface design is the narrowness of a human's attention, which tends to become more focused as the level of concentration increases. As a human becomes more engrossed in the task at hand, breaking that focus becomes more difficult. In 1972 a commercial aircraft crashed because the pilots became so absorbed with a landing gear problem (actually, with the process of changing the landing gear indicator light bulb) that they allowed the plane to fly into the ground, even though warnings were sounding in the cockpit.

Still another human characteristic that must be anticipated during interface design is the mind's limited capacity to deal with multiple facts simultaneously. In an article in *Psychological Review* in 1956, George A. Miller [1956] reported research indicating that the human mind is capable of dealing with only about seven details at once. Thus, it is important that an interface be designed to present all the relevant information when a decision is required rather than to rely on the human user's memory. In particular, it would be poor design to require that a human remember precise details from previous screen images. Moreover, if an interface requires extensive navigation among screen images, a human can get lost in the maze. Thus, the content and arrangement of screen images becomes an important design issue.

Although applications of ergonomics and cognetics give the field of human-machine interface design a unique flavor, the field also encompasses many of the more traditional topics of software engineering. In particular, the search for metrics is just as important in the field of interface design as it is in the more traditional areas of software engineering. Interface characteristics that have been subjected to measurement include the time required to learn an interface, the time required to perform tasks via the interface, the rate of user-interface errors, the degree to which a user retains proficiency with the interface after periods of nonuse, and even such subjective traits as the degree to which users like the interface.

The *GOMS* model, originally introduced in 1954, [http://en.wikipedia.org/wiki/GOMS] is representative of the search for metrics in the field of human-machine interface design. GOMS (goals, operators, methods, and selection rules) is a methodology that allows the actions of a human using an interface to be analyzed as sequences of elementary steps (press a key, move the mouse, make a decision). The performance of each elementary step is assigned a precise time period, and thus, by adding the times assigned to the steps in a task, GOMS provides a means of comparing different proposed interfaces in terms of the time each would require when performing similar tasks.

The design of human-machine interfaces promises to be an active field of research in the foreseeable future. Many issues dealing with today's GUIs are yet unresolved, and a multitude of additional problems lurk in the use of three-dimensional interfaces that are now on the horizon. Indeed, because these interfaces promise to combine audio and tactile communication with three-dimensional vision, the scope of potential problems is enormous.

14.8 Basic Developer Human Factors

Engineers in every discipline learn the limits of the tools and materials they work with. If you're an electrical engineer, you know the conductivity of various metals and a hundred ways to use a voltmeter. If you're a structural engineer, you know the load-bearing properties of wood, concrete, and steel.

If you're a software engineer, your basic building material is human intellect and your primary tool is you. Rather than designing a structure to the last detail and then handing the blueprints to someone else for construction, you know that once you've designed a piece of software to the last detail, it's done. The whole job of programming is building air castles—it's one of the most purely mental activities you can do.

Consequently, when software engineers study the essential properties and raw materials, they find that they're studying people; intellect, other attributes that are less tangible than wood, concrete, and steel [McConnell 2004, pp. 819-220]. Thus, in software engineering, the responsibility for "doing a good job" rests much more solidly and completely with the individual engineer. It is the responsibility of the engineer, and of the organization employing him/her, to ensure that the engineer has not only mastered the technology but has developed his/her capabilities to work in this human-centered profession.

14.9 Operating System Basics

An *operating system* is the software that controls the overall operation of a computer. It provides the means by which a user can store and retrieve files, provides the interface by which a user can request the execution of programs, and provides the environment necessary to execute the programs requested.

Perhaps the best known example of an operating system is Windows, which is provided in numerous versions by Microsoft and widely used in the PC arena. Another well-established example is UNIX, which is a popular choice for larger computer systems as well as PCs. In fact,

UNIX is the core of two other popular operating systems: Mac OS, which is the operating system provided by Apple for its range of Mac machines, and Oracle Solaris, which was originally a product of Sun Microsystems. Still another example of an operating system found on both large and small machines is Linux, which was originally developed non-commercially by computer enthusiasts and is now available through many commercial sources, including IBM.

To understand the composition of a typical operating system, we first consider the complete spectrum of software found within a typical computer system. Then we will concentrate on the operating system itself.

14.9.1 Classifying software. We can divide a machine's software into two broad categories: application software and system software. *Application software* consists of the programs for performing tasks particular to the machine's utilization. A machine used to maintain the inventory for a manufacturing company will contain different application software from that found on a machine used by an electrical engineer. Examples of application software include spreadsheets, database systems, desktop publishing systems, accounting systems, program development software, and games. In contrast to application software, *system software* performs those tasks that are common to computer systems in general.

Within the class of system software are two categories: one is the operating system itself and the other consists of software units collectively known as utility software. The majority of an installation's utility software consists of programs for performing activities that are fundamental to computer installations but not included in the operating system. In a sense, utility software consists of software units that extend (or perhaps customize) the capabilities of the operating system.

For example, the ability to format a magnetic disk or to copy a file from a magnetic disk to a CD is often not implemented within the operating system itself but instead is provided by means of a utility program. Other instances of utility software include software to compress and decompress data, for playing multimedia presentations, and for handling network communication.

Unfortunately, the distinction between application software and utility software can be vague. From our point of view, the difference is whether the package is part of the computer "software infrastructure." Thus a new application may evolve to the status of a utility if it becomes a fundamental tool. When still a research project, software for communicating over the Internet was considered application software; today such tools are fundamental to most PC usage and would therefore be classified as utility software.

The distinction between utility software and the operating system is equally vague. In particular, anti-trust lawsuits in the United States and Europe have been founded on questions regarding whether units such as browsers and media players are components of Microsoft's operating systems or utilities that Microsoft has included merely to squash competition.

14.9.2 Components of an operating system. Let us focus now on components that are within the domain of an operating system. In order to perform the actions requested by the computer's users, an operating system must be able to communicate with the users. The portion of an operating system that handles this communication is called the shell. Older shells communicate with users through textual messages using a keyboard and monitor screen. More modern shells perform this task by means of a *graphical user interface* (GUI) in which objects to be manipulated, such as files and programs, are represented pictorially on the monitor screen as icons.

An important component within today's GUI shells is the *window manager,* which allocates blocks of space on the screen, called *windows,* and keeps track of which application is associated with each window. When an application wants to display something on the screen, it notifies the window manager, and the window manager places the desired image in the window assigned to the application. In turn, when a mouse button is clicked, it is the window manager that computes the mouse's location on the screen and notifies the appropriate application of the mouse action.

In contrast to an operating system's shell, the internal part of an operating system is called the *kernel.* An operating system's kernel contains those software components that perform the very basic functions required by the computer installation. One such unit is the *file manager,* whose job is to coordinate the use of the machine's mass storage facilities. More precisely, the file manager maintains records of all the files stored in mass storage, including where each file is located, which users are allowed to access the various files, and which portions of mass storage are available for new files or extensions to existing files.

For the convenience of the machine's users, most file managers allow files to be grouped into a bundle called a *directory* or *folder.* This approach allows a user to organize his or her files according to their purposes by placing related files in the same directory. Moreover, by allowing directories to contain other directories called *subdirectories,* a hierarchical organization can be constructed. A chain of directories within directories is called a *directory path.* Paths are often expressed by listing the directories along the path separated by slashes.

Any access to a file by other software units is obtained at the discretion of the file manager. The procedure begins by requesting that the file manager grant access to the file through a procedure known as *opening the file.* If the file manager approves the requested access, it provides the information needed to find and to manipulate the file. This information is stored in an area of main memory called a *file descriptor.* It is by referencing the information in this file descriptor that individual operations are performed on the file.

Another component of the kernel consists of a collection of *device drivers,* which are the software units that communicate with the controllers (or at times, directly with peripheral devices) to carry out operations on the peripheral devices attached to the machine. Each device driver is uniquely designed for its particular type of device (such as a printer, disk drive, or monitor) and translates generic requests into the more technical steps required by the device assigned to that driver.

Still another component of an operating system's kernel is the memory manager, which is charged with the task of coordinating the machine's use of main memory. Such duties are minimal in an environment in which a computer is asked to perform only one task at a time. However, in multiuser or multitasking environments in which the computer is asked to address many needs at the same time, the duties of the memory manager are extensive. In these cases, many programs and blocks of data must reside in main memory concurrently. Thus, the memory manager must find and assign memory space and ensure that the actions of each program are restricted to the program's allotted space. Moreover, as the needs of different activities come and go, the memory manager must keep track of those memory areas no longer occupied.

The task of the memory manager is complicated further when the total main memory space required exceeds the space actually available in the computer. In this case the memory manager may create the illusion of additional memory space by rotating programs and data back and forth between main memory and mass storage (a technique called *paging*). The data is divided into uniform sized units called pages, which are typically a few KB in size. Then the memory manager shuffles these pages back and forth between main memory and mass storage so that the pages that are needed at any given time are actually present in the main memory. The result is that the computer is able to function as though it actually had more main memory than it actually has. This large "fictional" memory space created by paging is called *virtual memory*.

A CPU is designed so that its program counter starts with a particular predetermined address each time the CPU is turned on. It is at this location that the CPU expects to find the beginning of the program to be executed. Conceptually, then, all that is needed is to store the operating system at this location. However, for technical reasons, a computer's main memory is typically constructed from volatile technologies—meaning that the memory loses the data stored in it when the computer is turned off. Thus, the contents of main memory must be replenished each time the computer is restarted.

In short, we need a program (preferably the operating system) to be present in main memory when the computer is first turned on, but the computer's volatile memory is erased each time the machine is turned off. To resolve this dilemma, a small portion of a computer's main memory where the CPU expects to find its initial program is constructed from special nonvolatile memory cells. Such memory is known as *read-only memory* (ROM) because its contents can be read but not altered.

In a general-purpose computer, a program called the *bootstrap* is permanently stored in the machine's ROM. (A program stored in ROM is called *firmware,* reflecting the fact that it consists of software permanently recorded in hardware.) This, then, is the program that is initially executed when the machine is turned on. The overall process of executing the bootstrap and thus starting the operating system is called *booting* the computer.

In closing we should point out that understanding the bootstrap process as well as the distinctions between an operating system, utility software, and application software allows us to comprehend the overall methodology under which most general-purpose computer systems operate. When such a machine is first turned on, the bootstrap process loads and activates the operating system.

The user then makes requests to the operating system regarding the utility or application programs to be executed. As each utility or application is terminated, the user is put back in touch with the operating system; at that time the user can make additional requests. Learning to use such a system is therefore a two-layered process. In addition to learning the details of the specific utility of application desired, one must learn enough about the machine's operating system to navigate among the applications.

14.10 Database Basics and Data Management

The term *database* refers to a collection of data that is multidimensional in the sense that internal links between its entries make the information accessible from a variety of perspectives. This is in contrast to a traditional file system sometimes called a *flat file,* which is a one-dimensional storage system, meaning that it presents its information from a single point of view.

A 'flat file' is either a plain text or mixed text binary file that usually contains one record per line or 'physical' record (example on disc or tape). Strictly, a flat file database should consist of nothing but data and, if records vary in length, delimiters. More broadly, the term refers to any database that exists in a single file in the form of rows and columns, with no relationships or links between records and fields except the table structure [http://en.wikipedia.org/wiki/Flat _file#Flat_files].

14.10.1 The significance of database systems. Historically, as computing machinery found broader uses in information management, each application tended to be implemented as a separate system with its own collection of data. Payroll was processed using the payroll file, the personnel department maintained its own employee records, and inventory was managed via an inventory file. This meant that much of the information required by an organization was duplicated throughout the company, while many different but related items were stored in separate systems.

In this setting, database systems emerged as a means of integrating the information stored and maintained by a particular organization. With such a system, the same sales data could be used to produce restocking orders, create reports on market tends, direct advertisements and product announcements to customers who are most likely to respond favorably to such information, and generate bonus checks for members of the sales force.

Such integrated pools of information provided a valuable resource with which management decisions could be made, assuming the information could be accessed in a meaningful way. In turn, database research focused on developing techniques by which the information in a database could be brought to the decision-making process. Much progress has been made in this regard. Today, database technology, combined with data mining techniques, is an important management tool, allowing the management of an organization to extract pertinent information from enormous amounts of data covering all aspects of the organization and its environment.

Moreover, database systems have become the underlying technology that supports many of the more popular sites on the World Wide Web. The underlying theme of sites such as Google, eBay, and Amazon is to provide an interface between clients and databases. To respond to a client's request, the server interrogates databases, organizes the results in the form of a Web page, and sends that page to the client. Such Web interfaces have popularized a new role for database technology in which a database is no longer a means of storing a company's records but instead is the company's product. Indeed, by combining database technology with Web interfaces, the Internet has become a major worldwide information source.

14.10.2 The role of schemas. Among the disadvantages of the proliferation of database technology is the potential of sensitive data being accessed by unauthorized personnel. Someone placing an order at a company's website should not have access to the company's financial data; similarly, an employee in a company's benefits department may need access to the company's employee records but should not have access to the corporation's inventory or sales records. Thus the ability to control access to the information in the database is as important as the ability to share it.

To provide different users access to different information within a database, database systems often rely on schemas and subschemas. A *schema* is a description of the entire database structure that is used by the database software to maintain the database. A *subschema* is a description of only that portion of the database pertinent to a particular user's needs. For example, a schema for a university database would indicate that each student record contains such items as the current address and phone number of that student in addition to the student's academic record. Moreover, it would indicate that each student record is linked to the record of the student's faculty adviser. In turn, the record for each faculty member would contain the person's address, employment history, and so on. Based on this schema, a linkage system would be maintained that ultimately connected the information about a student to the employment history of a faculty member.

To keep the university's registrar from using this linkage to obtain privileged information about the faculty, the registrar's access to the database must be restricted to a subschema whose description of the faculty records does not include employment history. Under this subschema, the registrar could find out which faculty member is a particular student's adviser but could not obtain access to additional information about that faculty member. In contrast, the subschema for the payroll department would provide the employment history of each faculty member but would not include the linkage between students and advisers. Thus the payroll department could modify a faculty member's salary but could not obtain the names of the students advised by that person.

14.10.3 Database management systems. A typical database application involves multiple software layers, which we will group into two major layers—an application layer and a database management layer. The application software handles the communication with the user of the database and may be quite complex, as exemplified by applications in which users access a database by means of a website. In that case the entire application layer consists of clients throughout the Internet and a server that uses the database to fill the requests from the clients.

Note that the application software does not directly manipulate the database. The actual manipulation of the database is accomplished by the *database management system* (DBMS*).* Once the application software has determined what action the user is requesting, it uses the DBMS as an abstract tool to obtain the results. If the request is to add or delete data, it is the DBMS that actually alters the database. If the request is to retrieve information, it is the DBMS that performs the required searches. (Actually, this is done through the OS's File Manager, with which the DMBS interfaces. It appears to the user to be done through the DBMS but the DBMS actually interfaces with the File Manager.)

14.11 Network Communications Basics

The need to share information and resources among different computers has led to linked computer systems, called *networks,* in which computers are connected so that data can be transferred from machine to machine. In these networks, computer users can exchange messages and share resources—such as printing capabilities, software packages, and data storage facilities—that are scattered throughout the system. The underlying software required to support such applications has grown from simple utility packages into an expanding system of network software that provides a sophisticated network-wide infrastructure. In a sense, network software is evolving into a network-wide operating system. In this report, we will explore this expanding field of computer science.

A computer network is often classified as being either a *local area network* (LAN), a *metropolitan area network* (MAN), or a *wide area network* (WAN). A LAN normally consists of a collection of computers in a single building or building complex. For example, the computers on a university campus or those in a manufacturing plant might be connected by a LAN. A MAN is a network of intermediate size, such as one spanning a local community. A WAN network links machines over a greater distance—perhaps in neighboring cities or on opposite sides of the world.

Another means of classifying networks is based on whether the network's internal operation is based on designs that are in the public domain or on innovations owned and controlled by a particular entity such as an individual or a corporation. A network of the former type is called an *open* network; a network of the latter type is called a *closed*, or sometimes a *proprietary* network. Open network designs are freely circulated and often grow in popularity to the point that they ultimately prevail over proprietary approaches whose applications are restricted by license fees and contract conditions.

The Internet (a popular worldwide network of networks) is an open system. In particular, communication throughout the Internet is governed by an open collection of standards known as the TCP/IP protocol suite. (See [http://en.wikipedia.org/wiki/Internet_Protocol_Suite] and [http://en.wikipedia.org/wiki/TCP/IP_model] for an overview of TCP/IP). Anyone is free to use these standards without paying fees or signing license agreements. In contrast, a company such as Novell Inc. might develop proprietary systems for which it chooses to maintain ownership rights, allowing the company to draw income from selling or leasing these products. Still another way of classifying networks is based on the topology of the network, which refers to the pattern in which the machines are connected. Two of the more popular topologies are the bus, in which the machines are all connected to a common communication line called a bus, and the star, in which one machine serves as a central focal point to which all the others are connected.

14.12 Distributed and Parallel Computing

14.12.1 Distributed computing. With the success of networking technology, interaction between computers via networks has become common and multifaceted. Many modern software systems, such as global information retrieval systems, company-wide accounting and inventory systems, computer games, and even the software that controls a network's infrastructure itself are designed as distributed systems, meaning that they consist of software units that execute as processes on different computers.

Early distributed systems were developed independently from scratch. But today, research is revealing a common infrastructure running throughout these systems, including such things as communication and security systems. In turn, efforts have been made to produce prefabricated systems that provide this basic infrastructure and therefore allow distributed applications to be constructed by merely developing the part of the system that is unique to the application.

One result of such undertakings is the system known as Enterprise JavaBeans (developed by Sun Microsystems, now part of Oracle Corp.), which is a development environment that aids in the construction of new distributed software systems. Using Enterprise JavaBeans, a distributed system is constructed from units called beans that automatically inherit the enterprise infrastructure.

Thus, only the unique application-dependent portions of a new system must be developed. Another approach is the software development environment called ".NET" (read dot NET) Framework (developed by Microsoft). In the .NET terminology, the components of the distributed system are called *assemblies*. Again, by developing these units of the .NET environment, only characteristics that are unique to that particular application need to be constructed— the infrastructure is prefabricated.

14.12.2 Parallel computing. Suppose we were asked to design a program to produce animation for an action computer game involving multiple attacking enemy spaceships. One approach would be to design a single program that would control the entire animation screen. Such a program would be charged with drawing each of the spaceships, which (if the animation is to appear realistic) would mean that the program would have to keep up with the individual characteristics of numerous spaceships.

An alternative approach would be to design a program to control the animation of a single spaceship whose characteristics are determined by parameters assigned at the beginning of the program's execution. Then the animation could be constructed by creating multiple activations of this program, each with its own set of parameters. By executing these activations simultaneously, we could obtain the illusion of many individual spaceships streaking across the screen at the same time.

Such simultaneous execution of multiple activations is *called parallel processing* or *concurrent processing*. True parallel processing requires multiple CPUs, one to execute each activation. When only one CPU is available, the illusion of parallel processing is obtained by allowing the activations to share the time of the single processor in a manner similar to that implemented by multiprogramming systems.

Many modern computer applications are more easily solved in the context of parallel processing than in the more traditional context involving a single sequence of instructions. In turn, newer programming languages provide syntax for expressing the semantic structures involved in parallel computations. The design of such a language requires the identification of these semantic structures and the development of a syntax for representing them.

A more complex issue associated with parallel processing involves handling communication between threads. For instance, in our spaceship example, the threads representing the different spaceships might need to communicate their locations among themselves in order to coordinate their activities. In other cases one thread might need to wait until another reaches a certain point in its computation, or one thread might need to stop another one until the first has accomplished a particular task.

Such communication needs have long been a topic of study among computer scientists, and many newer programming languages reflect various approaches to thread interaction problems. As an example, let us consider the communication problems encountered when two threads manipulate the same data. If each of two threads that are executing concurrently need to add the value "3" to a common item of data, a method is needed to ensure that one thread is allowed to complete its transaction before the other is allowed to perform its task. Otherwise, they could both start their individual computations with the same initial value, which would mean that the final result would be incremented by only 3 rather than 6. Data that can be accessed by only one thread at a time is said to have mutually exclusive access.

One way to implement mutually exclusive access is to write the program units that describe the threads involved so that when a thread is using shared data, it blocks other threads from accessing that data until such access is safe. Experience has shown that this approach has the drawback of distributing the task of ensuring mutual exclusion throughout various parts of the program—each program unit accessing the data must be properly designed to enforce mutual exclusion, and thus a mistake in a single segment can corrupt the entire system. For this reason many argue that a better solution is to embody the data item with the ability to control access to itself. In short, instead of relying on the threads that access the data to guard against multiple accesses, the data item itself is assigned this responsibility. The result is that control of access is concentrated at a single point in the program rather than dispersed among many program units. A data item augmented with the ability to control access to itself is often called a *monitor*.

We conclude that the design of programming languages for parallel processing involves developing ways to express such things as the creation of threads, the pausing and restarting of threads, the identification of critical regions, and the composition of monitors.

In closing, we should note that although animation provides an interesting setting in which to explore the issues of parallel computing, it is only one of many fields that benefit from parallel processing techniques. Other areas include weather forecasting, air traffic control, simulation of complex systems (from nuclear reactions to pedestrian traffic), computer networking, and database maintenance.

14.13 Concepts of Programming Languages

In this section we consider some of the concepts found in imperative as well as object-oriented programming languages. (An *imperative language* is one that describes computation in terms of statements that change the program state [http://en.wikipedia.org/wiki/Imperative_programming]: *Object-oriented programming* is a "programming paradigm" using "objects"—data structures consisting of data fields and "methods" [processes] together with their interactions—to design applications and computer programs [http://en.wikipedia.org/wiki/Object-oriented_programming]).

Examples of programming languages are: C, a third-generation imperative language. C++, an object-oriented language that was developed as an extension of the language C. Java and C#, object-oriented languages derived from C++. (Java is a product of Sun Microsystems, now part of Oracle Corporation, whereas C# was developed by Microsoft.) FORTRAN and Ada, originally designed as third-generation imperative languages although their newer versions have expanded to encompass most of the object-oriented paradigm.

Generally, a program consists of a collection of statements that tend to fall into three categories: declarative statements, imperative statements, and comments. *Declarative statements* define customized terminology that is used later in the program, such as the names used to reference data items; *imperative statements* describe steps in the underlying algorithms; and *comments* enhance the readability of a program by explaining its esoteric features in a more human-compatible form.

Normally, an imperative program (or an imperative program unit within an object-oriented program) begins with a collection of declarative statements describing the data to be manipulated by the program. This preliminary material is followed by imperative statements that describe the algorithm to be executed. Comment statements are dispersed as needed to clarify the program.

14.13.1 Variables and data types. High-level programming languages allow locations in main memory to be referenced by descriptive names rather than by numeric addresses. Such a name is known as a *variable*, in recognition of the fact that by changing the value stored at the location, the value associated with the name changes as the program executes. Some languages require that variables be identified via a declarative statement prior to being used elsewhere in the program. These declarative statements also require that the programmer describe the type of data that will be stored at the memory location associated with the variable.

Such a type is known as a *data type* and encompasses both the manner in which the data item is encoded and the operations that can be performed on that data. For example, the type *integer* refers to numeric data consisting of whole numbers, probably stored using two's complement notation. Operations that can be performed on integer data include the traditional arithmetic operations and comparisons of relative size, such as determining whether one value is greater than another.

The type *real* (sometimes called *float*) refers to numeric data that might contain values other than whole numbers, probably stored in floating-point notation. Operations performed on data of type *real* are similar to those performed on data of type *integer*. Recall, however, that the activity required for adding two items of type real differs from that for adding two items of type integer.

Other common data types include *character* and *Boolean*. The type *character* refers to data consisting of symbols, probably stored using ASCII or Unicode. Operations performed on such data include comparisons such as determining whether one symbol occurs before another in alphabetical order, testing to see whether one string of symbols appears inside another, and concatenating one string of symbols at the end of another to form one long string. The type *Boolean* refers to data items that can take on only the values true or false. Operations on data of type Boolean include inquiries as to whether the current value is true or false.

The data types that are included as primitives in a programming language, such as *int* for integer and *char* for character, are called *primitive data types*. As we have learned, the types *integer, real/float, character,* and *Boolean* are common primitives. Other data types that have not yet become widespread primitives include *images, audio, video,* and *hypertext*. However, types such as GIF, JPEG, and HTML might soon become as common as integer and real.

14.13.2 Data structures. In addition to data type, *variables* in a program are often associated with data structure, which is the conceptual shape or arrangement of data. For example, text is normally viewed as a long string of characters, whereas sales records might be envisioned as a rectangular table of numeric values, where each row represents the sales made by a particular employee and each column represents the sales made on a particular day.

One common data structure is the *homogeneous array*, which is a block of values of the same type such as a one-dimensional list, a two-dimensional table with rows and columns, or tables with higher dimensions. To establish such an array in a program, most programming languages require that the *declaration statement* declaring the name of the array also specify the length of each dimension of the array.

Once a homogeneous array has been declared, it can be referenced elsewhere in the program by its name, or an individual component can be identified by means of integer values called *indices* that specify the row, column, and so on, desired.

In contrast to a homogeneous array in which all data items are the same type, a *heterogeneous array* is a block of data in which different elements can have different types.

We need to point out that structures such as arrays are actually implemented inside a computer. In particular, the data contained in an array might be scattered over a wide area of main memory or mass storage. This is why we refer to data structure as being the *conceptual shape* or *arrangement* of data. Indeed, the actual arrangement within the computer's storage system might be quite different from its conceptual arrangement.

14.13.3 Constants and literals. Sometimes a fixed, predetermined value is used in a program. For example, a program for controlling air traffic in the vicinity of a particular airport might contain numerous references to that airport's altitude above sea level. When writing such a program, one can include this value, say 645 feet, literally each time it is required. Such an explicit appearance of a value is called a *literal*.

Often, the use of literals is not good programming practice because literals can mask the meaning of the statements in which they appear. Moreover, literals can complicate the task of modifying the program should it become necessary.

14.13.4 Assignment statements. Once the special terminology to be used in a program (such as the variables and constants) has been declared, a programmer can begin to describe the algorithms involved. This is done by means of imperative statements. The most basic imperative statement is the *assignment* statement, which requests that a value be assigned to a variable (or more precisely, stored in the memory area identified by the variable). Such a statement normally takes the syntactic form of a variable, followed by a symbol representing the assignment operation, and then by an expression indicating the value to be assigned. The semantics of such a statement is that the expression is to be evaluated and the result stored as the value of the variable.

Much of the power of assignment statements comes from the scope of expressions that can appear on the right side of the statement. In general, any algebraic expression can be used.

Languages differ, however, in the manner in which algebraic expressions are interpreted. These ambiguities are normally resolved by the use of parentheses and the rules of operator precedence, meaning that certain operations are given precedence over others.

14.13.5 Control statements. A *control statement* is an imperative statement that alters the execution sequence of the program. Of all the programming statements, those from this group have probably received the most attention and generated the most controversy. The major "villain" is the simplest control statement of all, the "go to" statement. It provides a means of directing the execution sequence to another location that has been labeled for this purpose by a name or number. The problem with such a feature in a high-level programming language is that it allows programmers to write convoluted programs that are difficult to interpret and maintain.

To avoid such complexities, modern languages are designed with control statements that allow an entire branching structure to be expressed within a single lexical structure. The goal is to provide a language that not only allows algorithms to be expressed in a readable form but also assists the programmer in obtaining such readability. This is done by restricting the use of those features that have historically led to sloppy programming while encouraging the use of better-designed features. The result is the practice known as *structured programming*, which encompasses an organized design methodology combined with the appropriate use of the language's control statements. The idea is to produce a program that can be readily comprehended and shown to meet its specifications.

14.13.6 Comments. No matter how well a programming language is designed and how well the language's features are applied in a program, additional information is usually helpful or mandatory when a human tries to read and understand the program. For this reason, programming languages provide ways of inserting explanatory statements, called *comments*, within a program. These statements are ignored by a translator, and therefore their presence or absence does not affect the program from a machine's point of view.

14.14 Debugging Tools and Techniques

Debugging is a methodical process of finding and reducing the number of bugs, or defects, in a computer program or a piece of electronic hardware, making it operate as expected. Debugging tends to be more difficult when various subsystems are tightly coupled, as changes in one subsystem may cause bugs to emerge in another.

14.14.1 Debugging techniques. As software and electronic systems have become generally more complex, various common *debugging techniques* have expanded with more methods to detect anomalies, assess impact, and schedule software patches and full system updates. The words "anomaly" and "discrepancy" can be used as neutral terms to avoid the words "error," "defect," and "bug," especially to avoid the implication that all so-called *errors*, *defects* or *bugs* must be fixed (at all costs). Instead, an impact assessment can be made to determine if changes to remove an *anomaly* (or *discrepancy*) would be cost-effective for the system, or perhaps a scheduled new release might render the changes unnecessary. Not all issues are life-critical or mission-critical in a system.

14.14.2 Debugging tools. A *debugger* or *debugging tool* is a computer program used to test and debug other programs (the "target" program). The examined code might alternatively be running on an instruction set simulator (ISS), a technique that allows great power in its ability to halt operations when specific conditions are encountered, yet which will typically be slower than executing the code directly on the appropriate (or the same) processor. Some debuggers offer two modes of operation—full or partial simulation—to limit this impact [http://en.wikipedia.org /wiki/Debugging].

When the program "crashes" or reaches a preset condition, the debugger typically shows the position in the original code if it is a source-level debugger or symbolic debugger, commonly now seen in integrated development environments. A low-level debugger or a machine-language debugger shows the line in the disassembly (unless it also has online access to the original source code and can display the appropriate section of code from its assembly or compilation). A "crash" occurs when the program cannot continue because of a programming bug, for example, if the program tried to use an instruction not available on the current version of the CPU or it attempted access to unavailable or protected memory.

14.15 Secure Coding

Since the operating system oversees the activities in a computer, it is natural for it to play a vital role in maintaining security as well. In the broad sense, this responsibility manifests itself in multiple forms, one of which is *reliability*. If a flaw in the file manager causes the loss of part of a file, then the file was not secure. If a defect in the dispatcher leads to a system failure (often called a system crash) causing the loss of an hour's worth of typing, we would argue that our work was not secure. Thus the security of a computer system requires a well-designed, dependable operating system.

The development of reliable software is not a subject that is restricted to operating systems. It permeates the entire software development spectrum and constitutes the field of computer science known as software engineering. In this section we focus on security problems that are more closely related to the specifics of operating systems.

14.15.1 Attacks from the outside. An important task performed by operating systems is to protect the computer's resources from access by unauthorized personnel. In the case of computers used by multiple people, this is usually approached by means of establishing "accounts" for the various authorized users—an *account* being essentially a record within the operating system containing such entries as the user's name and password, and privileges to be granted to that user. The operating system can then use this information during each login procedure (a sequence of transactions in which the user establishes initial contact with a computer's operating system) to control access to the system.

Accounts are established by a person known as the super user or the *administrator*. This person gains highly privileged access to the operating system by identifying himself or herself as the administrator (usually by name and password) during the login procedure. Once this contact is established, the administrator can alter settings within the operating system, modify critical software packages, adjust the privileges granted to other users, and perform a variety of other maintenance activities that are denied normal users.

From this "lofty perch," the administrator is also able to monitor activity within the computer system in an effort to detect destructive behavior, whether malicious or accidental. To assist in this regard, numerous software utilities, called *auditing software,* have been developed that record and then analyze the activities taking place within the computer system. Another culprit that auditing systems are designed to detect is the presence of *sniffing software*, which is software that, when left running on a computer, records activities and later reports them to a would-be intruder.

With all the technical complexities associated with computer security, it is surprising to many that one of the major obstacles to the security of computer systems is the carelessness of the users themselves. They select passwords that are relatively easy to guess (such as names and dates), they share their passwords with friends, they fail to change their passwords on a timely basis, they subject off-line mass storage devices such as USB drives to potential degradation by transferring them back and forth between machines, and they import unapproved software into the system that might subvert the system's security. For problems like these, most institutions with large computer installations adopt and enforce policies that catalog the requirements and responsibilities of the users.

14.15.2 Attacks from within. Once an intruder (or perhaps an authorized user with malicious intent) gains access to a computer system, the next step is usually to explore, looking for information of interest or for places to insert destructive software. This is a straightforward process if the prowler has gained access to the administrator's account, which is why the administrator's password is closely guarded. If, however, access is through a general user's account, it becomes necessary to trick the operating system into allowing the intruder to reach beyond the privileges granted to that user.

References

Additional information on the *computing foundations* KA can be found in the following documents.

- **[Booch 2007]** Grady Booch, *Object-Oriented Analysis and Design with Applications*, Addison-Wesley, Reading, MA, 2007.

- **[Comer 1981]** Douglas Comer, "Principles of Program Design Induced from Experience with Small Public Programs," *IEEE Transactions on Software Engineering*, SW-7, March 1981, pp, 169-174.

- **[Curtis et al. 1986]** B. Curtis, E.M. Soloway, R.E. Brooks, J.B. Black, K. Ehrlich, H.R. Ramsey, "Software Psychology: The Need for any Interdisciplinary Program," *Proceeding of the IEEE,* 74(8), 1986, pp. 1092-1106.

- **[DeMarco & Lister 1985]** T. DeMarco and T. Lister, "Programming Performance and the Effects of the Workplace," *Proceedings of the 8th International Conference on Software Engineering,* Washington, DC, 1985, IEEE Computer Society Press, pp. 268-272.

- **[Dijkstra 1979]** Edsger Dijkstra, "Programming Considered as a Human Activity." (1979) *Classics in Software Engineering.* Yourdon Press, New York, 1982.

- **[GQM 2008]** "Goal-Question-Metric (GQM) Approach," *Software Tech News*, Vol. 11, No 4, December 2008. https://www.goldpractices.com/practices/gqm/ - 46 pages. (Recommended as a CSDP exam reference book by the IEEE Computer Society).

- **[Kan 2002]** Stephen H. Kan, *Metrics and Models in Software Quality Engineering* (Hardcover), 2nd Edition, Addison Wesley, Reading, MA, 2002, 560 pages. ISBN-13: 978-0201729153. (Recommended as a CSDP exam reference book by the IEEE Computer Society.)

- **[McConnell 2004]** Steve McConnell, *Professional Software Development.* Addison-Wesley, Boston, MA, 2004.

- **[McCue 1978]** Gerald McCue, "IBM's Santa Teresa Laboratory—Architectural Design for Program Development." *IBM System Journal,* 1978.

- **[McGarry, Waligora & McDermott 1989]** Frank McGarry, Sharon Waligora, and Tim McDermott, "Applying Software Measurement." *Proceedings of the Fourteenth Annual Software Engineering Workshop,* (November 29, 1989). Greenbelt, MD: Goddard Space Flight Center Software Engineering Laboratory (SEL), Document SEL-89-007, 1989.

- **[Mills 1983]** Harlan D. Mills, *Software Productivity*, Little & Brown, Boston, MA 1983.

- **[Miller1956]** George A. Miller, "The magical number seven, plus or minus two: Some limits on our capacity for processing information." *Psychological Review*, 63 (2), 1956, pp. 81–97.

- **[Montgomery 2007]** Douglas C. Montgomery and George C. Runger, *Applied Statistics and Probability for Engineers,* 4th Edition, John Wiley, Hoboken, NJ, 2007, 784 pages, ISBN: 978-0-471-74589-1. (Recommended as a CSDP exam reference book by the IEEE Computer Society.)

- **[Moore 2005]** James W. Moore, *The Road Map to Software Engineering: A Standards-Based Guide,* 1st Edition, John Wiley, Hoboken, NJ, 2005, 440 pages, ISBN-13: 978-0471683629. (Recommended as a CSDP exam reference book by the IEEE Computer Society.)

- **[Null & Lobur 2006]** Linda Null and Julia Lobur, *The Essentials of Computer Organization and Architecture* (Hardcover), 2nd Edition, Jones & Bartlett, Sudbury, MA, 2006, 700 pages, [Chapters 1-4, 9-12, also sections 8.1-8.4, 8.6, 8.7], 478 pages. (Recommended as a CSDP exam reference book by the IEEE Computer Society.)

- **[Parikh & Zvegintzov 1983]** *Tutorial on Software Maintenance*, IEEE Computer Society, Los Alamitos, CA, 1983.

- **[Polya 1973]** Geroge Polya, *How to Solve It,* Princeton University Press, Princeton, NJ, 1973.

- **[Sackman, Erikson, & Grant 1981]** H. Sackman, W.J. Erikson, and E.E. Grant, "Exploratory Experimental Studies Comparing Online and Offline Programming Performance," *Communications of the ACM,* 11(1) January 1968, pp. 3-11.

- **[Shneiderman 1975]** Ben Shneiderman, "Exploratory Experiments in Programmer Behavior," *International Journal of Parallel Programming,* Volume 5, Number 2, 1975, pp. 123-143.

- **[Sommerville 2007]** Ian Sommerville, *Software Engineering,* 8th Edition, Addison-Wesley, Harlow. England, 2007. (Recommended as a CSDP exam reference book by the IEEE Computer Society.)

- **[Thomas 1984]** Richard Thomas, "Using Comments to Aid Program Maintenance," *BYTE,* May 1884, pp. 415-422.

- **[Weinberg 1971]** Gerald M. Weinberg, *The Psychology of Computer Programming*, Dorset House Publishing, New York, 1971.

- **[Wikipedia]** Wikipedia is a free web-based encyclopedia which enables users to add and edit online content. Definitions cited from Wikipedia and other sources have been verified by the authors and other peer reviewers.

Chapter 14.2
Essentials of Computing

Richard Hall Thayer and Merlin Dorfman

This is the fourteenth chapter of a textbook to aid individual software engineers in a greater understanding of the IEEE SWEBOK [2013] and a guide book to aid software engineers in passing the IEEE CSDP and CSDA certification exams.

Each element of Computing Foundations listed below is defined. These software engineering features provide a greater understanding of SWEBOK as well as being useful in studying for the certificate exams.

Chapter 14 covers the CSDP exam specifications for the Computing Foundations Study Guide [Software Exam Specification, Version 2, 18 March 2009]. This list of exam specifications is reported to be the same list that the exam writers used to write the exam questions. Therefore it is the best source of help for the exam takers.

This section of the study guide involves:

1. Programming fundamentals

2. Algorithms, data structures/representation (static & dynamic), and complexity

3. Problem solving techniques

4. Abstraction use and support (for encapsulation, hierarchy, etc.)

5. Computer organization (architecture)

6. Basic concept of a system

7. Basic user human factors (i/o, error messages and robustness)

8. Basic developer human factors (comments, structure, and readability)

9. Operating system basics

10. Database basics and data management

11. Network communication basics

12. Distributed and parallel computing

13. Concepts of programming languages

14. Debugging tools and techniques

15. Secure coding

14.1 Programming Fundamentals

This section of the exam guide is based on a 334-page exam reference document that has been condensed into a twelve-page self-study guide [McConnell 2004, pp. 125-459]. Items of lesser importance have not been included. If a feeling of insecurity remains after reading and studying the condensed version, the authors recommend reading McConnell's book. It is easy to read and contains numerous examples that fully explain the programming concepts.

Programming fundamentals covers the following subjects [McConnell 2004, pp. 125-459]:

- Working classes (Section 14.1.1)

- High-quality routines (Section 14.1.2)

- Defensive programming (Section 14.1.3)

- Pseudocode programming process (Section 14.1.4)

- General issues when using variables (Section 14.1.5)

- The power of variable names (Section 14.1.6)

- Fundamental data types (Section 14.1.7)

- Unusual data types (Section 14.1.8)

- Organizing straight-line code (Section 14.1.9)

- Controlling loops (Section 14.1.10)

- Unusual control structures (Section 14.1.11)

- Table-driven methods (Section 14.1.12)

- General control issues (Section 14.1.13)

14.1.1 Working classes. In the dawn of computing, programmers thought about programming in terms of statements. Throughout the 1970s and 1980s, programmers began thinking about programs in terms of routines. In the 21st century, programmers approach programming in terms of classes.

A *class* is a collection of data and routines that share a cohesive, well-defined responsibility. A class might also be a collection of routines providing a cohesive set of services even if no common data is involved. The key to being an effective programmer is the maximization of the portion of a program that can be safely ignored while working on a particular section of code. Classes comprise the primary tool employed for accomplishing this objective.

This section of the study guide contains brief advice pertaining to the creation of high-quality classes. It contains the following subjects:

- Abstract data types (ADTs)

- Benefits of using abstract data types.

14.1.1.1 Abstract data types (ADTs). An abstract data type is a collection of data and operations that work with the data. The operations describe the data to the program and then allow the rest of the program to change the data. The term "data" in "abstract data type" is loosely used. An ADT may present itself in the form of a graphics window with all operations that affect it, a file and file operations. One example of an ADT is commonly viewed in the form of an insurance rate table with accompanying operations.

14.1.1.2 Benefits of using ADTs. An ad-hoc approach to programming practices is not necessarily problematic. However, if either desirable or necessary, the approach can be replaced with a stronger programming practice that produces these benefits:

- ***Hidden implementation details*** — Hiding information about font data type results in data type changes that can be modified in one place without affecting the entire program.

- *Changes that don't affect the entire program* — If richer fonts supporting more operations (such as switching to small caps, superscripts, strikethrough, etc.) are required, the program can be changed in one place. The change will not affect the entire program and can be tailored to specific segments of code.

- *An informative interface* — Code indicating, for example, *current font size* = 16, is ambiguous because *16* could refer to a size measured in either pixels or points. The context does not indicate the unit of measurement.

- *Improved performance* — In lieu of wading through an entire program, the recoding of a few well-defined routines will improve performance; for example, font performance.

- *An obviously correct program* — The tedious task of verifying correct programming statements is replaced with the easier task of verifying correct calls to the proper object.

- *The program becomes self-documenting* — Classes provide more readable code than programming statements.

14.1.2 High-quality routines. This document of the study guide examines routines and the characteristics that differentiate between preferable and non-preferable routines.

14.1.2.1 Valid reasons to create a routine. The following list contains valid reasons for creating a routine. The reasons overlap somewhat and are not intended to create an orthogonal set.

- *Reduce complexity* — The single most important reason to create a routine is to reduce a program's complexity. A routine hides information that can be easily retrieved.

- *Reliable code* — Code is more reliable when metadata is stored in one place. Modifications are more reliable because successive and slightly different modifications are avoidable under the mistaken assumption that identical ones have been made.

- *Support sub-classing* — Fewer lines of new code are needed to override a short, well-factored routine than one that is long and poorly factored.

- *Improved portability* — The use of routines isolates non-portable capabilities, explicitly identifying and isolating future portability work. Non-portable capabilities include non-standard language features, hardware dependencies, operating-system dependencies, and so on.

- *Improved performance* — Code can be optimized in one place instead of its inclusion in several locations within the program. Storing code in one place will enable easier profiling to detect inefficiencies.

14.1.3 Defensive programming. Defensive programming does not mean being defensive about one's programming. More generally, it refers to the recognition that programs will produce problems and require modifications, and that a smart programmer will develop code accordingly.

14.1.3.1 Protecting your program from invalid inputs. "Garbage in, garbage out." This expression is essentially software development's version of caveat emptor: "let the user beware." 'Garbage in, garbage out' is not sufficient for production software. A well written program never produces garbage, regardless of intake.

There are three general ways to handle the intake of garbage:

1. ***Check the values of all data from external sources*** — When retrieving data from a file, a user, the network, or some other external interface, check to be certain that the data falls within the allowable range.

2. ***Check the values of all routine input parameters*** — Checking the values of routine input parameters is essentially the same as checking data that comes from an external source, except that the data comes from another routine instead of an external interface.

3. ***Decide how to handle bad inputs*** — Once an invalid parameter has been detected, determine which different approaches are useful as an adjunct to the other quality improvement techniques.

14.1.3.2 Error-handling techniques. How does one handle expected errors that may occur in the code? Depending on the specific circumstances, options may include returning to a neutral value, substituting the next piece of valid data, returning a previous answer, substituting the closest legal value log, sending a warning message to a file, returning an error code, calling an error-processing routine or object, displaying an error message, or shutting down. A combination of these responses may be used.

14.1.4 Pseudocode programming process. The term "pseudocode" refers to an informal, English-style notation for describing the operation of an algorithm, a routine, a class, or a program. The *Pseudocode Programming Process* defines a specific approach that should be implemented when using pseudocode to streamline the creation of code within routines.

Because pseudocode resembles English, it is natural to assume that any English-like description that collects thoughts will have roughly the same effect as any other description. Pseudocode uses the syntax of a programming language and the semantics of the English language. In practice, some styles of pseudocode are more useful than others. English-like statements precisely describe specific operations.

14.1.5 General issues when using variables. Some languages require the declaration of variables. Other languages allow implicit variable declarations. The following four points are suggested when using variables in coding languages:

- ***Turn off implicit declaration***— Some compilers allow the disabling of implicit declarations. This forces the programmer to declare all variables before their use.

- ***Declare all variables***— Declare a new variable the moment it is typed, even though this step is not required by the compiler. This will catch some, but not all errors.

- ***Use naming convention*** — Establish a naming convention for common suffixes such as *Option Explicit* and *No* to avoid using two variables when only one is intended.

- ***Check variable names***— Use the cross-reference list generated by your compiler or another utility program. Many compilers list all variables contained in a routine, allowing one to spot, for example, both *acctNum* and *acctNo.* They also point out variables that are declared but not used.

14.1.6 The power of variable names. A variable and its corresponding assigned name are essentially the same. Consequently, the variable name determines the integrity of the variable. Choose variable names with care.

14.1.6.1 Naming consideration. The most important consideration in naming a variable is the entity it represents. An effective technique for selecting a good name is to state in words exactly what the variable represents. This statement is often the best variable name. It is easy to read because it does not contain cryptic abbreviations and is unambiguous. Because it contains a full description of the entity, it is less likely to be confused with another name or programming feature. Likewise, the statement is easy to remember because the name is similar to the concept.

14.1.7 Fundamental data types. Fundamental data types are the basic building blocks for all other data types. This paragraph contains tips for using numbers (in general), integers, floating-point numbers, characters and strings, Boolean variables, enumerated types, named constants, and arrays.

14.1.7.1 Integers. When using integers consider the following:

- *Check for integer division* — Ensure that the division method will produce the desired result. For example, 7/10 does not equal 0.7 when computed by a computer.

- *Check for integer overflow* — When calculating integer multiplication or addition, be aware of the largest possible integer in the computer system. Problems originate when results are larger than the largest possible integer.

14.1.7.2 Floating-point numbers. The main consideration when using floating-point numbers is that many fractional decimal numbers can't be accurately represented using the Os and 1s available in a digital computer. The following points present three specific guidelines pertaining to floating-point numbers:

1. *Addition and subtraction* — Avoid addition and subtractions for numbers that have greatly different magnitudes.

2. *Equality comparisons* — Avoid using equality comparison for floating-point numbers that should be equal but are not always identical.

3. *Rounding error problems* — Anticipate rounding error problems that do not differ from the problem of numbers with greatly different magnitudes.

14.1.7.3 Strings and characters. The following two points provide tips for using strings. The first applies to strings in all languages.

1. *Avoid the use of literal characters* — Use named constants when programming in a language that supports their use. Otherwise, use global variables.

2. *String literals tend to take up a lot of space* — String variables are used for menus, messages, help screens, entry forms, and so on. Excessive string variables may grow beyond control and cause memory problems. String space is not a concern in many programming environments. However, in embedded systems programming, and other applications in which storage space is at a premium, solutions to string-space problems are easier to implement if the strings are relatively independent of the source code.

14.1.7.4 Boolean variables. It is difficult to misuse logical or Boolean variables. Their thoughtful use produces a cleaner program.

- *Use Boolean variables to document the program* — Instead of merely testing a Boolean expression, assign the expression to a variable that makes the implication of the test unmistakable.

14.1.7.5 Named constants. A named constant is similar to a variable except that the constant's value cannot be changed once it has been assigned.

Using a named constant is a way of "parameterizing" the program. An aspect of the program that might change can be put into a parameter those changes in one place if the change needs to be made throughout the program.

14.1.7.6 Arrays. Arrays are the simplest and most common type of structured data. In some languages, arrays are the only type of structured data. An array contains a group of items that belong to the same type and that are directly accessed through the use of an array index. The following tips are useful when using arrays:

- *Make sure that all array indexes are within the bounds of the array* — Programming problems arise because array elements can be randomly accessed. The most common problem entails an attempt by a program to access an array element that is out of bounds. In some languages, this produces an error; in others, it simply produces bizarre and unexpected results.

14.1.8. Unusual data types. In addition to the data types discussed earlier, some languages support exotic data types.

14.1.8.1 Structures. The term "structure" refers to data constructed from various data types. In general, classes are created rather than structures. This allows the program to take advantage of privacy and functionality offered by classes in addition to public data supported by structures. However, directly manipulating blocks of data can be useful. Structures bundle groups of related items together.

14.1.8.2 Pointers. Pointer usage is one of the most error-prone areas of modern programming. Many modern languages such as Java, C+, C++, and Visual Basic do not provide pointer data types. Some programming groups forbid the use of pointers even if allowed by the language. Using pointers is inherently complicated, and using them correctly requires an excellent understanding of the compiler's memory-management scheme.

14.1.8.3 Global data. Global data is accessible anywhere in a program. Most experienced programmers have concluded that using global data is riskier than using local data. They have also concluded that access to data from several routines is useful. However, even if global variables are unlikely to produce errors, they are not a preferable programming practice.

14.1.9 Organizing straight-line code. Organizing straight-line code entails changes from a data-centered view of programming to a statement-centered view. The simplest kind of control flow is introduced: putting statements and blocks of statements in sequential order. Although organizing straight-line code is a relatively simple task, some organizational subtleties influence code quality, correctness, readability, and maintainability.

14.1.9.1 Statements must be in a specific order. The easiest sequential statements to prepare are those in which order counts. When statements have dependencies requiring placement in a certain order, take steps to make the dependencies clear.

14.1.9.2 Statements whose order does not matter. In certain cases, the order of a few statements or a few blocks of code may not seem to matter. One statement may not appear to depend on or to logically follow another statement. But ordering affects readability, performance, and maintainability, and in the absence of execution-order dependencies, secondary criteria can be used to determine the order of statements or blocks of code.

14.1.10 Controlling loops. A "loop" is an informal term that refers to any kind of iterative control structure—any structure that causes a program to repeatedly execute a block of code.

Common loop types in the C++ and Java languages include for, while, and do-while. Microsoft Visual Basic uses For-Next, While-Wend, and Do-Loop-While. Using loops is one of the most complex aspects of programming; knowing how and when to use each kind of loop is a decisive factor in constructing high-quality software.

14.1.10.1 Selecting the kind of loop. Most programming languages use a few kinds of loops:

- The *counted loop* is performed a specific number of times, perhaps once for each employee.

- The *continuously evaluated loop* does not predetermine how many times it will be executed. It tests whether or not each iteration has been completed. For example, the loop runs while money remains in the account, until the user selects "quit", or until an error is encountered.

- The *endless loop* continuously executes once it has started. This loop is found in embedded systems such as pacemakers, microwave ovens, and cruise controls.

- The interior loop performs its action once for each element in a container class.

Loops are first differentiated by flexibility—whether the loop executes a specified number of times or whether it tests for completion upon each iteration. Various kinds of loops are differentiated by the location of the test for completion. Testing can be set for the beginning, the middle, or the end of the loop.

Flexibility and the test location determine the kind of loop chosen as a control structure. Table 14.1 shows various loops in several languages and describes each loop's flexibility and test location.

14.1.11 Unusual control structures. Several control structures exist in a hazy twilight zone, simultaneously leading-edge, and discredited and disproved. The following useful constructs—recursion and GOTOs—are not available in all programming languages.

Table 14.1: The kinds of loops

Language	Kind of Loop	Flexibility	Test Location
Visual basic	*For-Next*	rigid	beginning
	While-Wend	flexible	beginning
	Do-Loop-While	flexible	beginning or end
	For-Each	rigid	beginning
C, C++, C#, Java	*For*	flexible	beginning
	While	flexible	beginning
	Do-While	flexible	end
	For each (Available only in C#, planned for other languages)	rigid	beginning

14.1.12 Table-driven methods. A table-driven method is a scheme that allows information to be presented in a table rather than via logic statements. Because virtually anything can be selected either with logic statements or by consulting a table, table-driven methods provide a second option for information presentation. In simple cases, logic statements are easier to read and are more direct.

As the logic chain becomes more complex, tables become increasingly attractive.

14.1.13 General control issues. No discussion about control would be complete unless it contained several general issues related to control constructs, including information storage and retrieval.

- There are three methods of retrieving information contained in tables: direct access, indexed access, and stair-step access.

- Secondly, what data should be stored in the table? Some tables store data while others store actions. The latter contains more complicated tables.

14.1.13.1 Boolean expressions. Except for the simplest control structure that calls for the execution of statements in sequence, all control structures depend on the evaluation of Boolean expressions.

14.1.13.2 Deep nesting. Excessive indentation or "nesting" has been pilloried in computing literature for 25 years and is still one of the chief culprits contained in confusing code. Studies have shown that the human mind has difficulty understanding and processing code containing more than three levels of "if" statements. Therefore, it is important to avoid more than three or four levels in indentation.

14.1.13.3 Structured programming. The term "structured programming" originated in a landmark paper titled "Structured Programming," presented by Edsger Dijkstra at the 1969 NATO Conference on Software Engineering [Dijkstra 1969].

The core essence of structured programming entails the simple idea that a program should use only one-in, one-out control constructs (also called single-entry, single-exit control constructs). A one-in, one-out control construct is a block of code with only one starting and one ending point. It has no other entries or exits. Structured programming is not the same as structured, top-down design. It only applies to the detailed coding level.

The central concepts of structured programming are still useful today and apply to considerations in using break, continue, throw, catch, return, and other topics.

14.1.13.4 Components of structured programming. The following sections describe the three constructs that constitute the core of structured programming.

1. *Sequence* — A sequence is a set of statements executed in order. Typical sequential statements include assignments and calls to routines.

2. *Selection* — A selection is a control structure that causes statements to be executed selectively. The if-then-else statement is a common example. Either the if-then clause or the else clause is selected for execution, but not both. A *case* statement is another example of selection control.

3. *Iteration* — An iteration is a control structure that causes a group of statements to be executed multiple times. An iteration is commonly referred to as a "loop." Kinds of iterations include *For-Next* in Visual Basic and *While* in C++ and Java.

4.2 Algorithms, Data Structures/Representation (Static and Dynamic), and Complexity

14.2.1 Algorithms. An *algorithm* is an effective method for solving a problem expressed as a finite sequence of instructions. Algorithms are used for calculation, data processing, and many other fields related to mathematics, computer science, and other scientific subjects. (In more advanced or abstract settings, the algorithm does not necessarily constitute a finite sequence or any type of sequence, and is therefore called a "nondeterministic algorithm.")

Each algorithm is a list of well-defined instructions written to complete a task. Starting from an initial state, the instructions describe a computation that proceeds through a well-defined series of successive states, eventually terminating in a final ending state. The transition from one state to the next is not necessarily deterministic; some algorithms known as randomized algorithms incorporate randomness.

An algorithm presents the basic idea of a program before code is actually written. The two most common algorithms are flowcharts and pseudocode. An experienced programmer can usually visually create a flowchart without the need for written documentation [http://en.wiki pedia org/wiki/Algorithm].

14.2.2 Data structures. A *data structure* is a particular way of storing and organizing data in a computer for its efficient use.

Different kinds of data structures are suited to different kinds of applications and some are highly specialized to perform specific tasks. For example, B-trees are particularly well suited for the implementation of databases, while compiler implementations usually use hash tables to reference identifiers.

Data structures are present in nearly every program or software system. Specific data structures are essential ingredients of many efficient algorithms and allow for the management of large amounts of data, such as large databases and internet indexing services. Some formal design methods and programming languages emphasize data structures rather than algorithms as the key organizing factor in software design.

There are two types of data structures: static and dynamic. *Static data structures* allocate memory at the time of compilation. *Dynamic data structures* apportion memory at run-time [http://en.wikipedia.org/wiki/Data_structure].

14.2.3 Complexity. Some theoretically solvable problems are so complex that their solutions lie beyond the realm of practicality. A simple problem requires a simple solution, whereas a complex problem does not contain a simple solution. However, not all programming problems are complex.

In the world of computer science, programmers are interested in problems that can be solved by computers. The solutions to these problems are first formulated as algorithms. A problem may have many solutions in which one or more of the solution algorithms is complex. The complexity of a problem can be measured by the complexity of the simplest solution to the problem [Brookshear 2009, pp. 275-281].

14.3 Problem Solving Techniques

Because of the elusive, artistic nature of problem solving, the following loosely defined problem-solving phases presented by the mathematician G. Polya [1973] in 1945 remain the basic principles to teach problem-solving skills are based today [Brookshear 2009, pp. 216-218].

Phase 1 — Understand the problem.

Phase 2 — Devise a plan for solving the problem.

Phase 3 — Carry out the plan.

Phase 4 — Evaluate the solution for accuracy and for its potential as a tool for solving problems.

Translated into the context of program development, these phases become

Phase 1 — Understand the problem.

Phase 2 — Get an idea of how an algorithmic procedure might solve the problem.

Phase 3 — Formulate the algorithm and represent it as a program.

Phase 4 — Evaluate the program for accuracy and for its potential as a tool for solving other problems.

Either of the two above approaches can be used to "solve" a problem.

14.4 Abstraction, Use, and Support

The term *abstraction* refers to the distinction between the external properties of an entity and the details of the entity's internal composition. Abstraction allows programmers to ignore the internal details of a complex device such as a computer, automobile, or microwave oven, and combine the internal details as a single, comprehensible unit, i.e., an abstraction. Moreover, it is by means of abstraction that such complex systems are designed and manufactured. Computers, automobiles, and microwave ovens are constructed using a series of components, each of which is created from smaller components. Each component represents a level of abstraction in which use is isolated from the details of its internal composition [Brookshear 2009, p. 11].

14.4.1 Encapsulation. Encapsulation refers to restricting access to an object's internal properties. An "encapsulated" object is one in which the object itself is capable of accessing internal properties. Encapsulation features are said to be "private." Features accessible from outside the object are said to be "public" [Brookshear 2009, p. 307].

14.4.2 Hierarchy. A *hierarchy* is an arrangement of items (objects, names, values, categories, etc.) in which the items are represented as being "above," "below," or "at the same level as" one another. These classifications are made with regard to rank, importance, seniority, power status, or authority. A hierarchy of power is called a power structure. Abstractly, a hierarchy is simply an ordered set or an acyclic graph.

A hierarchy can link entities either directly or indirectly, and either vertically or horizontally. For example, the only direct links in a hierarchy are to one's immediate superior or to the supervisor of a subordinate, although a system that is largely hierarchical can also incorporate alternative hierarchies. Indirect hierarchical links can extend "vertically" via multiple links in the same direction following a path.

All parts of the hierarchy that are not linked vertically to one another are nevertheless "horizontally" linked through a separate path. This is achieved by traveling up the hierarchy to find a common direct or indirect superior, and then down again. This is akin to two co-workers or colleagues who each report to a common superior, yet who have the same relative amount of authority [http://en. wikipedia.org/wiki/Hierarchy].

14.5 Computer Organization (Architecture)

The modern definition of a *computer* is an electronic device that performs calculations on data, presenting the results to humans or other computers in a variety of (hopefully useful) ways. *Computer organization* refers to the level of abstraction above the digital logic level, but below the operating system level. At this level, the major components are functional units or subsystems that correspond to specific pieces of hardware built from the lower level building blocks described in the previous module.

The generic computer contains *input* devices (keyboard, mouse, A/D [analog-to-digital] converter, etc.), a *computational unit*, and output devices (monitors, printers, D/A converters). The computational unit is the computer's heart and usually consists of a *central processing unit* (CPU), a *memory*, and an input/output (I/O) interface. I/O devices present on a given computer vary greatly. See Figure 14.1 [Johnson 2010].

A simple computer operates fundamentally in discrete time. Computers are *clocked* devices, in which computational steps occur periodically according to ticks of a clock. This description belies clock speed: When one has "a 1-GHz computer," the computer takes one nanosecond to perform each step. That is incredibly fast! A "step" does not, unfortunately, necessarily mean a computation like an addition; computers break such computations down into several stages, which means that the clock speed need not express the computational speed. Computational speed is expressed in units of millions of instructions/second (Mips). A one-GHz computer (clock speed) may have a computational speed of 200 Mips.

Computers perform integer (discrete-valued) computations. Computer calculations can be numeric (obeying the laws of arithmetic), logical (obeying the laws of an algebra), or symbolic (obeying any selected law). Each computer instruction that performs an elementary numeric calculation—an addition, a multiplication, or a division—does so only for integers. The sum or product of two integers is also an integer, but the quotient of two integers is likely to not be an integer. How does a computer access numbers that have digits to the right of the decimal point? This problem is addressed by using the so-called *floating-point* representation of real numbers. At its heart, however, this representation relies on integer-valued computations [http://cnx.org /content /m10263/latest/].

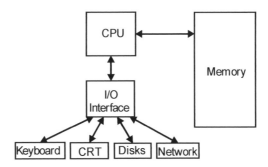

Figure 14.1: Generic computer hardware organization
[Johnson 2010]

14.6 Basic Concept of a System

A system is a universally used term. Computer systems, operating systems, payment systems, the educational system, and the system of government are all regularly referenced. Although variable in format, each shares the characteristic that somehow, the system is more than simply the sum of its parts.

An abstract system such as the system of government is beyond the scope of this book. Consequently, Sommerville [2007, pp. 21] has decided to focus on systems that include computers and that provide a specific service such as enabling communication, supporting navigation, and salary computation.

14.6.1 Definitions of a system. A *system* is a purposeful collection of interrelated components that work together to achieve an objective.

This general definition embraces a vast range of systems. For example, a very simple system such as a pen may only include three or four hardware components. By contrast, an air traffic control system includes thousands of hardware and software components in addition to human users who make decisions based on information transmitted via the computer system.

Systems that include software fall into two categories:

1. *Technical computer-based systems* include hardware and software components but not procedures and processes. Examples of technical systems include televisions, mobile phones, and most personal computer software. Individuals and organizations use technical systems for a particular purpose but knowledge of this purpose is not included in the system. For example, a word processor does not know it is writing a book.

2. *Socio-technical systems* include one or more technical systems with embedded knowledge relating how the system should be used to achieve a broader objective. These systems have defined operational processes, include operators as inherent parts of the system, are governed by organizational policies and rules, and may be affected by external constraints such as national laws and regulatory policies. For example, this book was created through a socio-technical publishing system that includes various processes and technical systems.

14.6.2 Essential characteristics of socio-technical systems. Socio-technical systems have emergent properties that belong to the system as a whole rather than being associated with individual parts of the system. Emergent properties depend on both the system components and the relationships between them. Due to complexity, the emergent properties can only be evaluated once the system has been assembled.

Socio-technical systems are often nondeterministic. When presented with a specific input they may not always produce the same output. The system's behavior depends upon human operators, and since people do not always react in the same way, system behavior can vary. Furthermore, use of the system may create new relationships between the system components and hence change their emergent behavior.

The extent to which the system supports organizational objectives does not depend merely on the system itself. It also depends on the stability of those objectives, the relationships and conflicts between organizational objectives, and how people in the organization interpret the objectives. New management may reinterpret the organizational objective that a system is designed to support, and a "successful" system may then become a "failure."

Properties and behavior of the system components are inextricably intermingled. The successful functioning of each system component depends on the functioning of other components. Thus, software will only operate if the processor is operational. The processor can only execute computations if the software system defining these computations has been successfully installed.

Systems are usually hierarchical and include other systems. For example, a police command and control system may include a geographical information system to provide details of incident locations. These ancillary systems are called sub-systems. Subsystems can operate as independent systems, a characteristic central to these systems. For example, the same geographical information system may be used in different systems.

Because software is inherently flexible, software engineers are able to solve unexpected system problems. For example, the siting of a radar installation produces ghosting of the radar image. Because it is impractical to move the radar to a site with less interference, system engineers have to find another way to remove this ghosting. A possible solution is to enhance the image-processing capabilities of the software to remove the ghost images. However, this may reduce the software processing speed, resulting in unacceptable software performance. The problem may then be characterized as a "software failure" versus a failure in the design process for the system as a whole.

Software engineers are commonly tasked with enhancing software capabilities without increasing hardware cost. Many so-called software failures are not a consequence of inherent software problems. Instead, software failures are the result of trying to alter software to accommodate modified system engineering requirements. A well-known example was the failure of the Denver airport baggage system [Swartz 1996], in which the controlling software was affected by the limitations of the equipment used.

Software engineering is therefore critical for the successful development of complex, computer-based socio-technical systems. Software engineers should not simply be concerned with the selected software, but should also have a broader awareness of how the software interacts with other hardware and software systems, and its intended usage. This knowledge helps to understand the limits of software, to design better software, and allows software engineers to participate as equal members of a system engineering group.

14.6.3 Emergent system properties. The complex relationships among system components reveal that a system is more than simply the sum of its parts. System component properties, also known as emergent properties, are properties of the system as a whole. These *emergent properties* cannot be attributed to any specific part of the system. Rather, they emerge once the system components have been integrated. Some of these properties can be derived directly from the comparable properties of sub-systems. However, they are often the result of complex sub-system interrelationships that cannot, in practice, be derived from the properties of individual system components.

Emergent properties are represented according to two types—functional and non-functional:

1. *Functional emergent properties* represent the sum of all parts of a system that work together to achieve an objective. For example, a bicycle, once assembled from its components, has the functional property of being a transportation device.

2. *Non-functional emergent properties* relate to the behavior of the system in its operational environment. Examples of non-functional properties are reliability, performance, safety,

and security. These are often critical for computer-based systems since failure to achieve a minimal defined level within these properties may make the system unusable. The system may be acceptable without all system functions because they are not needed by all users. However, a system that is unreliable or too slow is likely to be rejected by each of its users.

To illustrate the complexity of emergent properties, consider the property of system reliability. Reliability is a complex concept that must always be considered at the system level rather than at the individual component level. Because the components in a system are interdependent, failures in one component can be propagated throughout the system, consequently affecting the operation of other components. It is often difficult to anticipate how the consequences of component failures propagate throughout the system. Consequently, valid estimates of overall system reliability cannot be made from data pertaining to the reliability of system components [Sommerville 2007 pp. 21-25].

14.7 Basic User Human Factors
(I/O, Error Messages, and Robustness)

Human-computer interaction (HCI) is the study of interaction between people (both users and people affected by the system) and computers. It is often regarded as the intersection of computer science, behavioral sciences, design, and several other fields of study. Interaction between users and computers occurs at the user interface (or simply *interface*), which includes both software and hardware. Examples include characters or objects displayed (by software) on a personal computer's monitor, input received from users via hardware peripherals such as keyboards and mice, and other user interactions with large-scale computerized systems such as aircraft and power plants.

The Association for Computing Machinery (ACM) defines human-computer interaction as "a discipline concerned with the design, evaluation and implementation of interactive computing systems for human use and with the study of major phenomena surrounding them." An important facet of HCI is the securing of user satisfaction [http://en.Wikipedia.org/wiki/Human-computer_interaction].

Because human-computer interaction studies a human and a machine in conjunction with one another, it draws from supporting knowledge belonging both to the machine and to the human. On the machine side, techniques in computer graphics, operating systems, programming languages, and development environments are relevant.

On the human side, communication theory, graphic and industrial design disciplines, linguistics, social sciences, cognitive psychology, and human factors are pertinent. Engineering and design methods are also applicable. Due to the multidisciplinary nature of HCI, people with different backgrounds contribute to its success. HCI is also referred to as *man–machine interaction* (MMI) or *computer–human interaction* (CHI) [http://en.wikipedia.org/wiki/Human-compute interaction].

14.7.1 Input/Output (I/O). Input/Output or I/O refers to the communication between an information processing system (such as a computer), and the outside world – possibly a human or another information processing system. Inputs pertain to the signals or data received by the system, and outputs are the signals or data sent from the system. The term can also be used as part of an action; to "perform I/O" is to perform an input or output operation.

I/O devices are used by a person (or other system) to communicate via a computer. For instance, a keyboard or a mouse may be an input device for a computer, while monitors and printers are considered to be output devices. Input and output devices such as modems and network cards are typically used for communication between computers.

Note that the designation of a device as either *input or output* depends on the system perspective. A mouse and keyboards input physical movements that the human user outputs and converts into signals understood by a computer. The output from these devices is input to the computer. Similarly, printers and monitors input signals that a computer outputs. They then convert these signals into representations that human users can see or read. For a human user, the process of reading or seeing these representations is receiving input [http://en.wikipedia.org /wiki/Input /output].

14.7.2 Error-handling techniques. How are expected errors handled? Depending on the specific circumstances, consider returning a neutral value, substituting the next piece of valid data, returning the same answer as the previous one, substituting the closest legal value, logging a warning message to a file, returning an error code, calling an error-processing routine or object, displaying an error message, or shutting down. A combination of these responses may be used [McConnell 2004, pp. 194-196].

The following are details pertaining to the above options:

- ***Return a neutral value*** — The best response to unusable data is to continue operating and simply return a value that is known to be harmless. A numeric computation may return a value of 0. A string operation might return an empty string, and a pointer operation may return an empty pointer.

- ***Substitute the next piece of valid data*** — When processing a stream of data, some circumstances call for simply returning the next valid data. When a corrupted record is encountered while reading records from a database, simply continue reading until a valid record is found.

- ***Return the same answer as the previous time*** — If the thermometer-reading software skips a reading it might simply return the same value as the previous prompt. This of course depends upon the application.

- ***Substitute the closest legal value*** — In some cases, one might choose to return the closest legal value with an error code. This is often a reasonable approach when taking readings from a calibrated instrument.

- ***Log a warning message to a file*** — When bad data is detected, one may choose to log a warning message to a file and then continue with the process. This approach can be used in conjunction with other techniques.

- ***Return an error code*** — If it is decided that only certain parts of a system will handle errors, other parts will not be responsible for those situated locally. Other system parts will simply report that an error has been detected and expect an advanced routine belonging to the calling hierarchy to handle the error. The return of an error code should include the following:
  - Set the value of a status variable

o   Return the status as the function's return value

o   Define an exception by using the language's built-in exception mechanism

- ***Call an error-processing routine/object*** — Another approach is to centralize error handling in a global error-handling routine or error-handling object. The advantage of this approach is that error-processing responsibility can be centralized, which can make debugging easier. The tradeoff is that the entire program will be aware of this central capability and will be coupled to it.

- ***Display an error message wherever the error is encountered*** — This approach minimizes error-handling overhead. It has the potential to spread user interface messages throughout the entire application, which can create challenges when needing to create a consistent user interface, when seeking to clearly separate the user interface from the rest of the system, or when attempting to localize the software in a different language. Also, beware of providing too much information for a potential attacker of the system. Attackers sometimes use error messages to uncover how best to attack a system.

- ***Handle the error whichever way works best locally*** —Some designs call for handling all errors locally. The programmer responsible for designing and implementing the portion of the system encountering the error decides which specific error-handling method to use.

- ***Shut down***— Some systems shut down whenever an error is detected. This approach is useful in safety-critical applications.

14.7.3 Robustness. Robustness pertains to the qualities of being able to withstand stresses, pressures, or changes in procedure or circumstance. A system, organism or design may be said to be "robust" if it is capable of coping well with variations or unpredictable variations in its operating environment with minimal damage, alteration or loss of functionality [http://robus .moshe-online.com]. This capability is particularly important in military systems that might be damaged by overt action.

14.8 Basic Developer Human Factors

This section is derived from Steve McConnell's well-known book, *Code Complete* [2004].

Engineers in every discipline learn the limits of the tools and materials they work with. If you're a software engineer, your basic building material is human intellect and your primary tool is you. Rather than designing a structure to the last detail and then handing the blueprints to someone else for construction, you know that once you've designed a piece of software to the last detail, it's done. The whole job of programming is building air castles—it's one of the most purely mental activities you can do.

Consequently, when software engineers study the essential property and raw materials, they find that they're studying people; intellect, other attributes that are less tangible than wood, concrete, and steel.

14.8.1 Personal character. Programming work is essentially unsupervisable because no one evaluates what you're working on. We've all had projects in which we spent 80 percent of the time working on a small piece we found interesting and 20 percent building the other 80 percent of the program.

Your employer can't force you to be a good programmer; a lot of the time he or she isn't even in a position to judge whether you're good. If you want to be great, you're responsible for making yourself great. It's a matter of your personal character.

Good programmers constantly look for ways to become better. Consider the following professional development ladder used at McConnell's company and several others [McConnell 2004, p. 825].

- *Level 1: Beginning* — A beginner is a programmer capable of using the basic capabilities of one language. Such a person can write classes, routines, loops, and conditionals, and use many of the features of a language.

- *Level 2: Introductory* — An intermediate programmer who has moved past the beginner phase is capable of using the basic capabilities of multiple languages and is very comfortable in at least one language.

- *Level 3: Competency* — A competent programmer has expertise in a language, an environment or both. A programmer at this level might know all the intricacies of J2EE or have the *Annotated C++ Reference Manual* memorized. Programmers at this level are valuable to their companies, and many programmers never move beyond this level.

- *Level 4: Leadership* — A leader has the expertise of a Level 3 programmer and recognizes that programming is only 15 percent communicating with the computer and 85 percent communicating with people. Only 30 percent of an average programmer's time is spent working alone [McCue 1978]. Even less time is spent communicating with the computer.

  The guru writes code for an audience of people rather than machines. True guru-level programmers write code that's crystal-clear, and they document it too. They don't want to waste their valuable gray cells reconstructing the logic of a section of code that they could have read in a one-sentence comment.

14.8.2 Writing comments. Some good tips for writing inline comments [McConnell 2004, pp. 786-791]:

- *Repeat of the Code* — A repetitious comment restates what the code does in different words. It merely gives the reader of the code more to read without providing additional information.

- *Explanation of the Code* — Explanatory comments are typically used to explain complicated, tricky, or sensitive pieces of code. In such situations, they are useful, but usually that's only because code is confusing. If the code is so complicated that it needs to be explained, it's nearly always better to improve the code than it is to add comments. Make the code itself clearer, and then use summary or intent comments.

- *Marker in the Code* — A marker comment is one that isn't intended to be left in the code. It's a note to the developer that the work isn't done yet. Some developers type in a marker that's syntactically incorrect (******, for example) so that the compiler flags it and reminds them that they have more work to do. Other developers put a specified set of characters in comments that don't interfere with compilation so that they can search for them.

- *Summary of the code* — A comment that summarizes code does just that: it distills a few lines of code into one or two sentences. Such comments are more valuable than comments that merely repeat the code because a reader can scan them more quickly than the code. Summary comments are particularly useful when someone other than the code's original author tries to modify the code.

- *Description* **of** *the code's intent* — A comment at the level of intent explains the purpose of a section of code. Intent comments operate more at the level of the problem than at the level of the solution.

- *Information that cannot possibly be expressed by the code itself* — Some information can't be expressed in code but must still be in the source code. This category of comments includes copyright notices, confidentiality notices, version numbers, and other housekeeping details; notes about the code's design; references to related requirements or architecture documentation; pointers to online references; optimization notes; comments required by editing tools such as Javadoc and Doxygen; and so on.

The three kinds of comments that are acceptable for completed code are information that can't be expressed in code, intent comments, and summary comments.

14.8.3 Commenting efficiently. Effective commenting isn't that time-consuming. Too many comments are as bad as too few, and you can achieve a middle ground economically.

Following are guidelines for commenting efficiently:

- *Use styles that don't break down or discourage modification.* Any style that's too fancy is annoying to maintain.

- *Use pseudocode programming to reduce commenting time.* When you outline the code in comments before you write it; when you finish the code you have finished the comments.

- *Integrate commenting into your development style.* Develop comments as you develop your code. If you wait until the end you will have more work to do because you will have to go back and figure out or try to remember what the code is doing.

- *Performance is not a good reason to avoid commenting.* To improve the performance of operational code, run the commented code through a tool that strips out the comments as part of the build process.

14.8.4 Structure. Continuing on with McConnell's book [McConnell 2004, pp. 319-323], the term "structure" refers to data that's built up from other types.

You'll generally want to create classes rather than structures so that you can take advantage of the privacy and functionality offered by classes in addition to the public data supported by structures.

14.8.5 Readability. Another theme that runs throughout this book is an emphasis on *code readability*. Communication with other people is the motivation behind the quest for the Holy Grail of self-documenting code [McConnell 2004, pp. 841-843].

The computer doesn't care whether your code is readable. It's better at reading binary machine instructions than it is at reading high-level-language statements. You write readable code because it helps other people to read your code. Readability has a positive effect on all these aspects of a program:

- Comprehensibility

- Reviewability

- Error rate

- Debugging

- Modifiability

- Development time (a consequence of all of the above)

- External quality (a consequence of all of the above)

Readable code doesn't take any longer to write than confusing code does, at least not in the long run. It's easier to be sure your code works if you can easily read what you wrote. That should be a sufficient reason to write readable code. But code is also read during reviews. It's read when you or someone else fixes an error. It's read when the code is modified. It's read when someone tries to use part of your code in a similar program.

Making code readable is not an optional part of the development process, and favoring write-time convenience over read-time convenience is a false economy. You should go to the effort of writing good code, which you can do once, rather than the effort of reading bad code, which you'd have to do again and again.

14.9 Operating System Basics

An *operating system* is computer software that manages the way different programs use the hardware. The system regulates the various ways that a user can control the computer. Operating systems are found on almost any device that contains a computer with multiple programs—from cellular phones and video game consoles to supercomputers and web servers. Among several modern operating systems for personal computers are Microsoft Windows, Mac OS X, and Linux.

Because early computers were often built for a single task, operating systems did not exist in their proper form until the 1960s. As computers evolved into devices capable of running multiple programs in succession, programmers began installing libraries of common programs (in the form of computer code) directly onto computers in order to avoid duplication and to speed up the operating process. Eventually, computers were designed to automatically switch from one task to the next.

The creation of runtime libraries to manage processing and printing speed followed, which evolved into programs capable of interpreting different types of programming languages into machine code. When personal computers designed by companies such as Apple, Atari, IBM, and Amiga became popular in the 1980s, vendors began adding features such as software scheduling and hardware maintenance. These features had become widely used on mainframe and mini computers. Later, features such as *graphical user interface* were developed specifically for personal computer operating systems [http://en.wikipedia.org/wiki/Operating_system].

14.9.1 Components of an operating system. An operating system can be divided into many different parts. One of the most important parts is the kernel, which controls low-level processes that the average user usually cannot see. The kernel controls how memory is read and written, the order in which processes are executed, how information is received and sent by devices such as the monitor, keyboard and mouse, and it decides how to interpret information received by networks.

The user interface is the part of the operating system that interacts with the computer user directly, allowing him or her to control and use programs. The user interface may be graphical with icons and a desktop, or textual, with a command line. Another similar feature is an application programming interface, which is a set of services and code libraries that allow applications to interact with one another and the operating system itself. Depending on the operating system, many of these components may not be considered as an actual part. For example, Windows considers its user interface to be part of the operating system, unlike many versions of Linux which do not include the user interface in the operating system [http://en.wikipedia.org /wiki/Operating_system].

14.9.2 Other important aspects of an operating system. Operating systems can be extremely complicated, yet are useful. Prior to the modern operating system, a human operator controlled the use of the machine and provided interfacing to the world. Through the years, operating systems have provided greater capability for machine operations. Operating systems allow machines to operate at greater capacity. The following is a list of recent improvements [Brookshear 2009, pp. 124-145]:

- ***Real-time process*** — The computer system must respond and process external data and events in "real time."

- ***Time-sharing*** — Time sharing is the ability of the computer system to support multiple users or programs "simultaneously." Time-sharing uses a feature called multiprocessing. One of the earlier time-sharing machines was called JOSS (*JOHNNIAC Open Shop System*). The JOHNNIAC was named in honor of John von Neumann, the developer of the concept that computer instructions, or programs, could be presented and manipulated as data. The Open Shop System became known as "stored program computing." (Dr. Thayer was an early user and programmer of the JOSS system.)

- ***Applications software*** — Applications software refers to additional software that further enables the base software to accomplish a specific application or task; e.g., payroll, telephone operations, inventory, and correcting spelling. Application software is also called "apps."

- ***System software*** — System software performs tasks common to the computer system in general.

- ***Utility software*** — Utility software performs activities and basic functions such as computing the sine of an angle, compressing and decompressing data, and making a telephone connection.

- ***Kernel*** — The kernel is the part of the operating system that performs the basic functions required by the installation; e.g., file manager, device drivers, etc.

- ***Bootstrapping (or booting)*** — Bootstrapping refers to the initial operations installed on a computer enabling it to turn on and imitate operations.

- ***Data processing system*** — The data processing system is a system whose aim is to process large amounts of data. Examples are billing, invoice, and payment systems.

- **Dependability** — The dependability of a system is an aggregate property that takes into account the system's safety, reliability, availability, and security.

- **Distributed system** — A distributed system entails a software system in which the software sub-system or individual components execute on different processors.

14.10 Database Basics and Data Management

A *database* consists of an organized collection of data with one or more multiple uses. Classifying a database involves determining the type of content included in the database; for example: bibliographic, full-text, numeric, or image. Other classification methods start from examining database models or database architectures (see below). Once classified, software organizes the data in the database according to a database model [http://en.wikipedia/org/wiki/Database].

14.10.1 Types of databases

- **Operational database** — Operational databases store detailed data needed to support the operations of an entire organization. They are also called subject-area databases (SADB), transaction databases, and production databases. For example:

  o Customer database

  o Personal database

  o Inventory database

  o Accounting database

- **Analytical database** — Analytical databases (a.k.a. OLAP- On-Line Analytical Processing) are primarily static, read-only databases that store archived, historical data used for analysis. For example, a company will store ten years of sales records in an analytical database and use the contents of the database to analyze marketing strategies in relationship to demographics.

- **Data warehouse** — A data warehouse stores data extracted from various operational databases of an organization for the current and previous years. The data warehouse becomes the central source of data that has been screened, edited, standardized and integrated, and compiled for use by managers and other end-user professionals within an organization. Data warehouses are characterized as being slow to establish yet effective for retrieving data.

- **Distributed database** — A distributed database is a grouping of databases of local workgroups and departments at regional offices, branch offices, manufacturing plants, and other work sites. These databases can include segments of both common operational and common user databases, as well as data generated and stored on a user's home site.

- **End-user database** — End-user databases consist of a variety of data files developed by end-users at their workstations. Examples of these data bases are collections of documents in spreadsheets, word processing documents, and data contained in downloaded files.

- **External database** — External databases are compiled by commercial services and provide access to external, privately-owned data online available for a fee to end-users and organizations. Many Internet sources supply access to databases either for a fee or as a free service.

- ***Hypermedia databases on the web*** — Hypermedia databases are a set of interconnected multimedia pages housed at a web site. They consist of a home page and other hyper-linked pages of multimedia or mixed media such as text, graphics, photographic images, video clips, and audio.

- ***Navigational database*** — Navigational databases enable queries to find objects primarily by following references from other objects. Traditionally, navigational interfaces are pro-cedural, although modern systems such as XPath can be characterized as being simultane-ously navigational and declarative.

- ***In-memory databases*** — In-memory databases rely primarily on main memory for com-puter data storage. This contrasts with database management systems which employ a disk-based storage mechanism. Main memory databases are faster than disk-optimized da-tabases because the internal optimization algorithms are simpler and execute fewer CPU instructions. Accessing data in memory provides faster and more predictable performance than disk access. Main memory databases are often used for applications in which re-sponse time is critical, such as telecommunications network equipment that operate emer-gency systems.

- ***Document-oriented databases*** — Document-oriented databases are computer programs designed for document-oriented applications. These systems may be implemented as a layer above a relational database or an object database. Contrary to relational databases, document-based databases do not store data in tables with uniform sized fields for each record. Instead, they store each record as a document containing certain characteristics. Any number of fields of undetermined length can be added to a document. Fields can also contain multiple pieces of data.

- ***Real-time databases*** — A real-time database is a processing system designed to handle workloads whose state may constantly change. This differs from traditional databases con-taining persistent data mainly unaffected by time. For example, a stock market changes rapidly and dynamically. Real-time processing allows a transaction to be processed fast enough for the result to be immediately received and acted on. Real-time databases are useful for accounting, banking, law, medical records, multi-media, process control, reser-vation systems, and scientific data analysis. As computers increase in power and data stor-age capacity, real-time databases become integrated into society and are employed in more and more applications.

- ***Relational database*** — Relational databases are the most commonly used database. They utilize tables to structure information that can be readily and easily searched.

14.11 Network Communication Basics

A *computer network communication system* is often referred to as a network. The system is a collection of computers and devices connected by communication channels that facilitate com-munication among users and allow users to share resources with one another. Networks may be classified according to a wide variety of characteristics [Brookshear 2007, pp. 152-157].

A computer network allows sharing of resources and information among devices connected to the network. The Advanced Research Projects Agency (ARPA) funded the design of the Advanced Research Projects Agency Network (ARPANET) for the United States Department of Defense. It was the first operational computer network in the world. Development of the network began in 1969, based on designs created during the 1960s.

14.11.1 Advantages of a computer network. Computer networks can be used for several purposes [http://en.wikipedia.org/Computer_network]:

- ***Facilitating communications*** — Via a network, people can communicate efficiently and easily via e-mail, instant messaging, chat rooms, telephone, video telephone calls, and videoconferencing.

- ***Sharing hardware*** — In a networked environment, each computer belonging to a network can access and use hardware available on the network. Suppose several personal computers on a network each require the use of a laser printer. If each personal computer is connected to a network containing a laser printer, each user has the ability to print from the laser printer.

- ***Sharing files, data, and information*** — Any authorized user within a network environment can access data and information stored on other computers belonging to the network environment. The capability of providing access to data and information on shared storage devices is an important feature of many networks.

- ***Sharing software*** — Users connected to a network can access applications and common software on the network.

14.11.2 Classes of computer communications networks. A *computer communication network* is often classified as being either a local area network (LAN), a metropolitan area network (MAN), or a wide area network (WAN). A LAN normally consists of a collection of computers in a single building or building complex. For example, the computers on a university campus, or those in a manufacturing plant might be connected by a LAN. A MAN is a network of intermediate size, such as one spanning a local community. A WAN links machines over a greater distance—perhaps in neighboring cities or on opposite sides of the world.

Another means of classifying networks is whether the network's internal operation is based on designs that are in the public domain or on innovations owned and controlled by a particular entity such as an individual or a corporation. A network of the former type is called an *open network*; a network of the latter type is called a *closed* or sometimes a *proprietary network*. Open network designs are freely circulated and often grow in popularity, ultimately prevailing over proprietary designs whose applications are restricted by license fees and contract conditions.

The Internet (a popular worldwide network of networks) is an open system. In particular, communication throughout the Internet is governed by an open collection of standards known as the TCP/IP protocol suit. These standards are available to all without paying fees or signing license agreements. In contrast, a company such as Novell, Inc., might develop proprietary systems for which it chooses to maintain ownership rights, allowing the company to draw income from selling or leasing these products.

Still another way of classifying networks is based on the topology of the network, which refers to the pattern in which the machines are connected. Two of the more popular topologies are the *bus*, in which the machines are all connected to a common communication line called a *bus*, and the *star*, in which one machine serves as a central focal point to which all the others are connected. The bus topology was popularized in the 1990s when implemented under a set of standards known as Ethernet.

Ethernet networks remain one of the most popular networking systems in use today. The star topology dates to the 1970s. It evolved from the paradigm of a large central computer serving many users. As simple terminals employed by these users grew into small computers themselves, a star network emerged. Today, the star configuration is popular in wireless networks in which communication is conducted by means of radio broadcast and a central machine called the *access point* (AP). This serves as a focal point around which all communication is coordinated.

The difference between a bus network and a star network is not always obvious by the physical arrangement of equipment. The distinction is whether the machines in the network are designed to communicate directly with each other over a common bus or indirectly through an intermediary central machine. For instance, a bus network might not appear as a long bus from which computers are connected over short links. Instead, it may have a very short bus with long links to the individual machines, meaning that the network would take the format of a star. A bus network is created by running links from each computer to a central location at which point each is connected to a device called a *hub*. This hub is a very short bus that relays signals received (with perhaps some amplification) back to the machines connected to it. The result is visually a star network but operationally a bus network.

14.11.3 Protocols. For a network to function reliably, it is important to establish rules by which activities are conducted. Such rules are called *protocols*. By developing and adopting protocol standards, vendors are able to build products for network applications that are compatible with products from other vendors. Thus, the development of protocol standards is an indispensable process in the development of networking technologies.

As an introduction to the protocol concept, let us consider the problem of coordinating the transmission of messages among computers in a network. Without rules governing this communication, all computers included in the network might insist on transmitting messages at the same time, or fail to assist other machines when that assistance is required.

In a bus network based on the Ethernet standards, the right to transmit messages is controlled by the protocol known as *Carrier Sense, Multiple Access with Collision Detection* (CSMA/CD). This protocol dictates that each message be broadcast to all the machines on the bus. Each machine monitors every message but keeps only those addressed to itself. To transmit a message, a machine waits until the bus is silent and at this time it begins transmitting while continuing to monitor the bus.

If another machine also begins transmitting, both machines detect the clash and pause for a brief yet independently random period of time before attempting to retransmit. The result is a system similar to a conversation among a small group of people. If two people talk at once, they both stop. The difference is that a conversation may entail an exchange such as "I'm sorry, what were you going to say?," "No, no, please continue," whereas under the CSMA/CD protocol each machine merely tries again later.

Two or more machines may not be able to detect transmission collisions. For example, one machine may not 'hear' the other because its own signal drowns the signal of the other machine. Secondly, objects or distance can block signals from different machines even though they can all communicate using the central AP (a condition known as the *hidden terminal problem*.) The result is that wireless networks adopt the policy of trying to *avoid* collisions rather than trying to *detect* them.

Such policies are classified as *Carrier Sense, Multiple Access with Collision Avoidance*, (CSMA/CA), many of which are standardized by IEEE within the protocols defined in IEEE Standard 802.11 and commonly referred to as *WiFi*. We emphasize that collision avoidance protocols are designed to avoid collisions and may not eliminate them completely. When collisions do occur, messages must be retransmitted.

The most common approach to collision avoidance is offering an advantage to machines that have already been waiting for an opportunity to transmit. The protocol used is similar to Ethernet's CSMA/CD.

When a machine first needs to transmit a message and finds the communication channel silent, it does not start transmitting immediately. Instead, it waits for a short period of time and then starts transmitting only if the channel has remained silent throughout that period. If a busy channel is experienced during this process, the machine waits for a randomly determined period before trying again. Once this period is exhausted, the machine is allowed to claim a silent channel without hesitation. This means that collisions between "newcomers" and those that have already been waiting are avoided because a "newcomer" is not allowed to claim a silent channel until all machines that have been waiting are given the opportunity to start.

However, this protocol does not solve the hidden terminal problem. After all, any protocol based on distinguishing between a silent or busy channel requires that each individual station be able to hear other stations. To solve this problem, some WiFi networks require that each machine send a short "request" message to the AP and wait for an acknowledgement before transmitting an entire message.

If the AP is busy because it is negotiating with a "hidden terminal," it will ignore the request and the requesting machine will be signaled to wait. Otherwise, the AP will acknowledge the request and the machine will be prompted to transmit. Note that all machines belonging to the network will hear all acknowledgements sent from the AP. Therefore, each machine knows if the AP is busy at any given time even though it may not be able to hear the transmissions taking place.

14.12 Distributed and Parallel Computing

Distributed computing uses multiple autonomous computers that communicate through a computer network. The computers interact with each other in order to achieve a common goal. A computer program that runs in a distributed system is called a distributed program.

Parallel computing is a form of computation in which many calculations are carried out simultaneously. It operates on the principle that large problems can often be divided into smaller ones, which are then concurrently solved in parallel [http://en.wikipedia.org/wiki/Concurrency _(computer_science)].

14.12.1 Distributed computing. The word *distributed* contained in the terms "distributed system," "distributed programming," and "distributed algorithm" originally referred to computer networks in which individual computers were physically distributed within a geographical area. The terms are now used in a much wider sense, even when referring to autonomous processes that run on the same physical computer and interact with each other by message passing.

While there is no single definition of a distributed system, the following defining properties are commonly used:

- A *distributed system* contains several autonomous computational entities, each of which has its own local memory.

- The entities communicate with each other by message passing.

The computational entities are called *computers* or *nodes*.

A distributed system may have a common goal such as solving a large computational problem. Alternatively, each computer may have its own user with individual needs. The purpose of the distributed system is to coordinate the use of shared resources and/or to provide communication services to all users.

Other typical properties of distributed systems include the following:

- The system has to tolerate failures in individual computers.

- The structure of the system (network topology, network latency, number of computers) is not known in advance. The system may consist of different kinds of computers and network links, and the system may change during the execution of a distributed program.

- Each computer has only a limited, incomplete view of the system. Each computer may know only one part of the input [http://en.wikipedia.org/wiki/Distributed_computing].

14.12.2 Parallel computing. Parallel computing is a form of computation in which many calculations are carried out simultaneously, operating on the principle that large problems can often be divided into smaller ones, which are then solved concurrently, or "in parallel." There are several different forms of parallel computing: bit level, instruction level, data, and task parallelism. Parallel computers can be roughly classified according to the level at which the hardware supports parallelism—with multi-core and multi-processor computers having multiple processing elements within a single machine. Clusters, MPPs, and grids use multiple computers to work on the same task. Specialized parallel computer architectures are occasionally used alongside traditional processors for accelerating specific tasks.

Parallel computer programs are more difficult to write than sequential ones because concurrency introduces several new classes of potential software bugs, of which race conditions are the most common. Communication and synchronization between the different subtasks are typically one of the greatest obstacles to achieving acceptable levels of parallel program performance [http://en. wikipedia.org/wiki/Parallel_computing].

14.13 Concepts of Programming Languages

The text by Brookshear [2009] lists the following traditional programming concepts:

- Variable and data types

- Data structure

- Constraints and literals

- Assignment statements

- Control statements

14.13.1 Variables. Some languages, for instance, *high-level languages*, allow their location in the main memory to be referenced by descriptive names rather than by numerical address. This type of name is called a *variable* because the value of the data stored in that location can be changed as the program executes.

14.13.2 Data types. If the data stored in a memory location is a variable, then there is a need to describe the type of data that will be stored there. This is called a *data type*. Types of data include *integer, real* (not necessarily a whole number), *character,* and *Boolean*.

14.13.3 Data structures. A *variable* can also be associated with a data structure. A data structure is the conceptual shape or arrangement of data. For example, a *string,* a *matrix,* and a *homogeneous array* are several types of data structures.

14.13.4 Constants and literals. A *constant* is a fixed, predetermined value used in a computer program. This fixed value data is sometimes called a *literal.*

14.13.5 Assignment statements. An *assignment statement* requests the value of a variable to be stored in the memory location assigned to that variable.

14.13.6 Control statements. A *control statement* is an imperative statement that alters the execution sequence of the program. A "go to" statement is a much-maligned control statement that will transfer the execution sequence to another location; this can bring disastrous results because errors in "go to" are easy to make.

14.13.7 Comments. It is helpful, if not essential, to provide additional information to the human reader of the code to improve his or her understanding of the program. These statements are ignored by the translator and do not affect the operation of the program.

14.14 Debugging Tools and Techniques

Debugging is a methodical process of finding and reducing the number of bugs, or defects, in a computer program or a piece of electronic hardware, making it operate as expected. Debugging tends to be more difficult when various subsystems are tightly coupled, as changes in one subsystem may cause bugs to emerge in another.

14.14.1 Debugging techniques. As software and electronic systems have become generally more complex, various common *debugging techniques* have expanded with more methods to detect anomalies, assess impact, and schedule software patches and full system updates. The words "anomaly" and "discrepancy" can be used as neutral terms to avoid the words "error," "defect," and "bug," especially to avoid the implication that all so-called *errors, defects* or *bugs* must be fixed (at all costs). Instead, an impact assessment can be made to determine if changes to remove an *anomaly* (or *discrepancy)* would be cost-effective for the system, or perhaps a scheduled new release might render the changes unnecessary. Not all issues are life-critical or mission-critical in a system.

It is equally important to avoid a situation in which a change might be more upsetting to users in the long-term than continuing with the known problems where the "cure would be worse than the disease." The acceptability of some anomalies can avoid a culture demanding a "zero-defects" mandate, in which programmers might be tempted to deny the existence of problems resulting in the appearance of zero *defects.* Considering collateral issues such as a cost-versus-benefit impact assessment, broader debugging techniques should expand to determine the frequency of anomalies (how often the same "bugs" occur) and their severity to help assess their impact to the overall system.

14.14.2 Debugging tools. A *debugger* or *debugging tool* is a computer program used to test and debug other programs (the "target" program). The examined code might alternatively be running on an instruction set simulator (ISS), a technique that allows great power in its ability to halt operations when specific conditions are encountered, yet which will typically be slower than executing the code directly on the appropriate (or the same) processor. Some debuggers offer two modes of operation—full or partial simulation—to limit this impact.

14.15 Secure Coding

Two key strategies easily employed by developers to help secure their systems are to write code that can withstand attack and to properly use security features.

14.15.1 Writing insecure code. There are many ways to get into trouble when it comes to security. You can trust all code that runs on your network, give any user access to important files, and never bother to check that code on your machine has not changed. You can run without virus protection software, not build security into your own code, and give too many privileges to too many accounts. You can even use a number of built-in functions carelessly enough to allow break-ins, and you can leave server ports open and unmonitored. Obviously, the list continues to grow. What are some of the really important issues, the biggest mistakes you should watch out for right now so that you don't compromise your data or your system?

14.15.2 Writing secure code. Security is a multidimensional issue. Security risks can originate anywhere. A programmer can write negligent error-handling code or be too generous with permissions. One can forget what services are running on the server. All user input can be accepted. And the list goes on. Below are eleven tips to follow for a safer network strategy and to provide a head start for protecting machines, networks, and code [Howard & Brown 2002].

The following eleven approaches are essential to writing secure code. Ten are from Howard and Brown's article [2002] and the eleventh was a quote from Roger Fujii [2000].

14.15.2.1 Trust user input at your system's peril. Always remember one thing, "don't trust user input." If you regularly assume that data is well formed and valid, then your troubles are about to begin. Most security vulnerabilities revolve around the attacker providing malformed data to the server.

Trusting that input is well formed can lead to buffer overruns, cross-site scripting attacks, SQL injection attacks, and more.

14.15.2.2 Protect against buffer overruns. A buffer overrun occurs when the data provided by the attacker is a larger quantity than expected by the application, resulting in an overflow into the internal memory space. Buffer overruns are primarily a C/C++ issue. Although a menace, they are generally easy to correct. The authors have experienced only *two buffer overruns* which were not obvious and were difficult to fix. The developer did not anticipate receiving externally provided data that was larger in quantity than the internal buffer allowed. The overflow causes corruption of other data structures in the memory, and this corruption can often lead to the attacker running malicious code. Buffer underflows and buffer overruns caused by array indexing mistakes also occur, but are less common.

14.15.2.3 Prevent cross-site scripting. Cross-site scripting vulnerabilities are web-specific issues and can compromise a client's data through a flaw in a single web page.

14.15.2.4 Don't require system administrator permissions. Many developers write code requiring input to build SQL queries to communicate with a back-end data store, such as Microsoft® SQL Server™ or Oracle. *SQL injection* is a code injection technique that exploits a security vulnerability occurring in the database layer of an application. The vulnerability is present when user input is either incorrectly filtered for string literal escape characters embedded in SQL statements or user input is not strongly typed and therefore, unexpectedly executed. A more general class of vulnerabilities can occur whenever one programming or scripting language is embedded inside another. SQL injection attacks are also known as SQL insertion attacks.

14.15.2.5 Watch that crypto code! Perhaps the most common mistake is encryption code that is typically quite fragile and easy to decipher. The risks associated with creating one's own encryption code are too high. Don't think that by creating a cryptographic algorithm the encryption code will not be deciphered. Attackers have access to debuggers and have both the time and the knowledge to determine exactly how these systems work. They are often broken in a matter of hours. Use the CryptoAPI for Win32® applications. The System Security Cryptography namespace has a wealth of well-written and well-tested cryptographic algorithms.

14.15.2.6 Reduce the attack profile. If a feature is not required by most clients, then it should not be installed by default. If the feature is installed by default, it should operate under the principle of least privilege. In other words, do not require the application to run with administrative rights if they are not required.

14.15.2.7 Employ the principle of least privilege. The operating system and the common language runtime (CLR) both have security policies for several reasons. Many programmers believe the security policy exists to prevent users from intentionally accessing files they shouldn't be allowed to see, reconfiguring the network to suit their needs, and other dastardly deeds. While it's certainly true that insider attacks are common and need to be guarded against, a greater reason exists for keeping this security policy tight.

The security policy places walls around code as a precaution against intentional or, just as frequently, unintentional actions by users to avoid wreaking havoc on the network. For instance, an attachment downloaded via e-mail and executed on Alice's machine is restricted to only accessing resources that Alice can access. If the attachment contains a Trojan horse, a good security policy will limit the damage encrypted within this virus.

The principle of least privilege affirms that any given privilege should be granted to the least amount of code necessary, for the least amount of time necessary. In other words, at any given time, try to erect as many walls around the code as possible. When an unfortunate circumstance presents itself—as Murphy's Law guarantees it will—you will be glad these walls were in place.

14.15.2.8 Pay attention to failure modes. A piece of code can fail in multiple ways. Most programmers would much rather focus on the normal path of execution, the corpus of the project. The normal pattern is to complete the error handling as quickly and painlessly as possible and proceed to the next line of real code.

Sadly, this is not a safe frame of mind. The programmer needs to pay much closer attention to failure modes in code. These bits of code are often written with little attention to detail and often remain completely untested. When was the last time your debugger stepped through every single line of code in a function, including every single error handler?

Untested code often leads to security vulnerabilities. Three things can help alleviate this problem. First, pay as much attention to error handlers as to normal code. Think about the state of the system while the error-handling code is executing. Is the system left in a valid and secure state? Second, once a function is written, step the debugger through it several times, ensuring that every error handler is hit. Note that even this technique may not uncover subtle timing errors.

Bad arguments may need to be passed to the function. The state of the system may need adjustment in some way that causes the execution of error handlers. By taking the time to step through the code, you are slowing yourself down long enough to take at least a second look at the code and the state of the system while it is running. You can discover many flaws in your programming logic by carefully stepping through code in a debugger —it's a proven technique. Finally, make sure that test suites force functions to fail. Try to have test suites that exercise every line of code in the function. These can help to discover regression, especially if tests are automated and run after every build.

One last very important detail regarding failure modes: If your code fails, be certain it leaves the system in the most secure state possible.

14.15.2.9 Impersonation is fragile. When writing server applications, it is common to use, directly or indirectly, a convenient feature of Windows called impersonation. Impersonation allows each thread in a process to run in a distinct security context, typically the client's security context. For instance, when the file system redirector receives a request for a file via the network, it authenticates the remote client, verifies that the client's request does not violate the discretionary access control list (DACL) on the share, and attaches the client's token to the thread handling the request, thus impersonating the client.

This thread can then access the local file system on the server using the security context of the client. This is convenient since the local file system is already secure; it will do an access check that considers the type of access being requested, the DACL on the file, and the impersonation token on the thread. If the access check fails, the local file system reports this to the file system redirector, who then can send a fault back to the remote client. This is incredibly convenient for the file system redirector because it simply passes the responsibility to the local file system and lets the local file system perform its own access checking, just as if the client was local.

14.15.2.10 Write applications (apps) that non-administrators can actually use. This is a corollary of the principle of least privilege. If programmers continue to produce code that doesn't run well on Windows unless the user is an administrator, how can one expect to shake free of the stigma of targeting an "insecure" system? Windows has a very robust set of security features; however, if users are required to run as administrators to perform tasks, they are not receiving optimal benefit from these features.

14.15.2.11 Eliminate "dead" code. Dead code normally arises when a software system has to be fixed with what is called a "patch" This patch "fixes" the fault in the program by replacing the software that does not work with a "piece" of software that does. The "old," faulty code, is left in place in the system but is "isolated" with a pair of "go to" statements so it cannot be executed. This isolated area can be a secure location to hide viruses. Therefore, a good suggestion is to purge all "dead" code [Fujii 2000].

14.16 Conclusion

Computer science, or computer foundations, as it is referred to in this chapter, is the backbone of software engineering. Many of the best software engineers were schooled in a solid computer science and programming background. It is frequently believed that because these individuals are assuming the role of software engineers, they understand the *fundamentals of computing*.

However, the all software engineers s possess a solid background in computer science and programming techniques. The difference in mastery of concepts and performance is caused by the failure of the latter to truly assimilate the software engineering culture.

It is therefore clear that an accomplished software engineer and a skilled programmer must understand both the science and the engineering of computer technology.

References

Additional information on the *computing foundations* KA can be found in the following documents.

- **[Bishop 2002]** Matt Bishop, *Computer Security: Art and Science* (Hardcover)Addison-Wesley, Boston 2002, 1136 pages. ISBN-13: 978-0201440997 [Chapters 1, 4, 13, 16, 18, 19, 23, and 29].

- **[Brookshear 2008]** J. Glenn Brookshear, *Computer Science: An Overview* (Paperback), 10th Edition. Addison-Wesley, Boston, 688 pages. [Chapters 3, 6, and 9] (Recommended as a CSDP exam reference book by the IEEE Computer Society.)

- **[Dijkstra 1969]** E.W. Dijkstra, "Structured Programming," *Software Engineering Techniques*, J.N. Buxton, and B. Randell, (eds). Brussels, NATO Science Committee, 1969.

- **[Fujii 2000]** Roger U. Fujii, Lecture given at Sacramento State University, Department of Computer Science. Fall Semester, 2000. As Chair of the IEEE Verification and Validation Standard Committee, he elaborated on the subject of dead code as an ideal location to hide viruses or other malicious software. Consequently, dead code should not be left in a production software system.

- **[GQM 2008]** "Goal-Question-Metric (GQM) Approach," *Software Tech News*, Vol. 11, No. 4, December 2008. https://www.goldpractices.com/practices/gqm (46 pages). (Recommended as a CSDP exam reference book by the IEEE Computer Society.)

- **[Howard & Brown 2002]** Michael Howard and Keith Brown, "Defend Your Code with Top Ten Security Tips Every Developer Must Know." *MSDN Magazine*, September, 2002.

- **[Johnson 2010]** Don Johnson, "Computer Architecture" http://www.intelligentedu.com /intro duction_to_computer_organization.html, June, 2010.

- **[Kan 2002]** Stephen H. Kan, *Metrics and Models in Software Quality Engineering* (Hardcover), 2nd Edition, Addison-Wesley, Boston, 2002, 560 pages, ISBN-13: 978-0201729153. (Recommended as a CSDP exam reference book by the IEEE Computer Society.)

- **[McConnell 2004]** Steve McConnell, *Code Complete* (Paperback), 2nd Edition, revised, Microsoft Press, 2004, 960 pages. ISBN-13: 978-0735619678.

- **[Montgomery & Runger 2007]** Douglas C. Montgomery and George C. Runger, *Applied Statistics and Probability for Engineers,* 4th Edition, John Wiley, Hoboken, NJ, 2007, 784 pages, (Recommended as a CSDP exam reference book by the IEEE Computer Society.)

- **[Moore 2005]** James W. Moore, *The Road Map to Software Engineering: A Standards-Based Guide,* 1st Edition, John Wiley, Hoboken, NJ, 2005, 440 pages, ISBN-13: 978-0471683629. (Recommended as a CSDP exam reference book by the IEEE Computer Society.)

- **[Null & Lobur 2006]** Linda Null and Julia Lobur, *The Essentials of Computer Organization and Architecture* (Hardcover), 2nd Edition, Jones & Bartlett, Sudbury, MA, 2006, 700 pages, ISBN-13: 978-0763737696, Chapters 1-4, 9-12, also sections 8.1-8.4,

8.6, 8.7, 478 pages. (Recommended as a CSDP exam reference book by the IEEE Computer Society.)

- **[Somerville 2006]** Ian Sommerville, *Software Engineering*, 8th Edition, Addison-Wesley, Boston, 2006, 864 pages, ISBN-13: 978-0321313799. (Recommended as a CSDP exam reference book by the IEEE Computer Society.)

- **[Swartz 1996]** A.J. Swartz, "Denver Airport Baggage System," *ACM SIGSOFT Software Engineering Notes*, Volume 21, Issue 2, March 1996, pp. 79-83.

- **[Voland 2003]** Gerard Voland, *Engineering by Design*, (Paperback), 2nd Edition, Prentice Hall, Upper Saddle River, New Jersey, 2003, 640 pages, ISBN-13: 978-0131409194 (Sections 1.5, 1.6, 2, 3, 4, 5.3. 5.4, 6, 8, 9.3, 9.4, and 9.5 – 191 pages). (Recommended as a CSDP exam reference book by the IEEE Computer Society.)

- **[Wikipedia]** Wikipedia is a free web-based encyclopedia which enables users to add and edit online content. Definitions cited from Wikipedia and other sources have been verified by the authors and other peer reviewers.

Chapter 15.1

Discrete Mathematics for Software Engineers[6]

Compiled by Richard Hall Thayer and Merlin Dorfman

One of the foundation series in the CSDP/CSDA exam requirements is mathematics. The primary and most detailed reference for the Mathematics Foundation knowledge area (KA) is Kenneth H. Rosen [2007],Discrete Mathematics & Its Application with Combinatorics and Graph Theory. This readable text provides excellent coverage of this mathematics topic. This chapter summarizes some of the key ideas from Rosen's book that are applicable to software engineering and includes material from [http://en.wikipedia.org /wiki /Discrete mathematics].

In a recent conference on software engineering education and training [CSEE&T 2011], two presentations were given on the need to teach discrete mathematics instead of calculus in software engineering education. The two educators making this presentation were world famous educators—Drs. Barry Boehm and Richard (Dick) Fairley. Therefore, it is very appropriate for discrete mathematics to be one of the subjects in the CSDP/CSDA certification exam.

We would like to recommend Rosen's book as excellent reading material for present-day and future software engineers. It is recommended by the IEEE Computer Society as a reference book for the CSDP and CSDA exams.

Dr. Rosen said in the introduction to his book:

Students [of a discrete mathematics course] should learn a particular set of mathematical facts and how to apply them. More importantly, such a course should teach students how to think logically and mathematically. To achieve these goals, this text [Rosen] stresses mathematical reasoning and the different ways problems are solved. Five important themes are interwoven in this text: mathematical reasoning, combinatorial analysis, discrete structures, algorithmic thinking, and applications and modeling.

Discrete mathematics is the study of mathematical structures that are fundamentally discrete rather than continuous. In contrast to real numbers that have the property of varying "smoothly," the objects studied in discrete mathematics – such as integers, graphs, and statements in logic – do not vary smoothly in this way, but have distinct, separated values. Discrete mathematics therefore excludes topics in "continuous mathematics" such as calculus and analysis. Discrete objects can often be enumerated by integers.

More formally, discrete mathematics has been characterized as the branch of mathematics dealing with countable sets (sets that have the same cardinality as subsets of the natural numbers, including rational numbers but not real numbers). However, there is no exact, universally agreed,

---

6. This overview paper on *discrete mathematics* credits [http://en.wikipedia.org/wiki/Discrete _mathematics] as its primary source.

definition of the term "discrete mathematics." Indeed, discrete mathematics is described less by what is included than by what is excluded: continuously varying quantities and related notions.

Graphs like the one in Figure 1 are among the objects studied by discrete mathematics, for their interesting mathematical properties, their usefulness as models of real-world problems, and their importance in developing computer algorithms.

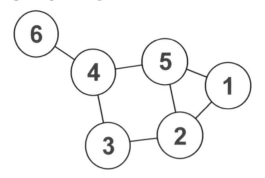

Figure 1: An example of a discrete graph

The set of objects studied in discrete mathematics can be finite or infinite. The term *finite mathematics* is sometimes applied to parts of the field of discrete mathematics that deals with finite sets, particularly those areas relevant to business.

Research in discrete mathematics increased in the latter half of the twentieth century, partly due to the development of digital computers, which operate in discrete steps and store data in discrete units. Concepts and notations from discrete mathematics are useful in studying and describing objects and problems in branches of computer science, such as computer algorithms, programming languages, cryptography, automated theorem proving, and software development. Conversely, computer implementations are significant in applying ideas from discrete mathematics to real-world problems, such as in operations research.

Although the main objects of study in discrete mathematics are discrete objects, analytic methods from continuous mathematics are often employed as well.

The following subject matters are contained in this article:

1. The grand challenges (past and present)

2. Theoretical computer science information theory

3. Logic

4. Set theory

5. Combinatorics

6. Graph theory Probability

7. Number theory

8. Algebra

9. Calculus of finite differences, discrete calculus or discrete analysis

10. Geometry

11. Topology

12. Operations research

13. Game theory, decision theory, utility theory, and social choice theory

14. Discretization

15. Discrete analogues of continuous mathematics

16. Hybrid, discrete and continuous mathematics

1. The Grand Challenges (Past and Present)

The history of discrete mathematics has involved a number of challenging problems that have focused attention within areas of the field. In graph theory, much research was motivated by attempts to prove the four-color theorem, first stated in 1852, but not proved until 1976 (by Kenneth Apple and Wolfgang Hake), using substantial computer assistance [http://en.wiki pedia.org/wiki/Discrete_mathematics].

A classic discreet variable problem involves coloring the regions of a map so that no two countries next to each other have the same color. The work done by Apple and Hake showed that four colors are sufficient. This problem is equivalent to the problem of coloring the vertices of the dual graph so that no two adjacent vertices in this graph have the same color.

The need to break German codes in World War II led to advances in cryptography and theoretical computer science, with the first programmable digital electronic computer being developed at England's Bletchley Park. At the same time, military requirements motivated advances in operations research. The Cold War meant that cryptography remained important, with fundamental advances such as public-key cryptography being developed in the following decades. Operations research remained important as a tool in business and project management, with the critical path method being developed in the 1950s.

The telecommunication industry has also motivated advances in discrete mathematics, particularly in graph theory and information theory. Formal verification of statements in logic has been necessary for software development of safety-critical systems, and advances in automated theorem proving have been driven by this need [http://en.wikipedia.org/wiki/Discrete_math ematics]:

- *Operations research* (also referred to as *decision science* or *management science*) is an interdisciplinary mathematical science that focuses on the effective use of technology from other mathematical sciences, such as mathematical modeling, statistical analysis, and mathematical optimization. Operations research arrives at optimal or near-optimal solutions to complex decision-making problems.[http://en.wikipedia.org/wiki/Operations_re search].

- *Critical Path Method* (a.k.a. CPM) is an algorithm for scheduling a set of project activities. The critical path, the longest necessary path through a network of activities, is an important tool for effective project management [http://en.wikipedia.org/wiki/Critical_Path].

2. Theoretical Computer Science

Theoretical computer science includes areas of discrete mathematics relevant to computing. It draws heavily on *graph theory* and *logic*. Included within theoretical computer science is the study of algorithms for computing mathematical results. *Computability* studies what can be computed in principle, and has close ties to logic, while complexity studies the time taken by computations. *Automata theory* and *formal language theory* are closely related to computability.

Petri nets and *process algebras* are used to model computer systems, and methods from discrete mathematics are used in analyzing very large scale integrated electronic circuits. *Computational geometry* applies algorithms to geometrical problems, while *computer image analysis* applies them to representations of images. *Theoretical computer science* also includes the study of various continuous computational topics [http://en.wikipedia.org/wiki/Discrete_mathematics].

3. Information Theory

Information theory involves the quantification of information. Closely related is coding theory which is used to design efficient and reliable data transmission and storage methods. Information theory also includes continuous topics such as: analog signals, analog coding, and analog encryption [http://en.wikipedia.org/wiki/Discrete_mathematics].

4. Logic

Logic is the study of the principles of valid reasoning and *inference*, as well as of *consistency*, *soundness,* and *completeness.* For classical logic, these principles can be easily verified with a *truth table.* The study of *mathematical proof* is particularly important in logic, and has applications to *automated theorem proving* and *formal verification* of software.

A *truth table* is a mathematical table used in logic—specifically in connection with Boolean algebra, Boolean functions, and propositional calculus—to compute the functional values of logical expressions on each of their functional arguments, that is, on each combination of values taken by their logical variables [Enderton 2001].

In particular, truth tables can be used to tell whether a propositional expression is true for all legitimate input values, that is, logically valid. Practically, a truth table is composed of one column for each input variable (for example, A and B), and one final column for all of the possible results of the logical operation that the table is meant to represent. Each row of the truth table therefore contains one possible configuration of the input variables (for instance, A=true B=false), and the result of the operation for those values [http://en.wikipedia.org/wiki/Truth _table].

Logical formulas are discrete structures, as are proofs, which form finite trees or, more generally, directed acyclic graph structures (with each inference step combining one or more premise branches to give a single conclusion). The truth-values of logical formulas usually form a finite set, generally restricted to two values: true and false, but logic can also be continuous-valued. Concepts such as infinite proof trees or infinite derivation trees have also been studied [http://en.wikipedia.org/wiki/Discrete_mathematics].

The rules of logic give precise meaning to mathematical statements. These rules are used to distinguish between valid and invalid mathematical arguments. In addition to its importance in understanding mathematical reasoning, logic has numerous applications in computer science. These rules are used in the design of computer circuits, the construction of computer programs, the verification of the correctness of programs, and in many other ways [Rosen 2007].

4.1 Propositions

We use letters to denote *propositional variables* (or *statement variables),* that is, variables that represent propositions, just as letters are used to denote numerical variables. The conventional letters used for propositional variables are *p, q, r, s* . . . The *truth value* of a proposition is true, denoted by T, if it is a true proposition and false, denoted by F, if it is a false proposition.

> **DEFINITION:** A proposition is a declarative sentence (a statement of fact) that is either *true* or *false*, but not both.

The area of logic that deals with propositions is called the *propositional calculus* or *propositional logic*.

> **DEFINITION:** Let p be a proposition. The negation of p is denoted by $\neg p$, or by a bar over p. (It is read "not p.") The truth value of the negation of p is the opposite of the truth value of p.

> **DEFINITION:** Let p and q be propositions. The conjunction of p and q is denoted by $p \wedge q$ (it is read "p and q."). The conjunction p and q is *true* when both p and q are *true* and is *false* otherwise.

> **DEFINITION:** Let p and q be propositions. The disjunction of p and q is denoted by $p \vee q$ (it is read "p or q)." The disjunction is *false* when both p and q are *false* and is *true* otherwise.

> **DEFINITION:** Let p and q be propositions. The *exclusive or* of p and q is denoted by $p \oplus q$ (it is also read "p or q"). The exclusive or is *true* when exactly one of p and q is *true* and is *false* otherwise.

> **DEFINITION:** A compound proposition that is *always* true no matter what the truth value of its variables is called a *tautology*. A compound proposition that is *always* false is called a *contradiction*. A compound proposition that is neither a tautology nor a contradiction is called a *contingency*.

4.2 Arguments

An *argument form* in propositional logic is a sequence of compound propositions involving propositional variables.

> **DEFINITION:** An *argument* in propositional logic is a sequence of propositions. All but the final proposition in the argument is called a *premise* and the final proposition is called the *conclusion*. An argument is *valid* if the truth of all its premises implies that the conclusion is true.

An *argument form* in propositional logic is a sequence of compound propositions involving propositional variables. An argument form *is valid* if no matter which particular propositions are substituted for the propositional variables in its premises, the conclusion is true if the premises are all true.

The key to showing that an argument in propositional logic is valid is to show that its argument form is valid. Consequently, we would like techniques to show that argument forms are valid. We will now develop methods for accomplishing this task.

5. Set Theory

Set theory is the branch of mathematics that studies *sets,* which are collections of objects, such as (blue, white, red) or the (infinite) set of all *prime numbers. Partially ordered sets* and sets with other *relations* have applications in several areas.

In discrete mathematics, *countable* sets (including *finite sets*) are the main focus. The beginning of set theory as a branch of mathematics that distinguishes between different kinds of *infinite sets,* is motivated by the study of trigonometric series, and further development of the theory of infinite sets is outside the scope of discrete mathematics. Indeed, contemporary work in *descriptive set theory* makes extensive use of traditional continuous mathematics [http://en.wiki pedia.org/wiki/Discrete_mathematics].

The set is the fundamental discrete structure on which all other discrete structures are built. Sets are used to group objects together. Often, the objects in a set have similar properties. The language of sets is a means to study such collections in an organized fashion.

> **DEFINITION:** A set is an unordered collection of objects.

> **DEFINITION:** The objects of a set are called *elements*, or members, of a set. A set is said to *contain* its *elements.*

We write $a \in A$ to denote that a is an element of the set A. The notation $a \notin A$ denotes that a is not an element of the set A. Note that lowercase letters are usually used to denote elements of sets.

> **DEFINITION:** Let A and *B* be sets. The *union* of the sets A and *B*, denoted $A \cup B$, *is* the set that contains those elements that are either in A or in *B*, or in both.

Two sets can be combined in many different ways.

An element x belongs to the union of the sets A and B if and only if x belongs to A or x belongs to B. This tells us that $A \cup B = \{x \mid x \in A \lor x \in B\}$.

> **DEFINITION**: Let A and B be sets. The *intersection* of the sets A and *B*, denoted $A \cap B$, *is* the set that contains those elements in both A and B.

An element x belongs to the intersection of the sets A and B if and only if x belongs to A and x belongs to B. This says that $A \cap B \quad \{x \mid x \in A \cap x \in B\}$

> **DEFINITION**: Two sets are called disjoint if their intersection is the empty set.

Let A = {1,3,5,7,9} and B = {2,4,6,8,10}. Because $A \cap B = 0$, A and B are disjoint.

6. Combinatorics

Combinatorics studies the way in which discrete structures can be combined or arranged. Enumerative combinatorics concentrates on counting the number of certain combinatorial objects.

Design theory is a study of combinatorial designs, which are collections of subsets with certain intersection properties. Partition theory studies various enumeration and asymptotic problems related to integer partitions, and is closely related to q-series, special functions and orthogonal polynomials. Originally a part of number theory and analysis, partition theory is now considered a part of combinatorics, or an independent field. Order theory is the study of partially ordered sets, both finite and infinite [http://en.wikipedia.org/wiki/Discrete_mathematics].

7. Graph Theory

Graphs are discrete structures consisting of vertices and edges that connect these vertices. Problems in almost every conceivable discipline can be solved using graph models.

DEFINITION: A *graph* G = (V, E) consists of V, a nonempty set of *vertices* (or *nodes*) and E, a set of *edges*. Each edge has either one or two *vertices* associated with it called *endpoints*. An edge is said to connect to the endpoints.

Tthe study of *graphs and networks*, is often considered part of combinatorics, but has grown large enough and distinct enough, with its own kind of problems, to be regarded as a subject in its own right. Graphs are one of the prime objects of study in discrete mathematics. They are among the most ubiquitous models of both natural and human-made structures. They can model many types of relations and process dynamics in physical, biological and social systems. In computer science, they represent networks of communication, data organization, computational devices, the flow of computation, etc. In mathematics, they are useful in geometry and certain parts of topology, e.g., *Knot Theory*. Algebraic graph theory has close links with group theory [http://en.wikipedia.org/wki/Discrete_mathematics].

8. Discrete Probability Theory

Discrete probability theory deals with events that occur in countable sample spaces. For example, count observations such as the numbers of birds in flocks comprise only natural number values {0, 1, 2, . . .}. On the other hand, continuous observations such as the weights of birds comprise real number values and would typically be modeled by a continuous probability distribution such as the normal distribution. Discrete probability distributions can be used to approximate continuous ones and vice versa. For highly constrained situations such as throwing dice or experiments with decks of cards, calculating the probability of events is basically enumerative combinatorics [http://en.wikipedia.org/wiki/Discrete_mathematics].

9. Number Theory

Number theory is concerned with the properties of numbers in general, particularly integers. It has applications to cryptography, cryptanalysis, and cryptology, particularly with regard to modular arithmetic, diophantine equations, linear and quadratic congruencies, prime numbers and primarily testing (i. e., whether a number is prime).

In mathematics, a *Diophantine equation* is an indeterminate polynomial equation that allows the variables to be integers only. Diophantine problems have fewer equations than unknown variables and involve finding integers that work correctly for all equations. In more technical language, they define an algebraic curve, algebraic surface, or more general object, and ask about the lattice points on it [http://en.wikipedia.org/wiki/Diophantine_equation].

Other discrete aspects of number theory include geometry of numbers. In analytic number theory, techniques from continuous mathematics are also used. Topics that go beyond discrete objects include transcendental numbers, Diophantine approximation, *p*-adic analysis and function fields [http://en.wikipedia.org/wiki/Discrete_mathematics].

An interesting application of number theory to software is *modular arithmetic*. In modular arithmetic we are only interested in the remainder. There is a notation to indicate that two integers have the same remainder when they are divided by the positive integer *m*.

> **DEFINITION:** If *a* and *b* are integers and *n* is a positive integer, then *a is congruent to b modulo n* if *n* divides *a* - *b*. We use the notation $a \equiv b$ (mod *n*) to indicate that *a* is congruent to *b* modulo *n*. If *a* and *b* are not congruent modulo *n* we write a $\not\equiv$ b (mod *n*).

10. Algebra

Algebraic structures occur as both discrete examples and continuous examples. Discrete algebras include: Boolean algebra used in logic gates and programming; relational algebra used in databases; discrete and finite versions of groups, rings and fields are important in algebraic coding theory; discrete semi-groups and monoids appear in the theory of formal languages [http://en.wikipedia.org/wiki/Discrete_mathematics].

A *semigroup* is an algebraic structure consisting of a set together with an associative binary operation. A semigroup generalizes a monoid in that there might not exist an identity element. It also (originally) generalized a group (a monoid with all inverses) to a type where every element did not have to have an inverse, thus the name semigroup [http://en.wikipedia.org/wiki/Semigroup].

In abstract algebra, a *monoid* is an algebraic structure with a single associative binary operation and an identity element. Monoids are studied in semigroup theory as they are naturally semigroups with identity [http://en.wikipedia.org/wiki/Monoid].

11. Calculus of Finite Differences, Discrete Calculus or Discrete Analysis

A *function* defined on an interval of the integers is usually called a sequence. A *sequence* could be a finite sequence from some data source or an infinite sequence from a discrete dynamical system. Such a discrete function could be defined explicitly by a list (if its domain is finite), or by a formula for its general term, or it could be given implicitly by a recurrence relation or difference equation.

Difference equations are similar to differential equations, but replace differentiation by taking the difference between adjacent terms; they can be used to approximate differential equations or (more often) studied in their own right. Many questions and methods concerning differential equations have counterparts for difference equations. For instance, where there are integral transforms in harmonic analysis for studying continuous functions or analog signals, there are discrete transforms for discrete functions or digital signals (e.g., the Z transform [http://en.wikipedia.orgwiki/Z_transform]). As well as the discrete metric there are more general discrete or finite metric spaces and finite topological spaces [http://en.wikipedia.org /wiki/Discrete_mathematics].

12. Geometry

Computational geometry applies computer algorithms to representations of geometrical objects [http://en.wikipedia.org/wiki/Discrete_mathematics].

- *Discrete geometry* and *combinatorial geometry* are about combinatorial properties of *discrete collections* of geometrical objects. A long-standing topic in discrete geometry is *tiling of the plane* (finding a geometric shape that can be replicated to cover a plane with no gaps and no overlaps [http://en.wikipedia.org/wiki/Tesselation]). Computational geometry applies algorithms to geometrical problems.

- *Computational geometry* is that part of discrete mathematics that studies computational problems involving geometric objects. Computational geometry is used extensively in computer graphics, computer games, robotics, scientific calculations, and a vast array of other areas.

13. Topology

Although *topology* is the field of mathematics that formalizes and generalizes the intuitive notion of "continuous deformation" of objects, it gives rise to many discrete topics; this can be attributed in part to the focus on topological invariants, which themselves usually take discrete values. Relevant topics include combinatorial topology, topological graph theory, topological combinatorics, computational topology, discrete topological space, and finite topological space.

In local area networks using a ring topology, messages are sent from device to device around the cycle until the intended recipient of a message is reached [http://en.wikipedia.org/wiki/Discrete_mathematics].

14. Operations Research

Operations research provides techniques for solving practical problems in business and other fields—problems such as allocating resources to maximize profit, or scheduling project activities to minimize risk. Operations research techniques include linear programming and other areas of optimization, queuing theory, scheduling theory, and network theory. Operations research also includes continuous topics such as continuous-time Markov process, continuous-time martingales, process optimization, and continuous and hybrid control theory.

In probability theory, a *martingale* is a model of a fair game where no knowledge of past events can help to predict future winnings [http://en.wikipedia.org/wiki/Discrete_mathematics].

15. Game Theory, Decision Theory, Utility Theory, and Social Choice Theory

Types of discrete methodical theories [http://en.wikipedia.org/wiki/Discrete_mathematics]:

- *Decision theory* is concerned with identifying the values, uncertainties and other issues relevant in a given decision, its rationality, and the resulting optimal decision.

- *Utility theory* is about measures of the relative economic satisfaction from, or desirability of, consumption of various goods and services.

- *Social choice theory* is about voting. A more puzzle-based approach to voting is ballot theory.

Game theory deals with situations where success depends on the choices of others, which makes choosing the best-recourse of action more complex. There are even continuous games [http://en.wikipedia.org/wiki/differential_game]. Topics include auction theory and fair division.

16. Discretization

Discretization concerns the process of transferring continuous models and equations into discrete counterparts, often for the purposes of making calculations easier by using approximations. Numerical analysis provides an important example [http://en.wikipedia.org/wiki/Discrete_mathematics].

17. Discrete Analogues of Continuous Mathematics

There are many concepts in continuous mathematics that have discrete versions, such as discrete calculus, discrete probability distributions, discrete Fourier transforms, discrete geometry, discrete logarithms, discrete differential geometry, discrete exterior calculus, discrete Morse theory, difference equations, discrete dynamical systems, and discrete vector measures.

In applied mathematics, discrete modeling is the discrete analogue of continuous modeling. In discrete modeling, discrete formulae are fit to data. A common method in this form of modeling is to use recurrence relations.

18. Hybrid, Discrete and Continuous Mathematics

The time scale calculus is a unification of the theory of difference equations with that of differential equations, which has applications to fields requiring simultaneous modeling of discrete and continuous data [http://en.wikipedia.org/wiki/Discrete_mathematics].

Some General and Cited References

Additional information on the *discrete mathematics* KA can be found in the following documents:

- Biggs, Norman L., *Discrete Mathematics*, Oxford University Press, Oxford, England, 2002.

- Brotherston, J., R Bornat, C. Calcagno, "Cyclic proofs of program termination in separation logic," *ACM SIGPLAN Notices*, Volume 43, Issue 1 (January 2008).

- Buss, Samuel R., *Handbook of Proof Theory* (Volume 137 of *Studies in logic and the foundations of mathematics*), Elsevier, Burlington, MA, 1998. ISBN 0444898409, p 13.

- Enderton, H., *A Mathematical Introduction to Logic*, Second Edition, Harcourt Academic Press, San Diego, CA, 2001.

- Hodkinson, Trevor R., and John A. N. Parnell, *Reconstructing the Tree of Life: Taxonomy and systematics of species rich taxa*, CRC Press, London, 2007, ISBN 0849395798, p. 97.

- Hopkins, Brian, *Resources for Teaching Discrete Mathematics*, Mathematical Association of America, 2008.

- Johnsonbaugh, Richard, *Discrete Mathematics*, Prentice Hall, Upper Saddle River, NJ, 2008.

- Millennium Prize Problems 2000-05-24. http://www.claymath.org/millennium/. Retrieved 2008-01-12.

- Mohar, Bojan, and Carsten Thomassen, *Graphs on Surfaces*, Johns Hopkins University Press, Baltimore, MD, 2001.

- Rosen, Kenneth H., *Discrete Mathematics & Its Application with Combinatorics and Graph Theory*, McGraw-Hill, New York, 2007. (Recommended as a CSDP exam reference book by the IEEE Computer Society.)

- Schulz, Stephan, "Learning Search Control Knowledge for Equational Theorem Proving," in *KI 2001: Advances in Artificial Intelligence: Joint German/Austrian Conference on AI, Vienna, Austria, September 19-21, 2001: Proceedings* (Volume 2174 of *Lecture Notes in Artificial Intelligence*), Franz Baader, Gerhard Brewka, and Thomas Eiter, eds., Springer, Berlin, 2001, ISBN 3540426124, p. 325.

- Troelstra, Sjerp, Helmut Schwichtenberg, *Basic Proof Theory*, Cambridge University Press, Cambridge, England, 2000, ISBN 0521779111, p. 186.

- Weisstein, Eric W., "Discrete mathematics" from *Math World*. (*MathWorld*™ is the web's most extensive mathematical resource, provided as a free service to the world's mathematics and internet communities as part of a commitment to education and educational outreach by Wolfram Research, makers of *Mathematica*.)

- Wikipedia is a free web-based encyclopedia enabling multiple users to freely add and edit online content. Definitions cited from Wikipedia and their related sources have been verified by the authors and other peer reviewers. Readers who would like to verify a source or a reference should search the subject on Google, and read the technical report found under Wikipedia.

Chapter 15.2

Essentials of Mathematics

Richard Hall Thayer and Merlin Dorfman

This is the fifteenth chapter of a textbook to aid individual software engineers in a greater understanding of the IEEE SWEBOK [2013] and a guide book to aid software engineers in passing the IEEE CSDP and CSDA certification exams.

This chapter studies some of the foundations of engineering mathematics. The purpose of requiring a basic understanding of mathematics for all software engineers is to enable the reading and understanding (comprehension) of mathematically-based papers and articles.

These software engineering features provide a greater understanding of SWEBOK as well as being useful in studying for the certificate exams to pass the mathematical portion of the CSDP exam. Interested engineers should delve deeper into this subject through self-study.

This chapter covers the CSDP exam мathematics Foundation module [Software Exam Specification, Version 2, 18 March 2009]. The primary and most detailed reference for the Mathematics Foundation knowledge area (KA) is Kenneth H. Rosen [2007] *Discrete Mathematics & Its Application with Combinatorics and Graph Theory*.

Table 1: Connections between the Mathematical Foundation CSDP/CSDA exam specification and the supporting paragraphs in the reference books

Mathematical Foundations	Source	Paragraphs
1. Functions, Relations and Sets	Rosen [2007]	Sections 2.3, 7.1
2. Basic Logic (prepositional and predicate)	Rosen [2007]	Sections 1.1 - 1.3
3. Proof Techniques (direct, contradiction, inductive)	Rosen [2007]	Sections 1.6, 1.7
4. Basic Counting	Rosen [2007]	Section 5.1
5. Graphs and Trees	Rosen [2007]	Sections 8.1, 9.1 - 9.2
6. Discrete Probability	Rosen [2007]	Chapter 6
7. Finite State Machines, regular expressions	Rosen [2007]	Sections 11.2, 11.4
8. Grammars	Rosen [2007]	Section 11.1
9. Numerical precision, accuracy, and errors	Cheney & Kincaid [2007]	Chapters 5 & 7
10. Number Theory	Rosen [2007]	Sections 3.4 - 3-7
11. Algebraic Structure	Rosen [2007] Lopez [1989]	Sections 9.1 - 9.2 All pages

15.1 Functions, Relations, and Sets

The first paragraph on mathematical foundations begins with a basic understanding of sets, relationships between sets, and functions. An outline of this paragraph is detailed in [http://www .cse.ohio-state.edu/~gurari/theory-bk/theory-bk-appendixse1.html; Gurari 1989]:

- Sets

- Set operations

- Relations

- Functions

- Countability

15.1.1 Sets. A *set* is a collection of elements. The order or repetition of the elements is immaterial. Notation of the form { x | x satisfies the property Q } is used for specifying the set of all elements x that satisfy property Q. Finite sets are also specified by explicitly listing their members between brackets.

The number of elements in set A, denoted |A|, is called the *cardinality* of the set. A set with no elements (i.e., cardinality equals 0) is called the *empty* set and is denoted by Ø.

Two sets labeled A and B are said to be *equal*, denoted A = B, if they have precisely the same members. A is said to be a *subset* of B, denoted A ⊆ B, if every element of A is also an element of B. A is said to be a *proper subset* of B, denoted A ⊂ B, if A is a subset of B and A is not equal to B.

The relationship between sets can be illustrated using *Venn diagrams*. A point in the plane represents each element of a given set. Each set is represented by a geometric shape enclosing only those points that represent the elements of the set (see Figure 15.1).

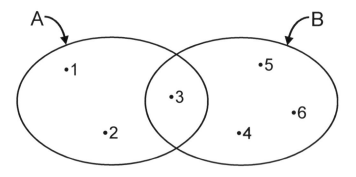

Figure 15.1: Venn diagram for the sets A = {1, 2, 3} and B = {3, 4, 5, 6} [Gurari 1989]

The *power set* of set A, denoted 2^A, is the set of all subsets of A, that is, the set {S | S is a subset of A}.

A *multiset* is a collection of elements in which the repetition of included elements is counted. The set of *natural numbers* is the set of all the nonnegative integers included in the multiset.

15.1.2 Set operations. The *union* of A and B, denoted A ∪ B, is the set {x | x is either in A or in B or in both}. The *intersection* of A and B, denoted A ∩ B, is the set {x | x is both in A and in B}. A and B are said to be *disjoint* if they have no elements in common and the intersection of A and B belong to an empty set, that is, if A ∩ B = Ø.

The *difference* between A and B, denoted A - B, is the set {x | x is in A but not in B}. If B is a subset of A, then A - B is said to be the *complement of B with respect to A*. When A is understood, A - B is simply said to be the *complement of* B, denoted B_c or B′. In such a case, A is called the *universe*.

15.1.3 Relations. A *relation* R from A to B is a subset of the Cartesian product A × B. If A = B, then R is said to be a *relation on* A.

The *domain* of R is the set {x | (x, y) is in R for some y in B}. If the domain of R is the set A, then R is said to be *total*. Otherwise, R is said to be *partial*.

The *range* of R is the set {y | (x, y) is in R for some x in A}. The *range of R at x*, denoted R(x), is the set {y | (x, y) is in R}.

15.1.4 Functions. A *function* f from A to B, denoted f: A → B is a relation from A to B, whose range f(x) at each x in A has cardinality 0 or 1. F(x) is said to be *defined* if it has cardinality 1, that is, if f(x) = {y} for some y. In such a case, f(x) is said to have the value of y, written f(x) = y. Otherwise, f(x) is said to be *undefined*.

A function f is said to be *one-to-one* if f(x) = f(y) implies x = y for all x and y in A. Function f is said to be *onto* if B is the range of f. Function f is said to be a *predicate*, or an *assertion*, if B = {false, true}.

| x | denotes the smallest integer that is not smaller than x. Mod (x, y) denotes the remainder of an integer division of x by y. Mins denotes the smallest value in S. Maxs denotes the biggest value in S. Gcd (x, y) denotes the greatest common divisor of x and y.

15.1.5 Countability. A set A is said to be *countable* if there exists an *onto function f* from the set of natural numbers to A. The set is said to be *countability infinite* if there exists a one-to-one *onto function f* from the set of natural numbers to set A. A set that is not countable is said to be *uncountable*.

15.2 Basic Logic

Logic is a language for reasoning. It is a collection of rules we use when doing logical reasoning. Human reasoning has been observed over centuries from at least the time of the Greeks, and patterns appearing in reasoning have been extracted, abstracted, and streamlined.

In logic we are interested in true or false statements, and how the truth/falsehood of a statement can be determined from other statements. However, instead of dealing with individual specific statements, we are going to use symbols to represent arbitrary statements so that the results can be used in many similar but different cases. The formalization also promotes the clarity of thought and eliminates mistakes.

There are various types of logic such as logic of sentences (propositional logic), logic of objects (predicate logic), logic involving uncertainties, logic dealing with fuzziness, temporal logic, etc. Here we are going to be concerned with propositional logic and predicate logic, which are fundamental to all types of logic [http://www.cs.odu.edu/~toida/nerzic/content/logic/intr_to_logic.html].

Logic first determines if a statement is true or false then decides if the truth/falsehood of the statement can be induced from other statements. Various types of logic include *propositional logic* (logic of sentences), *predicate logic* (logic of objects), logic involving uncertainties, logic concerning fuzziness, and temporal logic. Basic logic is concerned with propositional logic and predicate logic, both of which are fundamental to all types of logic. This paragraph describes the following [Toida 2009]:

- Propositional logic

- Predicate logic

15.2.1 Propositional logic. The *sentence* is the smallest unit observed without further inspecting sentence structure, nor analyzing and discussing meaning. Of interest is whether a sentence is true or false. This determination is followed by an interest into whether or not the truth or falsehood of a (certain) sentence is preceded by a set of sentences, and if so, the ensuing progression. Thus, sentences considered in basic logic are not arbitrary sentences; they are those that are either true or false and are called propositions. If a proposition is true, it has a truth-value of "true;" if a proposition is false, its truth-value is "false" [Toida 2009].

15.2.2 Predicate logic. *Propositional logic* does not completely represent every type of assertion used in computer science and mathematics. Nor can it express certain types of relationships between propositions such as equivalence. The predicate feature is introduced to cope with the deficiencies of propositional logic.

A *predicate* is a verb phrase template describing a property of objects, or a relationship among objects represented by variables. If B is adopted as the name for the predicate "is blue," sentences that assert an object 'is blue' can be represented as "B(x)", where x represents an arbitrary object. B(x) reads as "x is blue."

15.3 Proof Techniques

In the field of mathematics, a *proof* presents a convincing demonstration (within the accepted standards of the field) that a particular mathematical statement is necessarily true. Proofs are obtained from deductive reasoning rather than from general inductive or empirical arguments. That is, a proof must demonstrate that a statement is true in every case, without exception. An unproven proposition that is believed to be true is known as a *conjecture* [http://en.wikipedia .org/wiki/Mathematical_proof].

A proven statement is often called a *theorem*. Once a theorem is confirmed (i.e., proven), it can be used as the basis to prove further statements. A theorem may also be referred to as a *lemma*, especially when intended for use as a step in the proof of another theorem [http://en.wiki pedia.org/wiki/Lemma_(mathematics)].

Proofs employ logic, yet usually include natural language that usually allows for a certain level of ambiguity. The vast majority of proofs contained in written mathematics may be considered applications of rigorous informal logic. *Formal proofs*, written in symbolic language instead of natural language, are considered in proof theory. The distinction between formal and informal proofs has led to the examination of current and historical mathematical practices known as *quasi-empiricism* and *folk mathematics*.

The *philosophy of folk mathematics* is concerned with the role of language and logic in proofs.

This section of proof techniques covers the following types of proofs:

- Direct proof

- Proof by contradiction

- Proof by induction

15.3.1 Direct proof. *Direct proofs* establish a conclusion by logically combining axioms, definitions, and earlier theorems. For example, a direct proof can be used to establish that the sum of two even integers is always even:

> *Consider two even integers x and y. Being even, they can be written as x=2a and y=2b respectively for integers a and b, hence the sum x + y = 2a + 2b = 2(a + b). This equation clearly states that x + y contains the integer 2 as a factor, and therefore, the sum of any two even integers must be even.*

This proof uses the definition of even integers accompanied by the *distributive law*.

15.3.2 Proof by contradiction. In logic, *proof by contradiction* is a form of proof that establishes the truth or validity of a proposition by showing that the proposition being false would imply a contradiction. Since by the law of bivalence a proposition must be either true or false, and its falsity has been shown impossible, the proposition must be true [http://en.wikipedia.org/wiki /Proof_by_contradiction].

Proof by contradiction is also known as indirect proof, apagogical argument, *reductio ad impossibile*. It is a particular kind of the more general form of argument known as *reductio ad absurdum*.

This method is perhaps the most prevalent in mathematical proofs. Review the following example:

> *A classic proof by contradiction from mathematics is the proof that the square root of 2 is irrational. If it were rational, it could be expressed as a fraction a/b in lowest terms, where a and b are integers, at least one of which is odd. However, if a/b = √2, then $a^2 = 2b^2$. Therefore, a^2 must be even. Because the square of an odd number is odd, that in turn implies that a is even. This means that b must be odd because a/b is in lowest terms.*
>
> *On the other hand, if a is even, then a^2 is a multiple of 4. If a^2 is a multiple of 4 and $a^2 = 2b^2$, then $2b^2$ is a multiple of 4, and therefore b^2 is even, and so is b.*
>
> *Therefore, b is odd and even, a contradiction. Therefore, the initial assumption— that √2 can be expressed as a fraction—must be false.*

15.3.3 Proof by induction. The simplest and most common form of mathematical induction proves that a statement involving a natural number *n* holds for all values of *n*. The proof consists of two steps [http://en.wikipedia.org/wiki/Mathematical_induction]:

1. The *basis (base case):* showing that the statement holds when *n* is equal to the *lowest* value that *n* is given in the question. Usually, *n* = 0 or *n* = 1.

2. The *inductive step:* showing that *i*f the statement holds for some *n*, *then* the statement also holds when *n* + 1 is substituted for *n*.

The assumption in the inductive step that the statement holds for some *n* is called the *induction hypothesis* (or *inductive hypothesis*). To perform the inductive step, one assumes the induction hypothesis and then uses this assumption to prove the statement for *n* + 1.

The choice between $n = 0$ and $n = 1$ in the base case is specific to the context of the proof: If 0 is considered a natural number, as is common in the fields of combinatorics and mathematical logic, then $n = 0$. If, on the other hand, 1 is taken as the first natural number, then the base case is given by $n = 1$.

This method works by first proving the statement is true for a starting value, and then proving that the process used to go from one value to the next is valid. If these are both proven, then any value can be obtained by performing the process repeatedly. It may be helpful to think of the domino effect; if one is presented with a long row of dominoes standing on end, one can be sure that:

1. The first domino will fall

2. Whenever a domino falls, its next neighbor will also fall

so it is concluded that *all* of the dominoes will fall, and that this fact is inevitable.

15.4 Basic Counting

The *fundamental counting principle* is used to find the number of ways to complete a task with multiple parts. For example, if the first part of a two-part task can be done in *a* ways, and the second part can be done in *b* ways, then the total number of ways to complete the task can be calculated by multiplying *a* X *b*.

This fundamental counting principle is introduced with the following example highlighting choices one might make given many possibilities:

> *How many different outfits can be made from three different shirts, four different pairs of pants, and two different pairs of shoes?*
>
> *How many combinations (counts) are contained in the above information?*
>
> *The answer is A X B X C = 3 X 4 X 2 = 24 counts.*

15.5 Graphs and Trees

Graphical representations are widely used for displaying relations among informational units because they help readers to visualize the relations, thereby better understanding the information contained among the relations and within the units. Two general types of graphical representations are distinguished [TEI 2004]:

- Graphs

- Trees

15.5.1 Graphs. *Graphs,* in the strictly mathematical sense, consist of points and the connections among them. Points are often called *nodes* or *vertices* and connections are referred to as *arcs,* or under certain conditions, *edges*. Among the various types of graphs commonly used are *networks* and *trees*.

Broadly speaking, graphs can be presented as two formats or types: *undirected* and *directed*. An *undirected graph* contains a set of *nodes* (or *vertices*) together with a set of pairs of those

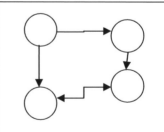

Figure 15.2: Directed Graph (for a undirected graph, remove arrow heads)

vertices, called *arcs* or *edges* (see Figure 15.2). Each node in an arc of an undirected graph is said to be *incident* with that arc, and the two vertices comprising an arc are said to be *adjacent*.

A *directed graph* is similar to an undirected graph except that the arcs are *ordered pairs* of nodes. In the case of directed graphs, the term *edge* is not used. Moreover, each arc in a directed graph is *adjacent from* the node from which the arc originates, and *adjacent to* the node to which the arc is directed. A graph containing no cycles is considered to be a tree.

5.5.2 Trees. A *tree* is a connected acyclic graph (see Figure 15.3). It is possible for a tree graph to follow a path from a vertex to any other vertex, yet there are no paths leading from a vertex to itself.

A *rooted tree* is a directed graph based on a tree, meaning the arcs in the graph correspond to the arcs of a tree such that there is exactly one node called the *root*, with a corresponding path from this root node to all other nodes in the graph. Nodes adjacent to the root node are called *children* and the node adjacent from a given node is referred to as the *parent*. Nodes with both a parent and children are called *internal nodes*. A node with no children is tagged as a *leaf* to crossing arcs.

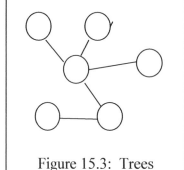

Figure 15.3: Trees

15.6 Discrete Probability

A *discrete probability distribution* is a function able to accommodate a discrete number of values that are not necessarily finite. This distribution is most often comprised of non-negative integers or some subset of non-negative integers. There is no existing mathematical restriction requiring that discrete probability functions be defined as integers. However, integers make practical sense. For example, a coin tossed 6 times may land 2 or 3 heads but will never land 2 ½ heads. Each discrete value has a certain probability of occurrence that is between zero and one. That is, a discrete function that allows negative values or values greater than one is not a probability function. The condition that the probabilities sum to one means that at least one of the values has to occur [eHSM 2012].

In contrast, a *continuous probability distribution* is a function containing an unlimited number of values.

15.7 Finite State Machines and Regular Expressions

A *finite-state machine* (FSM) or *finite-state automaton* (plural: *automata*), or simply a *state machine*, is a mathematical abstraction sometimes used to design digital logic or computer programs. It is a *behavior model* composed of a finite number of states, transitions between those states, and actions, similarly to a flow graph in which one can inspect the way logic runs when certain conditions are met. It has finite internal memory, an input feature that reads symbols in a sequence, one at a time without going backward; and an output feature, which may be in the form of a user interface, once the model is implemented. The operation of a FSM begins from one of the states (called a *start state*), goes through transitions depending on input to different states and can end in any of those available; however, only a certain set of states mark a success- ful flow of operation (called *accept states*) [http://en.wikipedia.org/wiki/Finite-state_machine].

In general, FSMs are one of the most widely used models in the field of computer program- ming. FSMs are particularly ubiquitous in programming embedded systems and for describing digital circuits. Modeling using FSMs has become so successful that the Unified Modeling

Language Standard by Object Management Group has adopted its use [http://Sakharov.net /fsmtutrial .html].

15.7.1 Finite automaton. The origin of FSMs is finite automata. More formal than a FSM, a *finite automaton* is defined as a quintuple (A, S, s, T, F), where [http://Sakharov.net/fsmtutorial .html]:

- A is a finite nonempty set of symbols (input alphabet)

- S is a finite nonempty set of states

- s is an initial state, an element of S

- T is the state transition function: T: S x A $\rightarrow$ S

- F is the set of final states, which is a subset of S

Finite automata are primarily used in parsing for recognizing languages. Input strings belonging to a given language should point an automaton toward final states. All other input strings should turn this automaton to states that are not final.

Finite automata that also generate output are called *transducers*. In order to define a transducer, an output alphabet and output function must be specified and added to the five components outlined earlier. The output function can be a function of a state or a function of both state and input symbols. If the output function depends on both a state and an input symbol, it is called a *Mealy automaton*. If the output function depends only on a state, it is called a *Moore automaton*.

15.7.2 Regular expression. In computing, a *regular expression* provides a concise and flexible means for matching *strings* of text, such as particular characters, words, or patterns of characters. A regular expression is written in a *formal language* that can be interpreted by a regular expression processor, a program that either serves as a *parser generator* or examines text and identifies parts that match the provided *specification.*

15.7.3 Finite state machines. The application of finite automata is mathematically rigorous. FSMs were introduced as a less rigorous and more suitable model for computer science. A FSM is defined by the following [http://sakharov.net/fsmtutorial.html]:

- a finite nonempty set of states

- an initial state

- a finite nonempty set of distinct input events or their categories

- state transitions

- actions

As opposed to input symbols for finite automata, any sequence of events can be a FSM input. In other words, any object can be an input entity. The only restriction regarding input is that all possible inputs should be classified as belonging to one of a finite number of distinct input categories (types and classes). Simpler modeling cases only allow a finite number of distinct input objects. It is assumed that input events are then processed synchronously, meaning the next event is processed only after the current event is fully consumed and a transition is executed when necessary. This may require queuing input events before their processing time.

Another important difference between finite automata and FSMs is that actions may be related to FSMs. The role of actions is to generate output. FSMs may also communicate with other processes by means of actions. Presumably, actions do not generate input events. In other words, FSMs consume external events only. Actions are stateless, and therefore unable to transmit information from one invocation to another. When actions are associated with transitions, a corresponding FSM is called a Mealy machine. Actions belonging to a FSM associated with states are called Moore machines. Because actions can be represented by virtually any program (code) and action input can be any object, the functionally of FSMs may be quite rich, extending far beyond the limits of finite automata.

15.7.4 State diagrams. FSMs are most commonly represented by *state diagrams* which are also referred to as *state transition diagrams*. A state diagram is a directed graph in which each vertex represents a state and each edge represents a transition between two states.

A state transition table presents a common representation of FSMs (See Figure 15.4). Every column included in the table corresponds to a state. Each row corresponds to an event category. Values contained in table cells provide states resulting from respective transitions. Table cells also can be used for specifying actions related to transitions.

FSM specifications are simple and 'flat.' The aim of this extension is to reduce the size of FSM specifications. In practice, the number of FSM transitions grows proportionally to the increase of states. This extension occurs because it is necessary to copy existing transitions replacing newly introduced states. The hierarchical FSMs solve this transition problem by allowing the possibility of encapsulating newly introduced states within a FSM that corresponds to one state belonging to the proceeding upper level. The next-level transitions are applied to the entire FSM of this lower level. Yet another extension of FSMs can be introduced by allowing sequences of events to define transitions [http://sakharov.net/fsmtutorial.html.

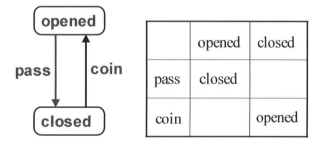

	opened	closed
pass	closed	
coin		opened

Figure 15.4: State transition diagram and state transition tables
[http://sakharov.net/fsmtutorial.html]

15.8 Grammars

A *grammar* is a formal definition of the syntactic structure (the syntax) of a language [http://dictionary.reference.com/browse/grammar].

A grammar is normally represented as a set of production rules that specify the order of constituents and their sub-constituents in a sentence (a well-designed string within the language). Each rule contains two symbols – a left hand side symbol and a right hand side symbol. The left-hand side symbol names a syntactic category such as a noun-phrase for a natural language grammar. The right-hand side symbol contains a sequence of zero or more symbols.

Each symbol may be either a terminal symbol or a non-terminal symbol. A terminal symbol corresponds to one lexeme, or a part of the sentence with no internal syntactic structure. A lexeme is known as an identifier or an operator in a computer language. A non-terminal symbol applies to the left-hand side of a rule.

One rule is normally designated as the top-level rule containing symbols that provide the structure for an entire sentence. A *parser*, which operates as a recognizer, uses a computer program to divide code into functional components.

In the realm of computing, a formal grammar such as a Backus-Naur-Form (BNF) can be used to parse a linear input stream, for example the source code of a program, into a data structure. Parsing expresses the established meaning or an inherent meaning of the input in a format that is easier for the computer to work with [http://en.wikipedia.org/wiki/Backus-Naur_Form].

15.9 Numerical Precision, Accuracy, and Errors

In the field of computer science, *precision* of a numerical quantity represents a measure of expressed detail. This is usually measured in bits although a measurement can be calculated using decimal digits. The measure is related to precision in mathematics, which describes the number of digits that are used to express a value [Cheney & Kincade 2008].

In the disciplines of engineering, industry, and statistics, the *accuracy* of a measurement system is determined by the degree of closeness of measurements of a quantity to its actual (true) value. The *precision* of a measurement system, also called *reproducibility* or *repeatability*, is the degree by which repeated measurements in unchanged conditions produce the same results (See Figure 15.5). Although accuracy and precision can be synonymous in colloquial use, they are deliberately contrasted in the context of the scientific method [http://en.wikipedia.org/wiki/Accuracy_and_precision].

In summary, *accuracy* indicates proximity of measurement results to a true value, while *precision* pertains to the repeatability or reproducibility of the measurement. (See Figure 15.5.) Therefore, a measurement system can be accurate but not precise, precise but not accurate, neither, or both. For example, if an experiment contains a systematic error, increasing the sample size generally augments precision but does not improve accuracy. Eliminating the systematic error improves accuracy but does not change precision.

A fault occurs when a human *error* results in a mistake within the software product. (The fault is the encoding of the human error). A *failure* is the deviation of the software from its required behavior. A wise man once said:

"A human error can lead to a fault which can lead to a computer failure."

A measurement system is considered *valid* if it is both *accurate* and *precise*. Terms related to validity are *bias* (non-random or directed effects caused by a factor or factors unrelated by the independent variable) and *error* (random variability). Generally, increasing precision does not improve accuracy.

In addition to accuracy and precision, measurements also contain a measurement resolution, which is the smallest change in the underlying physical quantity that produces a response in the measurement. Its precision however, may be low.

Human errors in computer programs are called "faults" instead of "errors" because they may or may not result in a computer failure.

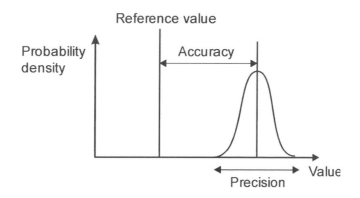

Figure 15.5: Accuracy versus precision
[http://en.wikipedia.org/wiki /Accuracy_and_precision]

15.10 Number Theory

Number theory is the branch of pure mathematics concerned with the properties of numbers in general and integers in particular, including the wider classes of problems that arise from their study [http://en.wikipedia.org/wiki/Number_theory].

The terms "arithmetic" or "the higher arithmetic" are also used to refer to number theory. These synonyms are older terms that have waned in popularity. However, the word "arithmetic" is popularly used as an adjective rather than the more cumbersome phrase "number-theoretic," as are "arithmetic of" rather than "number theory of," e.g., *arithmetic geometry, arithmetic functions*, and *arithmetic of elliptic curves*.

Number theory may be subdivided into several fields according to the employed methods and the genre of questions investigated. The following ten examples of fields are examined:

1. Elementary number theory
2. Analytic number theory
3. Algebraic number theory
4. Geometry of numbers
5. Combinatorial number theory
6. Computational number theory
7. Arithmetic algebraic geometry
8. Arithmetic topology
9. Arithmetic dynamics
10. Modular forms

15.10.1 Elementary number theory. *Elementary number theory* studies integers without the use of techniques borrowed from other mathematical fields. Elementary number theory is a branch of pure mathematics devoted primarily to the study of the integers. Number theorists study prime numbers (the building blocks of integers, i.e., all integers can be expressed uniquely as the product of prime numbers) as well as the properties of objects made out of integers (such as rational numbers) or defined as generalizations of the integers (such as, for example, algebraic integers) [http://en.wikipedia.org/wiki/Number_theory].

Integers can be considered either as themselves or as solutions to equations (Diophantine geometry). Questions in number theory are often best understood through the study of analytical objects (e.g., the Riemann zeta function) that encode properties of the integers, primes or other number-theoretic objects in some fashion (analytic number theory). One may also study real numbers in relation to rational numbers, e.g., as approximated by the latter (Diophantine approximation).

15.10.2 Analytic number theory. The *analytic number theory* employs the combined machinery of calculus and complex analysis to tackle questions relating to integers [http://en.wikipedia.org /wiki/Analytic_number_theory]. The prime number theorem (PNT, which describes how prime numbers are distributed among the positive integers) and the related Riemann hypothesis are examples of the analytic number theory.

15.10.3 Algebraic number theory. In *algebraic number theory*, the concept of a number is expanded to the algebraic numbers, which are roots of polynomials with rational coefficients. These domains contain elements analogous to integers known as algebraic integers. In this setting, the familiar features of the integers (e.g., unique factorization) are not necessarily required. The virtue of the machinery employed when using Galois theory, group cohomology, class field theory, group representations and L-functions is that it allows one to deal with new phenomena and yet partially recover the behavior of the usual integers [http://en.wikipedia.org /wiki /Algebraic_number_theory].

15.10.4 Geometry of numbers. The *geometry of numbers* incorporates basic geometric concepts, such as lattices, into number-theoretic questions. This theory incorporates two fundamental theorems in algebraic number theory. It begins with Minkowski's theorem [http://en.wikipe dia.org/wiki/Minkowski's_theorem] applying lattice points in convex sets and leads to basic proofs of the finiteness of the class number and Dirichlet's unit theorem [http://en.wikipedia.org /wiki/Dirichlet's_theorem].

15.10.5 Combinatorial number theory. *Combinatorial number theory* analyzes number theoretic problems that involve combinatorial ideas in their formulations or solutions. Paul Erdős is the main founder of this branch of number theory. Typical topics include covering systems, zero-sum problems, various restricted sum sets, and arithmetic progressions in a set of integers. Algebraic and analytic methods are powerful theories when integrated with combinatorial number theory. (See also arithmetic combinatorics and basic counting, Paragraph 15.4.)

15.10.6 Computational number theory. *Computational number theory* studies algorithms relevant to number theory. Fast algorithms used for prime testing and integer factorization have important applications in cryptography.

15.10.7 Arithmetic algebraic geometry. *Arithmetic algebraic geometry* is a branch of mathematics combining techniques of abstract algebra, especially commutative algebra, with the language and proofs of geometry. Occupying a central place in modern mathematics, it has multiple conceptual connections with such diverse fields as complex analysis, topology and number theory [http://en.wikipedia.org/wiki/Algebraic_geometry].

The fundamental objects of study in arithmetic algebraic geometry are algebraic varieties and geometric manifestations of solutions pertaining to systems of polynomial equations. Plane algebraic curves, which include lines, circles, parabolas, lemniscates, and Cassini ovals, form one of the best-studied classes of algebraic varieties.

15.10.8 Arithmetic topology. *Arithmetic topology* was developed from a series of analogies between number fields and 3-manifolds. Prime ideals and knots were pointed out by Barry Mazur and Yuri Manin in the 1960s [http://en.wikipedia.org/wiki/Prime_ideal].

15.10.9 Arithmetic dynamics. *Arithmetic dynamics* is a field that emerged in the 1990s that amalgamates two areas of mathematics: dynamical systems and number theory. Classically, discrete dynamics refers to the study of the iteration of self-maps belonging to a complex plane or real line. Arithmetic dynamics is therefore the study of the number-theoretic properties of integers, rationals, *p*-adics, and/or algebraic points under repeated application of a polynomial or rational function [http://en.wikipedia.org/wiki/Arithmetic_dynamics].

15.10.10 Modular forms. *Modular forms* are complex analytic functions on the upper half-plane satisfying a certain functional equation and growth condition. (The upper half-plane is associated with a common visualization of complex numbers with points in the plane endowed with Cartesian coordinates, with the Y-axis pointing upwards: the "upper half-plane" corresponds to the half-plane above the X-axis, i.e., complex numbers with positive imaginary parts.) The theory of modular forms therefore belongs to complex analysis. However, the primary importance of the theory has traditionally been its connections with number theory. Modular forms appear in other areas such as algebraic topology and string theory [http://en.wikipedia.org/wiki/Modular_form].

15.11 Algebraic Structure

An *algebraic structure* presents an introduction to abstract mathematical structures of modern algebra. Algebraic structures include [http://en.wikipedia.org/wiki/Algebraic_structure]:

- group

- ring

- field

- module

- vector space

- algebra over a field

15.11.1 Group. In the field of mathematics, a *group* is an algebraic structure consisting of a set and an operation that combine any two of their elements to form a third element. To qualify as a group, the set and the operation must satisfy a few conditions called group axioms, namely *closure, associativity, identity and invertibility*. For example: All the possible manipulations of a Rubik's Cube form a group [http://en.wikipedia.org/wiki/Group_(mathematics)].

While groups are familiar to many mathematical structures such as number systems—for example, the integers endowed with the group axioms form a group—the formulation of the axioms is detached from the concrete nature of the group and its operation. This detachment allows one to calculate entities of very different mathematical origins in a flexible way while retaining essential structural aspects of many objects related to abstract algebra and other algebraic functions. The ubiquity of groups in numerous areas—both within and outside the field of mathematics—makes them a central organizing principle of contemporary mathematics.

15.11.2 Ring. In mathematics, a *ring* is an algebraic structure consisting of a set with two binary operations (usually called addition and multiplication), where each operation combines two elements to form a third element. To qualify as a ring, the set together with its two operations must satisfy certain conditions, namely that the set must be an abelian group under addition and a monoid under multiplication such that multiplication distributes over addition [http://en .wikipedia.org/wiki/Ring_(mathematics)].

In abstract algebra, an *abelian group,* (also called a *commutative group*), is a group in which the result of applying the group operation to two group elements does not depend on their order (the axiom of commutativity). Abelian groups generalize the arithmetic of addition of integers [http://en.wikipedia.org/wiki/Abelian_group].

In abstract algebra, a branch of mathematics, a *monoid* is an algebraic structure with a single associative binary operation and an identity element. Monoids are studied in semi group theory as they are naturally semi-groups with an identity [http://en.wikipedia.org/wiki/Monoid].

15.11.3 Field. In abstract algebra, a *field* is an algebraic structure with notions of addition, subtraction, multiplication, and division, satisfying certain axioms. The most commonly used fields are the field of real numbers, the field of complex numbers, and the field of rational numbers, but there are also finite fields, fields of functions, various algebraic number fields, *p*-adic fields, and others.

As an algebraic structure, every field is a ring, but not every ring is a field. The most important difference is that fields allow for division, although not division by zero. A ring need not possess multiplicative inverses. In addition, the multiplication operation in a field is required to be commutative. A ring in which division is possible but commutativity is not assumed (such as the quaternion) is called a *division ring* or *skew field*. Historically, division rings were sometimes referred to as fields, while fields were called "commutative fields" [http://en.wikipedia.org /wiki/Field_(mathematics)].

15.11.4 Module. In abstract algebra, the concept of a *module* over a ring is a generalization of the notion of vector space. Instead of requiring the scalars to lie in a field, the "scalars" may be arranged in an arbitrary ring. Modules also generalize the notion of abelian groups, which are modules placed over the ring of integers [http://www.saylor.org/site/wp-content/uploads/2011 /04/Module-mathematics.pdf].

Thus, a module, like a vector space, is an additive abelian group. A product is defined between elements of the ring and elements of the module, and this multiplication is both associative when used with the multiplication of the ring, and distributive.

Modules are very closely related to the representation theory of groups. They are also one of the central notions of commutative algebra and homological algebra and are used widely in algebraic geometry and algebraic topology.

15.11.5 Vector space. A *vector space* is a mathematical structure formed by a collection of vectors: objects that may be added together and multiplied ("scaled") by numbers which are called *scalars* in this context. Scalars are often considered as real numbers, but one may also consider vector spaces with scalar multiplication by complex numbers, rational numbers, or even more general fields. The operations of vector addition and scalar multiplication must satisfy certain requirements called *axioms* [http://en.wikipedia.org/wiki/Vector_space].

15.11.6 Algebra over a field. In mathematics, an *algebra over a field* is a vector space equipped with a bilinear vector product. It is an algebraic structure consisting of a vector space together with an operation, usually called multiplication, that combines any two vectors to form a third vector. To qualify as an algebra over a field, this multiplication must satisfy certain compatibility axioms with the given vector space structure, such as distributivity. In other words, an algebra over a field is a set containing operations of multiplication, addition, and scalar multiplication according to elements within the field [http://en.wikipedia.org/wiki/Algebra_over_a_field].

References

Additional information on the *discrete mathematics* KA can be found in the following documents:

- **[Cheney & Kincaid 2007]** E. Ward Cheney and David R. Kincaid. *Numerical Mathematics and Computing* (Hardcover), 6th Edition. Thompson Brooks/Cole, Belmont, CA 784 pages [Chapter 2], 2007. (Recommended as a CSDP exam reference book by the IEEE Computer Society.)

- **[eHSM 2010]** *NIST/SEMATECH e-Handbook of Statistical Methods*. http://www.itl.nist .gov /div898/handbook. 2012.

- **[Gurari 1989]** Eitan Gurari, *An Introduction to the Theory of Computation*. Ohio State University: Computer Society Press, Los Alamitos, CA, 1989.

- **[Lopez 1998]** Alex Lopez-Ortiz, *Algebraic Structures*. 1998, http://www.cs.uwaterloo.ca /~alopez-o/math-faq/mathtext/node6.html. (Recommended as a CSDP exam reference book by the IEEE Computer Society.)

- **[Miller, at al. 2008]** Charles Miller,Vern E. Heeren, John Hornsby, and Margaret Morrow, *Mathematical Ideas*. Pearson, Boston, 2008, p. 682.

- **[Rosen 2009]** Kenneth H. Rosen, *Discrete Mathematics & Its Applications with Combinatorics and Graph Theory*, Tata McGraw-Hill, New Delhi, 2009. (Recommended as a CSDP exam reference book by the IEEE Computer Society.).

- **[Sinko 2005]** Patrick J. Sinko, *Martin's Physical Pharmacy & Pharmaceutical Sciences*; Fifth Edition, ISBN 0-7817-6426-2, Lippincott, Williams, & Wilkins, New York, 2005.

- **[TEI 2004]** Text Encoding Initiative; The TEI is a consortium that collectively develops and maintains a standard for the representation of texts in digital form, http://www.tei-c.org /index.xml and http://www.tei-c.org/release/doc/tei-p4-doc/html/GD.html. 2004.

- **[Toida 2009]** Shunichi Toida, *Discrete Structures/Discrete Mathematics Web Course Material*. Old Dominion University, Department of Computer Science, Norfolk, VA, 2009.

- **[Wikipedia]** Wikipedia is a free web-based encyclopedia that enables users to add and edit online content. Definitions cited from Wikipedia and other sources have been verified by the authors and other peer reviewers.

Chapter 16.1

An Introduction to Engineering[7]

Dr. Gerard Voland
Provost and Vice Chancellor
University of Michigan-Flint

Upon completion of this paper, the reader should be able to:

- *Identify some of the attributes that an engineer should possess in order to be successful*

- *Describe the stages of the engineering design process used to develop innovative solutions to technical problems*

- *Explain why engineers must be methodical when solving technical problems*

- *Discuss the reasons for such current practices in engineering as life-cycle design, design for quality, design for export, design for manufacturing and assembly, and "engineering without walls"*

- *Explain why modern engineers often work in teams, and why it is important to maintain a working environment of mutual trust, accountability, and respect*

- *Explain why engineering design—and the study of engineering—require that we be patient and diligent in our work (even if no apparent progress is visible on the surface), and that we persevere until success finally is achieved*

- *Explain the need for technical reports to be well organized and well written, and describe the general format often used for such reports*

1. Definitions of Engineering

Engineers apply science and technology to develop solutions to practical problems—problems that need to be solved for the benefit of humanity. The Accreditation Board for Engineering and Technology, Inc. (ABET) provides the following definition of engineering as a *profession:*

> *Engineering is the profession in which a knowledge of the mathematical and natural sciences, gained by study, experience, and practice, is applied with judgment to develop ways to utilize, economically, the materials and forces of nature for the benefit of mankind [ABET Accreditation Yearbook; New York: Accreditation Board for Engineering and Technology, Inc., 1993].*

Alternatively, our working definition of engineering as an *activity* is as follows:

> *Engineering is an innovative and methodical application of scientific knowledge and technology to produce a device, system or process, which is intended to satisfy human needs.*

Both definitions emphasize that engineering is *not* solely "inventing" (although certainly both engineering and inventing may result in a new device or process); the two activities differ in

---

7. Derived from Gerald Voland, *Engineering by Design,* Pearson Prentice Hall, Upper Saddle River, NJ, 2004. pp. 1-29. © 2004 Pearson Prentice Hall. (This book is recommended by the IEEE Computer Society as a reference book for the CSDP exam.) An easy-to-read book.

rather subtle ways. For example, inventors seek to develop a new (and usually patentable) idea, whereas engineers seek to solve a specific technical problem in the best possible manner—even if this solution is neither new nor patentable. In other words, the objectives of an engineer may differ from those of an inventor. Secondly, an engineer applies scientific knowledge and follows a methodical approach in developing designs, whereas an inventor may do neither.

We must quickly note that many engineers are *also* inventors, and that many inventors are both methodical and scientifically knowledgeable. However, engineers should *always* be methodical in their work and able to apply scientific principles as needed.

In an important survey [Summarized in R.B. Landis, *Studying Engineering: A Road Map to a Rewarding Career, Discovery,* Burbank, CA, 1995] representatives from industry were asked to prioritize a list of attributes that an engineer should possess. Their *prioritized* listing was as follows:

1. *Problem-solving skills.* Engineers must be able to:

    o   Identify and define the problem to be solved

    o   Develop alternative design solutions

    o   Implement the solution finally selected

2. *Effective communication skills.* Engineers must be able to convey ideas effectively in both written and oral form.

3. *Highly ethical and professional behavior.* Engineers must be able to recognize and resolve ethical dilemmas, and behave in a professional manner at all times and under all circumstances.

4. *An open mind and positive attitude.* If engineers are to be successful in solving challenging technical problems, they must be both imaginative and optimistic that their efforts will bear fruit.

5. *Proficiency in math and science.* Engineers must be adept in mathematical techniques and knowledgeable about science.

6. *Technical skills.* Engineers must acquire the appropriate set of technical skills if they are to perform well in their chosen profession.

7. *Motivation to continue learning.* Given that both technology and scientific knowledge are expanding at an incredibly rapid rate, engineers must be willing and able to acquire new skills and knowledge in their areas of expertise.

8. *Knowledge of business strategies and management practices.* Engineers must be familiar with such strategies and practices if they are to succeed in industry.

9. *Computer literacy.* Engineers must be familiar with the latest computer technology if they are to use it in effective ways in various engineering applications.

10. *Understanding of world affairs and cultures.* It is critical to understand cultural differences if one is to work in harmony with others from around the world, as today's engineers often do.

Engineering is a service profession. Virtually all engineered products and processes are responses to people's needs. A significant amount of engineering thought and effort can (and should) be devoted toward improving even such relatively common products as wheelchairs.

Each of us in this profession seeks to serve or assist others by providing them with a safer, happier, and more productive lifestyle.

Engineering can be divided into many distinct (but often overlapping) disciplines in which a particular problem focus or application area is of primary interest. For example,

- *Agricultural engineers* focus on the food and fiber industries, in which harvesters, milk processors, feed distributors, and other farm machinery are used to produce, process, and distribute food in an efficient and economical manner.

- *Chemical engineers* are often involved in the materials processing and production industries, in which fuels, plastics, insecticides, paints, cements, and other substances are developed for society's needs (and in which the recycling of wastes and the elimination of environmental pollutants are critical objectives).

- *Civil engineers* apply their knowledge of structures, surveying, and hydraulics to design and build dams, tunnels, bridges, roads, and other large-scale systems for densely populated areas.

- *Electrical engineers* develop better ways to generate, distribute, and utilize electrical energy, communications systems, and computer technology in order to improve people's lives.

- *Industrial engineers* integrate materials, equipment, and people to form systems that will generate high-quality products and services in a safe, productive, comfortable, profitable, and efficient manner.

- *Mechanical engineers* are involved in the design and development of such products as engines, aircraft, automobiles, pumps, refrigeration units, and solar energy systems.

In each of these disciplines, we find engineers striving to improve the quality of their customers' lives.

Of course, there are many other recognized disciplines and sub-disciplines within engineering; these include aerospace engineering, biomedical engineering, computer engineering, environmental engineering, manufacturing engineering, nuclear engineering, petroleum engineering, software engineering, and systems engineering.

It is also important to recognize that a problem or application area often overlaps several different engineering disciplines, thereby requiring engineers from various fields to pool their expertise in order to design and develop a viable solution. Engineers seldom work alone and seldom work only with people from their particular discipline. Every engineer should develop the skills necessary to communicate and work with people from other engineering disciplines and professions.

2. The Engineering Design Process

Mathematicians, physicists, chemists, and other scientists seek unique solutions to the problems that they investigate. In other words, each of these problems has a one-of-a-kind solution. In contrast, engineers focus on problems for which there are many practical solutions; they seek the best solution from among these many alternatives.

Of course, in order to determine the best solution from among a set of alternatives, engineers must first be able to recognize and develop each of these alternatives—a very formidable task!

To perform this task in an effective and efficient manner, engineers often follow a procedure known as the engineering design process.

Since the early 1960s, many versions of the engineering design process have been prescribed by authors. Some prescriptions of the process are very brief with only four separate stages, whereas others are decomposed into dozens of subtasks that are to be performed by the designer. However, most of these variations include the basic tasks of *problem formulation, synthesis, analysis,* and *implementation* (although the labels given to these tasks sometimes vary from author to author). We have chosen to include *needs assessment* and *abstraction* as distinct elements in the process, for we believe that the resulting five-stage process is a truly effective problem-solving algorithm.

1. **Needs assessment.** The need for a solution is first established.

   - *Identify the objectives to be achieved by a solution.*

   - *Identify who will benefit from the solution. In what ways? How do you know?*

   - *Begin with the end in mind; know where you are going.*

2. **Problem formulation.** The "real" problem to be solved is defined in the form of design goals that are to be achieved by any viable solution.

   - *Ask if the real problem differs from the problem as initially perceived or presented. In what ways?*

   - *What or who was the source of the original problem statement? Did this source bias the statement in some way because of a unique perspective? If so, is the statement then incorrect or incomplete? In what ways?*

   - *Structure the search for a solution. Identify as many different pathways leading to possible solutions as you can. Know where you are going and direct your search by pruning those paths that will (probably) not lead to a solution.*

   - *Acquire and apply technical knowledge as appropriate. In order to formulate the problem correctly and completely, and to structure the search for a solution, one must make informed—that is, knowledgeable—decisions.*

   - *Identify the design specifications (both explicit and implicit constraints or boundaries within which the solution must lie).*

   - *Identify the resources (time, money, personnel) that will be needed to obtain a solution.*

   - *Prioritize the design goals; continually review this list and modify it as needed during the remainder of the design process. Be aware that your initial prioritization may be incorrect. Be open to change in your goal list. Focus primarily on those goals deemed most important, but recognize that all goals should be achieved by the final solution.*

3. **Abstraction and synthesis.** Develop abstract (general) concepts or approaches through which the problem could be solved, and then generate detailed alternative solutions or designs for the problem.

   - *Recall related solved problems or experiences, pertinent theories, and fundamental approaches (if any exist) to solving this type of problem.*

- *Expand your thinking as to what is possible and what is not possible.*

- *Seek to develop solutions that are fully acceptable to all involved. What approaches can be taken to solve the problem? Which of these approaches is most valid? Why?*

- *Reconsider the problem statement: Is it still valid or must it be modified?*

- *Be creative; use established and appropriate techniques for generating as many detailed solutions as possible.*

- *Combine ideas for achieving each of the individual design goals into total solutions. Seek to make the whole (i.e., the complete design) greater than the sum of the parts (i.e., the individual ideas or sub-solutions).*

- *Once again, expand your thinking as to what is possible and what is not possible. Be adaptable.*

- *Again reconsider the problem statement: Is it still valid or must it be modified? Does your goal list need to be modified? If so, in what way?*

4. **Analysis. Compare and evaluate alternative designs.**

- *Choose a basis for comparing your alternative design solutions by establishing objective evaluation criteria.*

- *Be critical of your work. Try to see your designs objectively and recognize each of their weaknesses or shortcomings (as well as their strengths).*

- *Consider fabrication/implementation requirements for each solution—for example, raw materials and standard parts ("off-the-shelf" components) to be used; manufacturing processes needed to shape the raw materials into final form; the impact that production, distribution, operation, and disposal of the fabricated design may have upon the environment, etc. Compare and contrast the requirements for each proposed design.*

- *Is each of the proposed solutions ethical in concept and operation (safe, environmentally responsible, etc.)?*

- *Eliminate alternatives that do not satisfy critical design goals (i.e., those goals that must be satisfied for the problem itself to be solved).*

- *Anticipate and avoid failure by eliminating weaknesses in your designs; focus upon others and their needs and expectations. Are there any inherent hazards in your designs? Can these hazards be eliminated or minimized?*

- *Does each design alternative satisfy appropriate ergonomic requirements (human-machine system design goals and specs)? If not, why not? Improve and refine each of your proposed designs, if possible.*

- *Construct prototypes of the most promising designs (if possible) and test/evaluate/refine these solutions.*

- *Select the best alternative from among those designs that remain as viable solutions to the problem.*

- *Revise and refine this best design as appropriate; eliminate or minimize weaknesses and shortcomings of the design. Can this "best" design be improved by combining it with elements from any or all of the other (rejected) alternatives?*

5. **Implementation**. Develop the final solution and distribute it to your intended clients/customers/users.

- *After successfully fabricating, testing and evaluating a design prototype (if such testing is possible), proceed with full production.*

- *Distribute to user population and obtain feedback for the next-generation design.*

A sixth step in the process, reflection, may be included. During this step, one contemplates the lessons learned and the knowledge acquired as a result of the just-completed design effort. Most of us quickly shift our attention from one completed task to the next without stopping to consider the ways in which we have grown from the experience.

A period of formal reflection can be immensely helpful in clarifying those aspects of the experience that can be used to perform future tasks in a more effective manner. It is particularly valuable if all members of the design team can share their final thoughts and reflections about a project once it has been completed (and before the team is broken up and the team members reassigned) thereby encouraging each person to identify and assess the benefits of the experience.

Engineering design is a naturally iterative process. Iteration can occur between any and all of the stages in the design process. One does not necessarily complete the entire design cycle (traveling from needs assessment through implementation) before returning to one of the earlier stages of the process to correct and modify earlier results.

For example, the engineer may acquire a deeper understanding of the problem as he or she evaluates a set of alternative solutions during stage 4 in the process. Recognizing that the real problem to be solved is far different from the one originally described in the problem statement (during stage 1), the engineer revises both the problem statement and goal list to correctly reflect this new insight. With this now appropriate target (a correct problem statement and goal list) at which to aim, the engineer is more likely to be successful.

Iteration also may occur as a result of tests on various design prototypes, resulting in a gradual refinement of the basic solution concept.

3. Nth-Generation Designs

Engineering design does not end with an optimal solution. There is *no such thing as a "perfect" solution to an engineering problem* because of the compromises that one usually must make in order to resolve conflicts among the design goals. For example, maximizing the durability of a design while minimizing its production costs can be very difficult to achieve fully, in which case the engineer strives to obtain an acceptable balance between these two goals.

As a result, the search for a better Nth-generation design solution to a problem may continue endlessly (e.g., once a product is marketed, feedback about the design is collected from the users, and the product then undergoes redesign to better meet the users' needs). Thus, the design process is repeated again and again as new and better solutions are developed.

4. Current Practices in Engineering Design

4.1 The engineering profession.

Just as engineering solutions undergo change from one design generation to the next, so too does the engineering profession itself change as the years go by. Engineers change the world and in turn are affected by the very changes that they wrought. As a result, engineering is an extremely dynamic profession, continuously undergoing change in response to a changing world.

- *Life-cycle design.* Engineers increasingly focus upon the entire life cycle of a design—from conception through its manufacture and use to its final disposal—in order to ensure that the design will be successful. Manufacturing decisions can affect the economic viability and the functionality of a design. For example, attractive packaging for a consumer product might require that the retail price be raised beyond profitability, leading to commercial failure. Or a poorly chosen fabrication process might reduce the strength of a product, leading to functional failure.

  Most consumers dislike maintaining, servicing, or repairing their products, and designs that do not minimize or eliminate the need for such maintenance and repair are more likely to become commercial failures.

  Furthermore, materials and components should be recycled to protect the environment and to generate cost savings for the manufacturer (in terms of both materials and reduced service facilities).

- *Design for manufacture and assembly.* Design engineers should work to ensure that any proposed solution can be properly manufactured. Although this need to consider the manufacturability of a design may seem to be obvious, product concepts were once simply "thrown over the wall" from the design engineers to those in manufacturing. The manufacturing engineers then were faced with the challenge of fabricating the designs no matter how difficult or expensive that might be to accomplish.

  Today, design and manufacturing engineers work together to produce products that are innovative yet cost-effective and manufacturable. Components are combined when possible; if unnecessary, they are eliminated. Materials and fabrication processes are selected to maximize company resources while serving the needs of the consumer.

- *Design for quality.* The principles of quality assurance are applied to a design in order to ensure low failure rates coupled with high performance levels. These principles help the engineer to first identify and then eliminate manufacturing and design defects in a product. The result is a design that is safer for the consumer to use and more cost-effective for the manufacturer to produce.

- *Faster design cycles.* The need to produce engineering solutions quickly and effectively is being met through the use of computer technology and concurrent engineering. Computer-aided design (CAD), computer-aided manufacturing (CAM), finite element analysis (FEA), and microprocessor controls have allowed engineers to reduce significantly the time required for developing new designs. Concurrent engineering—in which different phases of engineering design, development, and manufacture are performed simultaneously—has further reduced this time by increasing effective communication between all those involved in the production of a design.

- ***Engineering without walls.*** Engineering departments within different companies often work together collaboratively to achieve a common goal. Companies are discovering that they sometimes can produce better designs more quickly and in a more cost-effective way by sharing expenses and pooling their resources.

   Virtual corporations are being formed in which engineers at remote sites work together via the Internet. By sharing their expertise, these engineers are better able to ensure that the needs of all those affected by a product (consumers, manufacturers, distributors, etc.) will be satisfied by the final design solution. In addition, they are better able to develop designs that will use the shared resources of their companies to full advantage.

- ***Design for export.*** Increasingly, products are developed for the international marketplace. Global product standards have been developed in many industries as companies seek to broaden their markets by working directly with foreign customers

4.2 Trends in engineering design.

Recognizing such trends in engineering design as they emerge is critical, for these trends usually reflect better ways in which to perform engineering tasks. However, although new tools may be developed and manufacturing methods may change, engineers should continue to be methodical, knowledgeable, collaborative, patient, and diligent in their work. Furthermore, the design process continues to provide a map for successful engineering work.

5. Teamwork

Modern engineering design usually depends upon people working together effectively across departmental lines in cross-functional teams. Such teams may include (in addition to engineers from a wide range of disciplines) individuals with expertise in finance, marketing, law, psychology, manufacturing, distribution, and other areas that relate directly to the project under development. Technical problems of current interest can be quite complex and multidimensional, often requiring broad interdisciplinary solutions. Working in formal design teams, engineers and others from various disciplines can more effectively devote and coordinate their diverse skills and knowledge to develop innovative solutions quickly and efficiently.

Each member of the team will view the problem and prioritize the goals to be achieved somewhat differently because of the unique experiences, training, and disciplinary expertise that she or he brings to the project. These variations in perspective and problem-solving methodologies are more likely to lead to a truly creative and effective design solution than if all members of the team had similar backgrounds and training. The challenge, then, is to establish a working climate in which all members of the team can contribute meaningfully to the effort in collegial and positive ways while sharing differences in opinion and perspective.

5.1 Common Goals.

To be successful, all members of a design team first must agree upon a single problem formulation and a set of initial expectations so that everyone will be moving in the same general direction as the work progresses.

5.2 Equitable workloads.

The overall workload for developing a final design should be shared equitably among all members of the team. The project work should be divided into general and then more specific activities. Some of the general or more global activities will require a coordinated effort by the entire team or by special subgroups, whereas the more specific or focused activities will best be completed by specific individuals. Responsibilities assigned to each individual should divide the entire workload fairly among team members while ensuring that the expertise of each individual will be properly utilized throughout the project. Also, recognize that the work—like the project plan itself—will be dynamic in nature, ever-changing, and likely necessitating changes in the initial individual and group assignments.

5.3 Mutual accountability.

There also must be mutual accountability; that is, all members of the team must share responsibility for the completion of all tasks and the development of the final design. Leadership and decision-making responsibilities should be shared—either formally or informally—among all members in order to increase each person's motivation and commitment to the project, and to enhance the quality of the final design.

The team should establish expectations for individual and group performance, recognizing that each person may be able to contribute in varying ways throughout the project. It can be helpful to use some form of peer appraisal, in which each member of the team assesses the performance of all other members and of the team as a whole. Peer appraisals can be narrative in format (with written comments generated on specific topic areas), numerical (which allows for more quantitative comparisons among team members), or both.

These appraisals should be performed anonymously, and the results can be shared by the team leader with each member individually and in a confidential manner. The overall results can be distilled into general themes in which individual and team performances are highly rated and other areas in which it needs to be improved. Sometimes, low performance scores will reflect a lack of communication among team members, or misperceptions about the expectations that individuals have of one another. The key is to provide each individual and the team with sufficient feedback on performance that corrective actions can be taken in a timely manner.

5.4 Collegial Environment.

Teamwork is built upon mutual trust and respect among all members of the group. The working environment must be one in which everyone feels comfortable about sharing an idea or opinion. Every individual's contributions must be seen as important to the entire group effort. Nevertheless, conflicts will occur: each person must realize that his or her ideas may be justly criticized (and perhaps ultimately rejected) by the team. However, all criticisms must be constructive in nature and respectful of the person whose work is being criticized.

5.5 Being Effective as a Team Member.

Teamwork requires that all members remain able and willing to collaborate and help one another to succeed. Each person must participate fully in the project work, listening to others and contributing whenever the opportunity to do so arises. One needs to be willing to learn new skills, perform both small and large tasks when necessary, and support others in a cooperative (not competitive) manner. In addition, each member should periodically self-assess his or her performance and take corrective action as needed.

All members of the team should, as a minimum, be able to:

- Apply the engineering design process effectively throughout the life of the project

- Contribute his or her disciplinary knowledge and expertise to the project, and to reports and presentations as needed

- Explain the roles and responsibilities of all members of the team

- Appreciate the contributions that each individual can provide to the effort, and the value of multiple disciplinary perspectives and problem-solving methodologies

- Provide appropriate perspective on various project issues with clarity, good humor, and supporting documentation

- Recognize and identify ethical issues as they occur

- Acquire some new skills and knowledge as the project progresses

- Use appropriate models and formats (e.g., written, graphical, mathematical) to communicate with all members of the team

5.6 Being Effective as a Team Leader.

Depending upon the nature of the work to be performed and other factors, the leadership of a team may remain with one individual throughout the life of a design project, or it may rotate from one person to another as the work progresses. In either case, the leader of a team must act as a facilitator and establish a collegial working climate in which all individuals participate fully and effectively, and trust in one another. She or he must motivate and encourage the team as a whole, and each of its members, to succeed. Leaders are responsible for resolving problems, whether they be related to the technical aspects of the project under investigation or to the personal dynamics among members of the team.

Working in a team environment, especially as the leader of the group, requires courage and daring since one is then open to increased scrutiny and public criticism from other members of the team. A domineering or overly critical approach by the leader is likely to discourage people from participating fully in the effort. Instead, leaders should help each member of the team to strengthen his or her skills and ability to contribute, while keeping the entire group on track toward achieving the final objective in a timely manner.

A leader of a design team should, as a minimum, be able to:

- Establish a collegial environment in which all members can interact comfortably with one another

- Motivate all members to contribute in meaningful ways to the team

- Delegate and coordinate tasks, as necessary

- Help others to synthesize and evaluate ideas

- Establish a cohesive team structure and mutually supportive group dynamics

- Organize, coordinate, monitor, and assess progress of all activities

- Lead the team in resolving ethical issues

- Encourage all members of the team to develop new skills and become more proficient in project management and collaboration

Finally, a leader should exhibit humility, admitting mistakes whenever they occur and stating "I don't know" when asked a question that he or she cannot answer (after which the answer should then be sought).

6. Writing Technical Reports

6.1 Technical reports.

Technical reports should conform to the traditional format for such documents, such as:

- *Title page*

- *Contents*

- *List of figures*

- *List of tables*

- *Abstract (or Summary).* The abstract or summary provides the reader with a very brief overview of the most important elements of the report; for example, the problem targeted for solution, the final design developed, conclusions, and recommendations for subsequent action. The abstract must be very concise and direct, and is therefore usually no longer than two or three paragraphs. Abstracts sometimes appear as the only published record of a report, thereby providing a public source of information for others who may be interested in acquiring the entire report.

- *Introduction.* The introduction is an opportunity to describe the system or situation under investigation, provide a succinct statement of the problem to be solved, and summarize the needs of the potential clients/users in terms of the corresponding goals that are sought in an optimal design solution.

- *Relevant background information.* The writer should provide the reader with more detailed descriptions of:

  o The user populations to be served

  o The environment in which the design solution will be used

  o The design specifications or constraints within which a solution must be developed

  o Prior art in the field (e.g., patented and/or marketed designs) and other aspects of the work to be performed

  o When appropriate, this information should be summarized in tabular or graphical form for both clarity and brevity.

- *Methodology.* The process or procedure that was followed in developing the final design solution should be described in sufficient detail so that the reader will be able to appreciate the care with which the work was carried out. All assumptions and decision points, together with the rationale for each decision, should be included. Again, use charts, diagrams, and tables as appropriate.

- *Alternative solutions developed.* Summarize each of the alternative solutions that were developed. Provide sufficient detail so that the reader will be able to understand the composition of each design (i.e., what it is), together with its functioning (how it works). (This section could be included as an appendix to the report, unless otherwise specified by your instructor or supervisor.)

- *Final design solution.* The final design solution should be described in sufficient detail so that the reader will be able to recognize both its strengths and its weaknesses. Detail drawings of the final design may be included as an appendix, unless otherwise specified.

Also include a summary of the evaluation and comparison effort that led to your choice of the final design (for example, you might summarize your evaluation in the form of a decision matrix.

Be certain that all of the decisions that you made in developing and selecting your final solution are clearly stated in the report. Justify each of these decisions with supporting arguments and data. Also, a feedback table summarizing the reactions of various groups (e.g., potential users, components or materials suppliers, manufacturing personnel, marketing specialists, financial analysts) to the proposed design should be included in this section. Finally, include details of any economic evaluations of the designs that were performed.

6.2 The need to communicate effectively. As in other professions, engineers must be able to convey ideas effectively in formal reports [Partially based upon Edward G. Wertheim, *Guide for Written Communication*, College of Business Administration, Northeastern University, 1995]. On April 2, 1995, the *Wall Street Journal* published a survey in which the ten most critical business writing problems were identified as:

1. Poor organization

2. Spelling and capitalization

3. Grammar and punctuation

4. Misused words

5. Redundancy

6. Hedging; sometimes called "weasel wording" (i.e., being noncommittal and/or unwilling to clearly state or write about one's position on an issue)

7. Lengthy paragraphs

8. Lengthy sentences

9. Passive language (e.g., "it is recommended that . . ." instead of "I recommend . . .")

10. Inappropriate tone

Engineering design proposals, technical reports, and other documents should avoid these weaknesses to be of a truly professional caliber and to reflect careful thought and preparation. A well-written and organized presentation can lead to implementation of a design concept, whereas a poorly-written report can have the opposite effect. Of course, a design concept must have intrinsic merit and value; a well-written document will not be able to overcome an essentially weak concept.

The following general guidelines may be helpful in preparing a technical report.

- *Purpose*. First ask, what is the purpose of this report? Write a one-sentence statement of the report's purpose focusing on the problem to be solved, the task to be performed, or the response that is sought from your intended audience. What is the main idea that must be conveyed? Include a statement of this purpose—in some appropriate form—in your introduction.

    Remember that the introduction should generate enough interest in the reader so that he or she will continue reading the remainder of the report. It should briefly describe the situation under consideration ("Numerous tasks must be performed in hospital emergency rooms, such as . . ."), the difficulties or problems to be solved ("Often these tasks either conflict with one another or are impeded by the physical layout of the facility"), and the proposed solution ("Our proposed layout includes partitioning the facility according to each of the tasks that must be performed . . ."). These descriptions must be coherent and brief, perhaps stated in as little as one or two paragraphs, if appropriate.

- *Audience.* Be certain that you are satisfying the needs of the audience. Consider the audience for your report: What do they need to know and understand in order to respond properly to your work?

- *After the first draft of the report has been written.* Ask if you have made the presentation truly accessible to readers. Have you obscured the essence of the report by relying upon technical language and terminology that may be unfamiliar to the reader? The comedian Milton Berle would tell his television comedy writers to make a joke more "lappy" if he believed it might go over the heads of the audience—that is, he wanted to ensure that the joke would land directly in the lap of each audience member and evoke laughter in response. A technical presentation similarly must be "lappy:" the reader must understand the significance of the work being reported, and the report recommendations must be stated clearly in terms of the actions to be taken by the reader.

- *Organization.* Next, begin with a general overview of the presentation and its organization. Prepare an outline of the main points to be covered and the underlying arguments for each statement or conclusion in the report.

  Based upon the initial outline, does it appear that the report will be organized properly for the benefit of the reader? Will the presentation flow from one section to another (and within each section) without abrupt changes or discontinuities that might confuse the reader?

  After the first draft of the report has been written, once again consider the organization of the presentation but at a more detailed level. Are the paragraphs linked in a meaningful and logical manner? Have you provided appropriate transitions between paragraphs and between sections? Do you use signposts such as subheadings and bold or italic fonts to help guide the reader through the material? Should paragraphs be added? Should some be deleted or modified? Is each paragraph self-contained (i.e., do later sentences in a paragraph support or expand upon the initial sentence)? Is each paragraph of an appropriate length? Are tables/diagrams/figures self-explanatory? Do they serve a useful purpose? Are they effectively integrated into the report? Could other information (currently in text form) be summarized in a table or figure that is missing from the report? How should such a table or figure be designed? Are titles and captions properly included in each table or figure?

  Has each of the conclusions and other statements contained in the report been properly justified by supporting discussion, data, and documentation? Are there generalizations included in the report that are too vague or meaningless?

- *Grammar, syntax, and punctuation.* Have you used correct grammar, syntax, and punctuation in your report?

  Spelling is easily checked electronically via a word-processor. However, not all spelling errors will be corrected by a computer *(form* instead of *from, affect* instead of *ef-*

fect, there instead of *their,* and so forth). Manually check all spellings and words in your final draft. Syntax and grammar can sometimes be more difficult to correct, yet it must be done! Ask a colleague to review your draft for clarity and correctness, if possible.

- **Rewrite.** All reports require a substantial amount of editing and rewriting. Winston Churchill, renowned for his eloquent and meaningful speeches, believed that a speech was not ready for presentation until it had been rewritten (at least) seven times!

  Is the message lost in unnecessarily dense, technical, or long-winded verbiage? Are the main points easily recognizable or are they lost among less important concerns?

  Have you justified each of your statements? Have you addressed all issues of importance? Are all sections in the report truly worth the reader's time or should some be eliminated?

  Has each idea been fully developed and expressed in clear, easily understood language? Have you included all supporting evidence for your conclusions and recommendations? Finally, is the entire paper coherent?

- **Conclusions.** Comment upon whether the final solution satisfies the original design goals that were sought. In particular, respond to the questions: will the needs of the users be satisfied by the design? Should the design be implemented? Why or why not? Justify your statements with pertinent data, logical reasoning, and references to appropriate discussions elsewhere in the report.

  Also, identify the risks associated with the implementation of your solution (and with the failure to implement). Do not be defensive about your work; instead, be honest in your evaluation and conclusions!

7. Summary

A summary of the paper:

- An engineer should possess a number of attributes to be successful. Included are:
  - o Effective communication skills
  - o Highly ethical and professional behavior
  - o An open mind and positive attitude
  - o Proficiency in math and science
  - o Technical skills
  - o Motivation to continue learning
  - o Knowledge of business strategies and management practices
  - o Computer literacy
- Understanding of world affairs and cultures
- Five stages of the engineering design process are used to develop innovative solutions to technical problems:
  - o Needs assessment
  - o Problem formulation

- o Abstraction and synthesis
- o Analysis
- o Implementation
- Current engineering practices include:
  - o Life-cycle design
  - o Design for quality
  - o Design for export
  - o Design for manufacturing and assembly
  - o Engineering without walls
  - o Faster design cycles
- Engineers usually work in teams, which require mutual trust, accountability, and respect among all members.
- Both engineering design and the study of engineering require that we be patient and diligent in our work, and that we persevere until success finally is achieved.
- Technical reports must be well organized and well written and serve the needs of the intended audience.

Chapter 16.2

Essentials of Engineering

Richard Hall Thayer and Merlin Dorfman

This is the sixteenth chapter of a textbook to aid individual software engineers in a greater understanding of the IEEE SWEBOK [2013] and a guide book to aid software engineers in passing the IEEE CSDP and CSDA certification exams.

> *There is a major attempt to integrate more "engineering" into software engineering. This chapter explains the engineering terminology essential to understand software engineering.*

Chapter 16 covers the CSDP exam specifications for the Engineering Foundations Knowledge Area (KA) [Software Exam Specification, Version 2, 18 March 2009]. This list of exam specifications is reported to be the same list that the exam writers used to write the exam questions. Therefore it is the best source of help for the exam takers:

1. Empirical methods and experimental techniques

2. Statistical analysis

3. Measurement

4. System development

5. Engineering design

6. Theory of measurement

7. Simulation, modeling and conceptual prototyping

8. Goal-question-metric (GQM) paradigm

9. Standards

10. Tool and platform selection

11. Root cause analysis

16.1 Empirical Methods and Experimental Techniques

Empirical denotes information gained by means of observation, experience, or experiment. A software engineering tool or technique can be developed from observed data. For example, the cost model COCOMO, created by Dr. Barry Boehm [1981], was developed using empirical data. Empirical quantities are those computed from observed values, as opposed to those derived from theoretical considerations. Empirical considerations are included in the scientific method, yet are often mistakenly assumed to be synonymous with the experimental method.

An experiment is a study of *cause and effect.* The *experimental* method (a.k.a. experimental technique or scientific method) is usually regarded as the most scientific of all research methods and is consequently called the "method of choice." The experimental method involves a "controlled" experiment—the deliberate manipulation of a variable selected for observation while striving to keep all other variables constant. The main obstacle associated with the non-experimental or empirical method is a lack of control over the particular situation under study or observation. The experimental method attempts to correct for this lack of control by studying cause and effect [http://en.wikipedia.org/wiki/Empirical_method].

Other topics related to engineering foundations include:

- Computer-related measuring techniques for the CPU
- Computer-related measuring techniques for memory usage.

16.1.1 Computer-related measuring techniques for the CPU. The measuring of process speed (through experimentation), and the throughput of data in a computer central processing unit (CPU) for the purpose of developing better processes are collectively referred to as computer-related measuring techniques for the CPU.

16.1.2 Computer-related measuring techniques for memory usage. The measuring of memory capacity and the throughput of data (though experimentation) by (using) a computer manager for the purpose of developing better processes is described as a computer-related measuring technique for memory usage.

16.2 Statistical Analysis

Statistical analysis is defined as the collection, examination, summarization, manipulation, and interpretation of quantitative data to discover its underlying causes, patterns, relationships, and trends [http://en.wikipedia.org/wiki/Statistical_analysis].

Other subjects related to statistical analysis include:

- Simple hypothesis testing
- Estimating
- Regression
- Correlation.

16.2.1 Simple hypothesis testing. *A statistical hypothesis test* is a method of making decisions using experimental data. In statistics, a result is called *statistically significant* if it is unlikely to have occurred by chance. A *simple hypothesis test* is a hypothesis which specifies the population distribution completely. This is in contrast to a composite hypothesis, which does not specify the population distribution completely [http://www.stats.gla.ac.uk/steps/glossary/hypothesis_testing .html#simplehyp].

Setting up and testing hypotheses is an essential part of statistical inference. In order to formulate such a test, usually some theory has been put forward, either because it is believed to be true or because it is to be used as a basis for argument, but has not been proven, for example, claiming that a new drug is better than the current drug for treatment of the same symptoms.

In each problem considered, the question of interest is simplified into two competing claims/hypotheses between which we have a choice; the null hypothesis, denoted H0, against the alternative hypothesis, denoted H1. These two competing claims/hypotheses are not, however, treated on an equal basis—special consideration is given to the null hypothesis [Easton & McCall 2006].

16.2.2 Estimating. *Estimating* is the process by which sample data are used to indicate the value of an unknown quantity in a population. Sometimes it is simply an "educated guess." Results of estimation can be expressed as a *single value*, known as a point estimate, or a range of values, known as a *confidence interval* [Easton & McCall 2006].

16.2.3 Regression. In statistics, *regression analysis* includes any techniques for modeling and analyzing several variables, when the focus is on the relationship between a dependent variable and one or more independent variables. More specifically, regression analysis helps us understand how the typical value of the dependent variable changes when any one of the independent variables is varied, while the other independent variables are held fixed. Most commonly, regression analysis estimates the *conditional expectation* of the dependent variable given the independent variables—that is, the average value of the dependent variable when the independent variables are held fixed.

In probability theory, a *conditional expectation* (also known as *conditional expected value* or *conditional mean*) is the expected value of a real random variable with respect to a conditional probability distribution [http://en.wikipedia.org/wiki/Conditional_expectation].

- *Regression analysis* is widely used for prediction and forecasting, where its use has substantial overlap with the field of machine learning. Regression analysis is also used to understand which among the independent variables are related to the dependent variable, and to explore the forms of these relationships. In restricted circumstances, regression analysis can be used to infer causal relationships between the independent and dependent variables.

- A large body of techniques for carrying out *regression analysis* has been developed. Familiar methods such as linear regression and ordinary least squares regression are parametric, in that the regression function is defined in terms of a finite number of unknown parameters that are estimated from the data [http://en.wikipedia.org/wiki/Regression _analysis].

16.2.4 Correlation. In the field of statistics, *correlation* refers to the simultaneous change in value of two numerical and random variables. Correlation between two variables can be subject to error based on the type of data used. A useful technique for verifying the data correlation is scatter diagrams. *Scatter diagrams* (also call *scatter plots*) can illustrate the correlation between plotted variables. Outliers or extreme values can have a major effect on the results of the collected data [Kan, 2002, pp. 76-78].

- A *scatter plot is* used when a variable exists that is under the control of the experimenter. If a parameter exists that is systematically incremented and/or decremented by the other, it is called the *control parameter* or independent variable and is customarily plotted along the horizontal axis. The measured or dependent variable is customarily plotted along the vertical axis.

- A *scatter plot* can suggest various kinds of correlations between variables with a certain confidence interval. Correlations may be positive (rising), negative (falling), or null (uncorrelated). If the pattern of dots slopes from lower left to upper right, it suggests a positive correlation between the variables being studied. If the pattern of dots slopes from upper left to lower right, it suggests a negative correlation.

    A line of best fit (alternatively called "*trendline*") can be drawn in order to study the correlation between the variables. An equation for the correlation between the variables can be determined by established best-fit procedures. For a linear correlation, the best-fit procedure is known as *linear regression* and is guaranteed to generate a correct solution (i.e., a "best fit line") in a finite time.

- One of the most powerful aspects of a *scatter plot*, however, is its ability to show nonlinear relationships between variables. Furthermore, if the data is represented by a mixture model of simple relationships, these relationships will be visually evident as superimposed patterns.

- The *scatter diagram* is one of the basic tools of quality control.

16.3 Measurement

A *measurement* is a process. *Measuring* represents the actual activity of assigning a number or a symbol to an entity. For instance, the height of a six-foot tall person is assigned the number six; a grade of C is assigned to a college course paper fulfilling minimum requirements. The term *metric* is defined as the quantitative measure of degree for which a system component or process possesses a given attribute.

A *direct measurement* is the mapping of a "real world entity" to a specific measurement. The following are two examples of direct measurement:

The length of source code (e.g., 10,498 lines of object code), or the number of defects (e.g., 1,010 defects), found in a computer program during software testing.

Indirect measurements are calculated from an input of direct measurements. For example, program productivity is calculated as the ratio of lines of code (e.g., 2,000) produced by a programmer, divided by the number of months of work (e.g., 10) resulting in a calculation of 200 lines of code per staff month (2,000 / 10 = 200). Error density usually refers to the number of defects per module size. A more common example of error density is the number of defects per line of code; e.g., in current software development there are approximately 0.1 defects per thousand lines of code (KLOC) [Fenton & Pfleeger, 1997, pp. 39-42].

> *An important note: Some software engineers use measure for direct measure and metric for indirect (computed) measure.*

16.4 System Development

System development encompasses all activities undertaken from the moment a potential requirement is identified until the resulting system is fully implemented and accepted by the end user.

System development can include, *but is not limited to,* the following activities:

- Requirement analysis
- Design
- Implementation
- Testing
- Performance
- Quality attributes
- Availability
- Reliability
- Maintainability

- Security

- Safety

- Operations and maintenance

16.4.1 Requirements analysis. In systems engineering and software engineering, *requirements analysis* encompasses those tasks that go into determining the needs or conditions to meet for a new or altered product, taking account of the possibly conflicting requirements of the various stakeholders [http://en.wikipedia.org/wiki/Requirements_analysis]. Requirements must be: *complete, consistent, correct, clear (unambiguous), parsimonious, concise, modifiable, verifiable, traceable and traced, implementation-free, and feasible* [Thayer & Dorfman 2008].

16.4.2 System design. In *system design*, the design functions and operations are described in detail, including screen layouts, business rules, process diagrams and other documentation. The output of this stage will describe the new system as a collection of modules or subsystems [http://en.wikipedia.org/wiki/Systems_development_life-cycle].

16.4.3 Implementation. Modular and subsystem programming code will be *implemented* during this stage. Unit testing and module testing are also done in this stage by the developers. This stage is intermingled with the next in that individual modules will need testing before integration to the main project [http://en.wikipedia.org/wiki/Systems_Development_Life_Cycle].

16.4.4 Testing. The code is tested at various levels in software testing. Unit, system and user acceptance testing are often performed. This is a gray area as many different opinions exist as to what the stages of testing are and how much if any iteration occurs. Iteration is not generally part of the waterfall model, but usually some occurs at this stage [http://en.wikipedia.org/wiki/Systems_Development_Life_Cycle].

16.4.5 Performance. Performance engineering as a subset of systems engineering encompasses the set of roles, skills, activities, practices, tools, and deliverables applied at every phase of the system development life cycle. The application of performance engineering ensures that an adequate solution will be designed, implemented, and operationally supported to meet the performance requirements defined for the system [http://en.wikipedia.org/wiki/Performance_engineering].

16.4.6 Quality attributes. Within systems engineering, *quality attributes* are non-functional requirements used to evaluate the performance of a system. These are sometimes named "ilities" after the suffix many of the words share. Notable quality attributes include:

- *Availability* — *Availability* is the readiness of a system to deliver services when requested. Availability is usually expressed as a decimal number, e.g., so an availability of 0.999 means that the system can deliver services for 999 out of 1000 times or tries. If system availability is a critical requirement, the architecture should be designed to include redundant components, making it possible to replace the updated components without stopping the system [Sommerville 2007, pp. 243, 795].

- *Reliability* — *Reliability* is the ability of a system to deliver services as specified. Reliability can be specified quantitatively as a probability of failure on demand or as a rate of occurrence [Sommerville 2006, p. 801].

- *Maintainability* — *Maintainability* is a measure of the ease and rapidity with which a system or equipment can be restored to operational status following a failure.

- *Security* — When considered during the system life cycle, security requirements tend to be documented within general lists of security features such as password protection, firewalls, virus detection tools, and so forth. *These are in fact not security requirements but rather implementation mechanisms (designs) intended to satisfy unstated requirements such as authenticated access.* As a result, security requirements specific to a given system and providing protection of essential services and assets are often neglected. In addition, the attacker (hacker) potential is not considered, increasing the likelihood that security requirements, when they are in place during operational conditions, are likely to be incomplete. A systematic approach to security requirements engineering will help to avoid the problem of generic lists of features and to take into account the attacker perspective.

  A systematic approach to implementing security requirements engineering will help to avoid the problem of inadequate generic lists of features, and will take into account the attacker (hacker) potential. Several approaches to security requirements engineering are described in the Homeland Security article [*Build Security In* 2010].

- *Safety* — *Safety* is the state of being "safe," the condition of being protected against physical, social, spiritual, financial, political, emotional, occupational, psychological, educational or other types or consequences of failure, damage, error, accidents, harm or any other event that could be considered non-desirable. Safety can also be defined to be the control of recognized hazards to achieve an acceptable level of risk. This can take the form of being protected from the event or from exposure to something that causes health or economic losses. It can include protection of people or of possessions [http://en.wikipedia.org/wiki/Safety].

  o *Safety engineers* ideally study an early design of a system, analyze it to determine what faults can occur, and then propose safety requirements for implementation in the design specifications. Safety requirements typically state what a system should *not* do.

  o Rather than actually influencing the design, safety engineers are often assigned to "prove" that a completed design is safe from a design faults that can cause system failures that would make the system "unsafe." If significant safety problems are discovered late in the design process, correcting them can become very expensive.

16.4.7 Operations and maintenance. *Operations and maintenance* takes place after the deployment of the system and includes changes and enhancements before the decommissioning or sunset of the system. Maintaining the system is an important aspect of SDLC. As key personnel change positions in the organization, new changes will be implemented, which will require system updates [http://en.wikipedia.org/wiki/Systems_development_life-cycle].

16.4.8 Effects of scaling. There are two effects of scaling – *economies of scale* and *diseconomies of scale*. *Economies of scale* is a concept referring to reductions in unit cost commensurate with the increase in size of a facility or scale. *Diseconomies of scale* pertain to economic forces that cause firms to produce goods and services at increased per-unit costs. [Boehm 1981, pp. 189-190].

16.4.9 Feature interaction. A feature interaction is a software engineering concept occurring when the interaction of two features modifies the behavior of one or both features [http://en.wikipedia.org/wiki/Feature_interaction_problem].

16.5 Engineering Design

The *engineering design process* is a formulation of a plan or scheme to assist an engineer in creating a product. The engineering design is defined as [Eratas & Jones 1996]:

> *. . . the process of devising a system, component, or process to meet desired needs. It is a decision-making process (often iterative) in which the basic sciences, mathematics, and engineering sciences are applied to convert resources optimally to meet a stated objective. Among the fundamental elements of the design process are the establishment of objectives and criteria, synthesis, analysis, construction, testing and evaluation.*

The engineering design process is a multi-step process including the research, conceptualization, feasibility assessment, establishing design requirements, preliminary design, detailed design, production planning and tool design, and finally production [http://en.wikipedia.org/wiki/Engineering_design_process]. The sections to follow are not necessarily steps in the engineering design process, for some tasks are completed at the same time as other tasks.

16.5.1 Research. A lot of time is spent on research or locating information. Consideration should be given to the existing applicable literature, problems and successes associated with existing solutions, costs, and marketplace needs [Eide, Jenison, Mashaw, & Northup 2002].

The source of information should be relevant, including existing solutions. Reverse engineering can be an effective technique if other solutions are available on the market [http://en.wikipedia.org/wiki/Engineering_design_process]. Other sources of information include the Internet, local libraries, available government documents, personnel organizations, trade journals, vendor catalogs and individual experts available [Eide, Jenison, Mashaw, & Northup 2002]

16.5.2 Conceptualization. Once an engineering issue is clearly defined, solutions must be identified. These solutions can be found by using ideation, or the mental process by which ideas are generated. The following are the most widely used techniques [Eratas & Jones 1996]:

- *Trigger word* — A word or phrase associated with the issue at hand is stated, and subsequent words and phrases are evoked. For example, to *move* something from one place to another may evoke *run, swim, roll*, etc.

- *Morphological chart* — Independent design characteristics are listed in a chart, and different engineering solutions are proposed for each solution. Normally, a preliminary sketch and short report accompany the morphological chart.

- *Synectics* — The engineer imagines him or herself as the item and asks, "What would I do if I were the system?" This unconventional method of thinking may find a solution to the problem at hand

- Brainstorming — This popular method involves thinking of different ideas and adopting these ideas in some form as a solution to the problem.

16.5.3 Feasibility assessment. The purpose of a feasibility assessment is to determine whether the engineer's project can proceed into the design phase. This is based on two criteria: the project needs to be based on an achievable idea, and it needs to be within cost constraints. It is of utmost importance to have an engineer with experience and good judgment involved in this portion of the feasibility study, for he/she knows whether the engineer's project is possible or not [Eratas & Jones 1996]

16.5.4 Establishing the design requirements. Establishing design requirements is one of the most important elements in the design process, and this task is normally performed at the same time as the feasibility analysis. The design requirements control the design of the project throughout the engineering design process. Some design requirements include hardware and software parameters, maintainability, availability, and testability [Eratas & Jones 1996].

16.5.5 Architectural design. The *architectural design* (sometimes incorrectly call "preliminary design") bridges the gap between the design concept and the detailed design phase. The design architectural phase is also called "embodiment" design. In this task, the overall system configuration is defined, and schematics, diagrams, and layouts of the project will provide early project configuration. During detailed design and optimization, the parameters of the part being created will change, but the architectural design focuses on creating the general framework on which to build the project [Eratas & Jones 1996].

16.5.6 Detailed design. The *detailed design* portion of the engineering design process is the task where the engineer can completely describe a product through solid modeling and drawings. Some specifications include [Eratas & Jones 1996]:

- Operating parameters
- Operating and non-operating environmental stimuli
- Test requirements
- External dimensions
- Maintenance and testability provisions
- Materials requirements
- Reliability requirements
- External surface treatment
- Design life
- Packaging requirements

The advancement of computer-aided design, or CAD, programs have made the detailed design phase more efficient. This is because a CAD program can provide optimization, where it can reduce volume without hindering the part's quality. It can also calculate stress and displacement using the finite element method to determine stresses throughout the part. It is the engineer's responsibility to determine whether these stresses and displacements are allowable, so the part is safe [Widas 1997].

16.5.7 Production planning and tool design. The production planning and tool design is nothing more than planning how to mass produce the project and which tools should be used in the manufacturing of the part. Tasks to complete in this step include selecting the material, selection of the production processes, determination of the sequence of operations, and selection of tools, such as jigs, fixtures, and tooling. This task also involves testing a working prototype to ensure the created part meets qualification standards [Eratas & Jones 1996

6.5.8 Production. With the completion of qualification testing and prototype testing, the engineering design process is finalized. The part must now be manufactured, and the machines must be inspected regularly to make sure that they do not break down and slow production [Eratas & Jones 1996].

16.6 Theory of Measurement

Measurement of some attribute of a set of things is the process of assigning numbers or other symbols to the things in such a way that relationships of the numbers or symbols reflect relationships of the attribute being measured. A particular way of assigning numbers or symbols to measure something is called a *scale* of measurement.

Measurement theory is concerned with the connection between data and reality.

The theory of measurement, also called the criteria for valid measurement, defines a hierarchy (levels) of measurement. Consider the following examples:

- The basic *nominal or categorizing* metrics assign a number or perhaps a symbol such as a letter, to a category. For example, the assignment of a country to a citizen of the world – American, English, Scottish, German, and so forth. Note that ranking is not implied, e.g., Americans are not better than Englishmen.

- An *ordinal* measure reflects a ranking accompanied by categorization. For example, Sears used to rank its appliances as good, better, and best.

- An *interval* measurement implies a fixed interval between numbers or symbols. For example, the assignment of a size to a person. A six-foot man is two inches taller than a 5 foot-10-inch man.

- A *ratio* measure implies a starting point. A basketball team can win with a score that is 50% better than another team because both teams started with a score of zero score.

- An *absolute* is the assignment of a measure to an artifact, normally by counting. There are 55 persons in the class.

The question, "What is good data?" must be answered. Do not confuse correct, accurate, and precise. *Correct* data follows the rules for which the metrics collection process was organized. *Accurate* data reflects the actual value of the item measured with acceptable *precision* recording exactness. Showing a metric with many decimal points—an implied precision—does not in itself make it more precise or accurate.

The consistency of the data must be known. If the process is repeated the following day, will it produce the same answer? Data that cannot be replicated are potentially inaccurate.

The next question to ask is "How to collect data?" There are two ways to collect data—manually and automatically. Books such as Fenton and Pfleeger [1997] recommend that data be collected automatically if possible, since this method is more reliable. Just remember that manual recording is subject to bias as well as human error.

If the data is collected manually, keep the procedures simple. Avoid unnecessary recording. Do not ask for unnecessary data. Do not ask for details unlikely to be received or used. Train staff to accurately record data. When returning the results of captured data to the original providers, ensure it is recorded in a form useful to their work. There is nothing worse than collecting data for an unknown reason for which you, the collector, receive no benefit.

The last question to be asked is, "When is the appropriate time to collect data?" Data should be collected as soon as possible after an event takes place. Lastly, data collection should be an integral part of the software engineering process.

16.7 Simulation, Modeling, and Conceptual Prototyping

16.7.1 Simulation. A *simulation* is based on the process of imitating a real phenomenon with a set of mathematical formulas. It is essentially a computer program that allows the user to observe an operation without actually performing the operation. Simulation software is widely used when designing equipment to prepare a final product as close to design specifications as possible without expensive in-process modifications.

In contrast, an *emulator* in computer science duplicates (provides a bit-for-bit replication of) the functions of one system using a different system, so that the second system behaves like (and appears to be) the first system. This focus on exact reproduction of external behavior is in contrast to some other forms of computer simulation, which can concern an abstract model of the system being simulated [http://en.wikipedia.org/wiki/Emulator].

Simulation software with real-time response is often used in gaming and as a component of important industrial applications. When the penalty for improper operation is costly—for projects involving airplane pilots, nuclear power plant operators, or chemical plant operators—a mockup of the actual control panel is connected to a real-time simulation of the physical response, providing valuable training experience without fear of a disastrous outcome. A *physical response* means some action or reaction in the "real world" that is caused by an input or output to or from the simulation system.

General simulation packages fall into two categories: discrete event simulations and continuous simulations. *Discrete event simulations* are used to model statistical events such as customers forming queues at a bank. By properly correlating arrival probabilities with observed behavior, a model determines optimal queue count to maintain wait times at a specified level. *Continuous simulations* are used to model a wide variety of physical phenomena such as ballistic trajectories, human respiration, electric motor response, radio frequency data communication, steam turbine power generation, etc. Simulations are used in the creation of initial system designs to optimize component selection and controller gains. Real-time operation of continuous simulation is used for operator training and off-line controller tuning [http://en.wikipedia.org/wiki/Simulation _software].

16.7.2 Model. A *model* is an abstraction of reality or a representation of a real object or situation. In other words, a model presents a simplified version of something. It may be as simple as a drawing of house plans, or as complicated as a miniature but functional representation of a complex piece of machinery. A model airplane may be assembled and glued together from a kit by a child, or it actually may contain an engine and a rotating propeller that allows it to fly like a real airplane.

A more useable concept of a model is that of an abstraction, from the real problem, of key variables and relationships. These are abstracted in order to simplify the problem itself. Modeling allows the user to better understand the problem and presents a means for manipulating the situation in order to analyze the results of various inputs ("what if" analysis) by subjecting it to a changing set of assumptions. models are replicas of the physical properties (relative shape, form, and weight) of the object they represent.

Others are physical models but do not have the same physical appearance as the object of their representation. A third type of model deals with symbols and numerical relationships and expressions. Each of these fits within an overall classification of four main categories: physical models, schematic models, verbal models, and mathematical models [http://www.reference for-business.com/management/Mar-No/Models-and-Mode ling.html].

16.7.3. Conceptual prototyping. *Conceptual prototyping* is a partial implementation of a product expressed either logically or physically with all the external interfaces presented. Other types of prototypes in existence are:

- Rapid (Throwaway) prototypes

- Evolutionary prototypes

The conventional purpose of a prototype is to allow a software user to evaluate a developer's proposed design of the eventual product. A prototype is physically tested rather than relying on interpretation and evaluation based on design descriptions. Prototyping can also be used by end users to describe and prove requirements not considered by the developers. If successfully proven, these requirements can then be added to the prototype. Therefore, controlling the prototype can be a key factor in the commercial relationship between solution providers and their clients.

16.7.4 Throwaway (Rapid) prototyping. Also called close-ended prototyping, throwaway or rapid prototyping refers to the creation of a model that will eventually be discarded rather than being integrated into the final delivered software. After the gathering of preliminary requirements, a simple working model of the system is constructed. This basic working model provides users with a visual example of system requirements when compiled into a finished system.

This type of prototyping is called *rapid prototyping* because it involves a short investigation of necessary requirements followed by the creation of a working model of various parts of the system at a very early stage. The method used in building the working model, or prototype, is usually quite informal, the most important factor being the speed in which the model is developed. The model then becomes the starting point from which users can re-examine expectations and clarify requirements. Once operational and tested, the prototype model is discarded and the system is formally developed based on the identified requirements.

The most obvious reason for using throwaway prototyping is its ability to be quickly tested. If users obtain quick feedback about requirements, they may be able to refine them early in the software development stage (phase). Making changes early in the development life cycle is extremely cost effective since there are no components that need rewriting or restructuring. If a project is changed after considerable progress has been made, small changes could require great efforts due to the many dependencies contained within software systems. Speed is crucial in implementing a throwaway prototype. Minimal time and limited financial resources are expended on a prototype intended to be discarded [http://en.wikipedia.org/wiki/Software_proto typing].

16.7.5 Evolutionary prototype. *Evolutionary prototyping* differs from throwaway prototyping in that the main goal when using the former is to build a very robust prototype in a structured manner. This prototype is then constantly refined. The evolutionary prototype, when built, forms the heart of the new system, providing a basis for future improvements and requirements.

When developing a system using evolutionary prototyping, that system is continuously refined and rebuilt. Evolutionary prototyping acknowledges that neither the customer nor the developer understands each requirement, and consequently, will build only those recognized as essential for the program's operation. This technique allows the development team to add features and make changes that could not be conceived during the requirements and design phase [http://en.wikipedia.org/wiki/Software_prototyping].

16.8 Goal Question Metric (GQM) Paradigm

GQM is the acronym for the Goal, Question, Metric Paradigm. GQM defines a measurement model according to three levels:

- ***Conceptual level (goal)*** — A goal is defined for an object under a variety of reasons, with respect to various models of quality, from various points of view, and relative to a particular environment.

- ***Operational level (question)*** — A set of questions is used to define models representing the object of study, focusing on that object to characterize the assessment or achievement of a specific goal.

- ***Quantitative level (metric)*** — A set of metrics, based on the models, is associated with every question in order to provide a measurable answer.

Technical literature typically describes GQM in terms of a six-step process. The first three steps focus on developing and implementing business goals to identify the correct metrics. The last three steps gather measurement data and effectively use the measurement results to assist with decision making and suggested improvements. Basili described his six-step GQM process as follows [http://en.wikipedia.org/wiki/GQM]:

1. Develop a set of corporate, division and project business goals and associated measurement goals for productivity and quality.

2. Generate questions based on models that define those goals as completely as possible in a quantifiable way.

3. Specify the measures that must be collected to answer those questions and track process and product conformance to the goals.

4. Develop mechanisms for data collection.

5. Collect, validate and analyze the data in real time to provide feedback to projects for corrective action.

6. Analyze the data in a post-mortem fashion to assess conformance to the goals and to make recommendations for future improvements.

16.9 Standards

A *standard* is an approved, documented, and available set of criteria used to specify and evaluate adequacy of an action or object. Selecting the appropriate software engineering standards involves:

- *Identifying* which standards are appropriate to the process or object at hand.

- *Evaluating* the capability of the standards to support the process or object.

- *Selecting* the appropriate standards that provide the most benefit to the process or object.

- *Adapting* the appropriate standard to the situation at hand through tailoring or modification to fit the process or object.

A standard can be either a *process standard* or a *product standard*. A software engineering *process standard* is a set of procedures that define the software engineering process; a software engineering *product standard* contains descriptions of software work products.

Standards also establish a process for institutionalizing successful project experiences and best practices.

Well-written standards improve communication among project personnel, which in turn allows for more efficient work reviews concerning progress and maintenance of the finished product. A good standard also eases the transfer of personnel between projects, thereby minimizing the need for training or retraining. Standards provide usable tools for the software quality assurance process and reduce the cost of developing software. Most importantly, software engineering standards provide top-level control of the development project.

Because standards aim to cover a wide variety of situations, they usually require tailoring to be suitable for individual projects. Tailoring means adapting the standards to the project environment and system requirements. It does *not* mean eliminating processes essential to the project's well-being under the guises of saving money and time.

Tailoring must be done with the assistance and approval of the imposing agent (e.g., higher management, the customer, the law courts, and/or the authority that imposed the standards in the first place).

16.10 Tool and Platform Selection

A *programming tool* or *software development tool* is a program or application used by software developers to create, debug, maintain, or otherwise support other programs and applications. The term usually refers to relatively simple programs that can be combined to accomplish a task, similar to using multiple hand tools to fix a physical object.

Many software tools are simple (i.e., stand-alone). Others are integrated into more powerful tools called integrated development environments (IDEs). These environments consolidate functionality into one place, sometimes increasing ease of use and productivity, other times sacrificing flexibility and extensibility [http://en.wikipedia.org/wiki/Programming_tool].

The distinction between tools and applications is not always clear. One person's tool is another's application software.

In the 1980s, CASE tools were very popular. CASE (computer-aided software engineering) tools are the scientific application of a set of tools and methods to a software system which is meant to result in high-quality, defect-free, and maintainable software products. They have since become less common. IDEs currently represent the most successful examples of these tools.

In relation to computing, a *platform* describes hardware architecture and software frameworks (system and application frameworks) necessary to run a software application. Typical platforms include a computer's architecture, operating system, programming languages, and related user interface.

A platform is a crucial element in software development. Simply defined as a place to launch (and run) software, it is an agreement between the platform provider and the software developer. The platform ensures the consistent interpretation of logic code as long as the platform is running on top of other platforms. Logic code includes byte code, source code, and machine code http://en.wikipedia.org/wiki/Computing_platform].

The ability to productively use a variety of tools is the hallmark of a skilled software engineer.

16.10.1 Categories of tools. Software development tools can be roughly divided into the following categories [Sommerville, 2007, p. 87]:

- *Planning tools* — PERT tools, estimation tools, spreadsheets

- *Editing tools* — Text editors, diagram editors, word processor functions

- *Change management tools* — Requirements traceability tools, change control systems

- *Configuration management (CM) tools* — Version management systems, system building tools

- *Prototyping tools* — Very high-level languages, user interface generators

- *Method support* — Design editors, data dictionaries, code generators

- *Language supporting tools* — Compilers and interpreters

- *Problem analysis tools* — Cross-reference generators, static analyzers, dynamic analyzers

- *Testing tools* — Test data generators, file comparators

- *Debugging tools* — Interactive debugging systems

- *Documentation tools* — Page layout programs, image editors

- *Reengineering tools* — Cross-reference systems, program restructuring systems

16.10.2 Platform selection. A *platform* is a combination of hardware and software used to run software applications. A platform can be described simply as an operating system, computer architecture, or the combination of both. Probably the most familiar platform is Microsoft Windows running on the x86 architecture system. Other well-known desktop computer platforms include Linux/Unix and Mac OS X. There are, however, many commonly-used devices such as cellular telephones ("Smartphones") that are effectively computer platforms. Application software can be written to depend on the features of a particular platform – the hardware, operating system, or virtual machine on which it runs. The commonly-used Java platform is a virtual machine platform that runs on many operating systems and hard-ware types [http://en.wikipedia.org/wiki/Cross-platform].

In computing, a *cross-platform*, or *multi-platform*, is an attribute conferred to computer software or computing methods and concepts that are implemented and inter-operate on multiple computer platforms. Cross-platform software may be divided into two types; one requires individual building or compilation for each platform that it supports, and the other one can be directly run on any platform without special preparation, e.g., software written in an interpreted language or pre-compiled portable bytecode for which the interpreters or run-time packages are common or standard components of all platforms.

For example, a cross-platform application may run on Microsoft Windows on the x86 architecture, Linux on the x86 architecture and Mac OS X on either the PowerPC or x86 based Apple Macintosh systems. A cross-platform application may run on as many as all existing platforms, or on as few as two platforms [http://en.wikipedia.org/wiki/Cross-platform].

16.10.2.1 Hardware platform. A *hardware platform* refers to either a computer's architecture or processor architecture. For example, the x86 and x86-64 CPUs comprise one of the most commonly used computer architectures in general-purpose home computers. These machines commonly run Microsoft Windows, although they are able to run other operating systems including Linux, OpenBSD, NetBSD, Mac OS X, and FreeBSD.

16.10.2.2 Software platform. *Software platforms* can be an operating system, a programming environment, or a combination of both. A notable exception to this is Java, which uses an operating-system independent, virtual machine for its compiled code, known in the world of Java as "bytecode."

16.11 Root Cause Analysis

Root cause analysis (RCA) is a class of problem-solving methods aimed at identifying the root causes of problems or events. The practice of RCA is predicated on the belief that problems are best solved by attempting to correct or eliminate root causes, as opposed to merely addressing the immediately obvious symptoms.

By directing corrective measures at root causes, it is hoped that the likelihood of problem recurrence will be minimized. However, it is recognized that complete prevention of recurrence by a single intervention is not always possible. Thus, RCA is often considered to be an iterative process, and is frequently viewed as a tool of continuous improvement [http://en.wikipedia.org /wiki/Root_cause_analysis].

16.11.1 Root cause analysis. RCA was initially a reactive method of problem detection and problem solving. When applying the reactive method, the analysis is done after an event has occurred. By gaining expertise in RCA it becomes a proactive method. This means that RCA is able to forecast the possibility of an event even before it could feasibly occur.

Quality engineers distinguish between *corrective action* (fixing a problem and ensuring that it does not recur) and *preventive action* (anticipating other problems that might have the same root cause, and ensuring that they do not occur) [ISO 9001:2008, Sections 8.5.2 and 8.5.3].

Root cause analysis is not a single, sharply defined methodology; there are many different tools, processes, and philosophies of RCA in existence. However, most of these can be classified into five very-broadly defined schools named according to their basic fields of origin: safety-based, production-based, process-based, failure-based, and systems-based [http://www.innova tionmanagement.org/Wiki/index.php?title=Root_Cause_Analysis].

16.11.2 General principles of root cause analysis.

- The primary aim of RCA is to identify the root cause of a problem in order to create effective corrective actions intended to prevent the problem from ever re-occurring. This is otherwise known as the "100 year fix".

- To be effective, RCA must be performed systematically as an investigation, with well documented evidence of the root cause and conclusions.

- There is always root causes for any given problem; the ability to locate the root causes may present a challenge.

- To be effective, the analysis must establish a sequence of events or a timeline to understand the relationships between contributory factors, the root cause, and the defined problem.

- Root cause analysis can help to transform an old culture that reacts to problems into a new culture that solves problems before their escalation. More importantly, root cause analysis reduces the instances of problems occurring over time within the environment in which the RCA process is operational.

16.11.3 General process for performing and documenting an RCA-based corrective action. Notice that RCA (in steps 3, 4, and 5) forms the most critical part of successful corrective action because it directs this action toward the true root causes of the problem. The root causes are secondary to the goal of problem prevention. Yet without knowing the root causes one cannot determine an effective corrective action for the defined problem. Therefore, the software developer must [http://en.wikipedia.org/wiki/Root_cause_analysis]:

- Define the problem

- Gather data/evidence

- Ask why the problem exists and identify the true root causes associated with the defined problem

- Identify corrective actions that will prevent recurrence of the problem (the 100-year fix)

- Identify effective solutions that prevent recurrence, remain under control, meet goals and objectives, and do not cause other problems

- Implement the recommendations

- Observe the recommended solutions to ensure project and product effectiveness

- Validate methodology for problem solving and problem avoidance

References

Additional information on the *engineering foundations* KA can be found in the following documents:

- **[Boehm 1981]** Barry Boehm, *Software Engineering Economics.* Prentice-Hall, Englewood Cliffs, N.J., 1981. ISBN 0-13-822122-7.

- **[Build Security In 2012]** https://buildsecurityin.us-cert.gov/bsi/home.html, US Department of Homeland Security, National Cyber Security Division, 2012.

- **[Easton and McCall 2006]** V.J. Easton & J.H. McCall, *Statistic Glossary*, Google, 2006.

- **[Eide, Jenison, Mashaw, & Northup 2002]** A. Eide, R. Jenison, L. Mashaw, L. Northup. Engineering: Fundamentals and Problem Solving. McGraw-Hill Companies Inc., New York, 2002.

- **[Eratas & Jones 1996]** A. Eratas and J. Jones, *The Engineering Design Process.* 2nd ed. John Wiley & Sons, Inc, New York, 1996.

- **[Fenton and Pfleeger 1997]** Norman E Fenton and Shari Lawrence Pfleeger, *Software Metrics: A Rigorous & Practical Approach*, 2nd edition, PWS Publishing Company, London, 1997.

- **[Grubb 2003]** Penny Grubb and Armstrong A. Takang, *Software Maintenance: Concepts and Practice* (Paperback), 2nd Edition. World Scientific Publishing, Singapore, 2003, 350 pages. ISBN-13: 978-9812384263.

- **[ISO 9001:2008]** ISO 9001:2008 Quality management systems — Requirements. International Organization for Standardization, 2008.

- **[Kan 2002]** Stephen Kan H. *Metrics and Models in Software Quality Engineering* (Hardcover), 2nd Edition. Addison Wesley, Boston, 2002, 560 pages.

- **[Somerville 2007]** Ian Sommerville, *Software Engineering*, 8th Edition. Addison-Wesley, Harlow, England, 2006, 864 pages. ISBN-13: 978-0321313799.

- **[Thayer & Dorfman 2008]** R.H. Thayer and Merlin Dorfman, *IEEE Software Engineering Standards and Examples: Guide for Implementing a Software Requirements Specification,* ReadyNotes, Version 1.1, IEEE Computer Society Press, Los Alamitos, CA, 2008.

- **[Widas 1997]** P. Widas, *Introduction to finite element analysis.* Retrieved from http://www.sv.vt.edu/classes/MSE2094_NoteBook/97ClassProj/num/widas/history.html, 1997.

- **[Wikipedia]** Wikipedia is a free web-based encyclopedia enabling multiple users to freely add and edit online content. Definitions cited from Wikipedia and their related sources have been verified by the authors and other peer reviewers.

Notes

Notes

Notes

Notes

Made in the USA
Lexington, KY
17 December 2014